Testimonials

"The world is finally waking up to the importance of green . . . including entrepreneurs! They understand and appreciate the importance of going green, but few have the practical roadmap to make it happen. If they are to succeed, green businesses must not ignore the fundamentals of planning, marketing, and raising money in addition to their impact on the environment. Croston gives entrepreneurs and small businesses an incredible blueprint on how to join the green revolution, be successful, profitable, and make a difference!"

—JIM HORAN, AUTHOR, CONSULTANT, SPEAKER, AND PRESIDENT
OF THE ONE PAGE BUSINESS PLAN COMPANY

"Glenn Croston's Starting Green *is the indispensable guide for the entrepreneur of the 21st century. The book is eerily prescient as it comes at a time we need it most. Croston's extensive research and incredible examples will illuminate the incredible opportunities within green business. Even as a green business owner for the past two decades, I drew countless ideas and inspiration from this book."*

—ERIC COREY FREED, PRINCIPAL OF ORGANICARCHITECT, AUTHOR OF
GREEN BUILDING & REMODELING FOR DUMMIES

"We face great challenges today in our economy and environment, but the shift toward sustainability offers even greater opportunities. Starting Green *gives you the tools to join this revolution with a business of your own. The business case for sustainability is clear; what we need now is action. This book will help you pave the way forward and thrive."*

—HUNTER LOVINS, CO-AUTHOR OF *NATURAL CAPITALISM*, CO-FOUNDER OF THE
ROCKY MOUNTAIN INSTITUTE, AND PRESIDENT AND FOUNDER OF
NATURAL CAPITALISM SOLUTIONS

An Ecopreneur's Toolkit for Starting a Green Business

Starting Green

From Business Plan to Profits

Glenn Croston, Ph.D.

EP
Entrepreneur.
Press

Editorial Director: Jere L. Calmes
Cover Design: Kaochoy Saeteurn
Production and Composition: Eliot House Productions

This publication is designed to provide accurate and authoritative information in regard to the subject matter covered. It is sold with the understanding
that the publisher is not engaged in rendering legal, accounting, or other professional services. If legal advice or other expert assistance is required, the
services of a competent professional person should be sought.

Library of Congress Cataloging-in-Publication Data
Croston, Glenn E., 1964–.
    Starting green/by Glenn Croston.
    p.   cm.
    ISBN–10: 1-59918-355-2 (alk. paper)
    ISBN–13: 978-1-59918-355-8
    1. Green products. 2. Green movement—Economic aspects. 3. New
business enterprises. I. Title.
    HD9999.G772C77 2009
    658.1'1—dc22   2009015373

Printed in Canada
13 12 11 10 09   10 9 8 7 6 5 4 3 2 1

Contents

v

CHAPTER 5

How to Green Your Business
Operations and Facilities **97**

CHAPTER 6

Green Marketing and Communications **139**

How to Join the Great Green Upswing

We live in a world of incredible opportunity. While our economy is going through wrenching turmoil and the world faces immense environmental challenges like climate change, these problems are also opportunities to provide solutions. This book gives you the tools to take on these challenges and become one of the eco-entrepreneurs creating the prosperous green world of tomorrow.

Entrepreneurs and businesses around the world are unleashing their creativity and passion in search of practical environmental solutions that lead to a better world. The transformation of our economy is at hand, opening the door to the new, environmentally sound businesses being created in every industry. Entrepreneurial startups are inventing new ways to deliver clean, renewable energy, moving away from fossil fuels and reshaping the multitrillion-dollar energy industry to fight climate change, reduce pollution, revitalize the economy, and protect our security. Entrepreneurs are building and renovating millions of energy-efficient homes, helping people save money and save the planet. Our auto industry is at a crossroads, and whoever produces innovative, attractive, and more efficient cars to meet the demands of the new world will emerge on top. "Those who recognize this opportunity will be the first to the future and the billionaires of tomorrow," says Hunter Lovins, one of the visionary co-authors of *Natural Capitalism*.

Whoever you are, whatever your background, or wherever you are today, there is an opportunity waiting for you to start and grow a successful green business and be part of this profound transformation. You don't need to be a lifelong environmentalist or invent a new energy technology to join in. You need a vision and commitment to making it happen. If you are a plumber, you can be a green plumber, helping people save water with energy-efficient fixtures. If you are an electrician, you can start a business in solar power. If you are a contractor, you can start making our buildings more energy efficient. Teachers, landscapers, engineers, mechanics, carpenters, salespeople, restaurant owners, clothing producers, and stay-at-home moms have all started green businesses. And you can too.

It's not always easy. There are plenty of preconceptions and doubts that keep people from starting their own green business. Some people who are deeply committed to helping the environment remain uneasy about linking environmental progress to profit. "Businesses can't solve this problem—they are the ones that created it," some people say. I've heard it more than once. The green business movement has its roots in the environmental movement of the 1960s, a countercultural movement, and there is still a current of this thinking running through the green business world today. I call this group Green 1.0; they are where the green wave started and tend to focus on conservation and "shoulds." You should drive a smaller car. You should live in a smaller house. You should avoid eating meat. (That's right, I'm pointing at you.)

THE FOUR STAGES OF GREEN BIZ HISTORY

The four stages of green business growth that I refer to in this book are:

1. *Green 1.0: Conservation.* The origins of the environmental movement focused on the virtue of preservation of resources.

2. *Green 2.0: The First-Generation Green Business Leaders.* Growing out of the environmental movement, the first wave of green business leaders worked to build viable businesses that remain true to their owners' environmental beliefs.

3. *Green 3.0: Green Goes Mainstream.* Breaking out of the green niche, some products and businesses work to appeal more broadly to consumers for whom the environment is not their highest concern.

4. *Green 4.0: Everything Is Green.* The world of the future, in which there are no green businesses because all businesses are green, making money without harming natural systems.

Green 1.0 is right about many things. We really should drive smaller cars, or at least more efficient ones. If everyone in America would drive cars that get 40 miles per gallon, it would greatly reduce our dependence on foreign oil, fight pollution, and slow climate change, all without waiting years and years for new technology to be developed. But we haven't done this. We should also use energy more efficiently, insulating and sealing every house in the country, but we haven't done this either. Why not? Do people hate the planet?

No, of course not. But there's more to it than that. A small percentage of people, maybe 5 percent, make the environment their top priority when making purchasing decisions. About 5 percent of the people respond to "You shoulds" and do the green thing even if it costs more. This includes the people who are already in the environmental movement and have been for many years. The challenge now—and the opportunity—is to get the other 95 percent involved. A fresh perspective may help you to move forward where others have run up against the wall and break through to a larger market.

There are some who say it can't be done, that going green is an expensive luxury that we just can't afford, that it's impractical. They are wrong. People like Gary Hirshberg at Stonyfield Farm and Ray Anderson and his team at Interface have been working for years to build successful businesses that are also sustainable. These green leaders are the essence of Green 2.0, in which pioneers proved they could build profitable businesses that also do the right thing for the planet. If they can do it, so can you.

For the most part, green business is not yet mainstream. But it will be, and the process has started. The transition to mainstream is where we are today, in Green 3.0. In Green 3.0, green businesses are growing up and evolving to reach the other 95 percent of the people. To do so, these businesses must connect with a far larger group than most have so far, challenging those who believe that being authentically green requires that a business stay small. They must do more than talk about the benefits for polar bears; they must be relevant to everyday life, to ordinary people who are worried about their mortgages and their kids. They must sell products at competitive prices that make sense to people on a budget. For most people, being green alone is not enough to make them buy a product, whatever it is. Most people buy products that work, they can afford, that make them feel good, that fill a need (or want), that provide good value, and that, all other things being equal, are also good for the planet. The environmental benefit is the green icing on the cake.

Information is key for green to go mainstream. Green entrepreneurs I speak with in every industry consistently bring up education and information as central aspects of their business. This is true for a number of reasons. One is that people have many preconceptions about green products and businesses that are only partially true or are just plain wrong. For example, many people assume that green products are expensive and don't work very well. They think that going green means you have to shiver in the dark and cold. These assumptions are barriers to change that need to be overcome with good information.

THE SEVEN DEADLY ASSUMPTIONS ABOUT GOING GREEN

Among the many misconceptions consumers and businesses have about going green, here are seven that you need to know and address.

1. *Green products don't work as well.* Most green products today, such as office products, clothes, or cleaning products, work as well as their conventional counterparts.

SEVEN DEADLY ASSUMPTIONS, CONTINUED

2. *Going green always costs a great deal more.* There are some green products that cost a little more than their less green counterparts, but many green products cost far less, like reconditioned toner cartridges or re-used clothing.

3. *Green is for the elite few.* With economies of scale and falling prices for green energy, organic food, and green consumer products, green is becoming more accessible for a wide range of consumers and businesses.

4. *To go green you have to be uncomfortable.* There might have been some unfortunate burlap experiences along the way, but today's green products must attract customers with more than their environmental attributes.

5. *Going green is an expensive, unaffordable luxury for businesses.* Green business practices save money and resources, and increase productivity. Far from being a luxury they can't afford, businesses have found they can't afford not to go green—the money saved may make or break the company.

6. *Green is a fad that will pass.* Green is not a fashion trend. It has strong, long-term drivers in its favor, like the ten trends I list in Chapter 1. Government support, business fundamentals, and changing markets will keep green growing for decades to come.

7. *Green is for environmentalists and liberals.* Going green is not the domain of any political party. A growing number of voices across the political spectrum have voiced the need to take action on environmental issues, including people like James Woolsey, former director of the CIA, who view green as a national security issue.

Information also helps people, businesses, and governments value the environment, recognizing the essential role of the environment in our economic prosperity and quality of life. Sure, we *like* the environment (who doesn't?), but how much is it worth to all of us? How much are we willing to spend on it? The more we realize the value of the environment and build this into our buying decisions and the more that government creates incentives that factor in this value, the more rapidly green businesses will move from a niche to the default way of doing business.

For all of their growth, green businesses have just scratched the surface and have huge growth ahead still. Solar power has been growing 30 to 40 percent a year, but still supplies less than 1 percent of our power. Organic food has grown 15 to 21 percent a year for many years, but still accounts for only 3 to 4 percent of the food we eat. The relatively small proportion of businesses that are green today leaves an opportunity for a much greater role for green business in the future. Someday there won't be any green businesses because they will all be green. That is Green 4.0, the end game, the complete greenification of the economy when all energy will be renewable, all buildings green, and all farming organic.

This book gives you the tools to get started building your own green venture so you can become part of this transformation of our economy. Need a green business vision and a plan? See Chapters 1 and 2. Need ideas for marketing, or for raising money? It's all here. Step by step, piece by piece, you'll form your own successful green enterprise. There are many lessons throughout this book from green leaders who have been down this path already and have been generous enough to share the lessons they have learned. From their experiences we can gather valuable insights on meeting the challenges of planning, marketing, and raising money. From their examples we can gain confidence that we can build successful green businesses as well.

From their wisdom we can find a better path for the world to follow.

Still, we cannot rely on the green leaders alone. You have an important role to play as well. Your role is unique, one that only you can play as you start and build your own green business. What starts small will take root, grow and spread. The possibilities ahead are boundless as you begin down the path, contributing to a better world.

Let's get started.

Introduction

There are many great reasons why green businesses are not a fad or a fashion, but one of the most important business trends of the 21st century. The green economy is a bright point in the economy, a source of hope for our world and an inspiration for the many people eagerly seeking a new and better direction in their lives and their businesses. Perhaps if he were here today, Horace Greeley would advise "Go Green,

Young Man" (or woman) to the many who are seeking the new frontier of hope, renewal, and opportunity.

So let's get to it. But where to begin?

Everything starts with a vision, with seeing a problem that needs to be solved and discovering a business solution that addresses it. And there are plenty of problems to be solved. Giant ones. But there is another way to look at things. Instead of looking at the world and seeing only problems, try to turn things around to find opportunities. As big as climate change, resource depletion, habitat loss, and our economic problems are, they also provide opportunities for the millions of entrepreneurs and dreamers in the world searching for the next big thing and yearning to make a difference in the world, for a way to leave their mark. There is no lack of opportunity. The only questions really are which one to pursue and how to do it.

Finding Opportunity

For more information about *75 Green Businesses*, check out the book's website or Amazon. The book describes opportunities almost anyone can pursue to build environmentally friendly businesses in energy, building, food, water, services, transportation, farming, biomimicry, and waste reduction.

I describe a variety of opportunities in *75 Green Businesses You Can Start to Make Money and Make a Difference*. While there is no lack of opportunity in the world, the trick is finding the opportunity that works for you, the path that unlocks your own potential. Maybe the answer is closer than you think. You might have already had the business idea that could change the world and your life, but dismissed it as silly. Think about all you have to offer, and don't underestimate yourself. You can do far more than you imagine.

How to Succeed in Green Business without Really Trying

Once you have an idea for a green business, how can you make it a reality? Inspiration and a vision are necessary to get started, but the vision needs to be realized. The initial idea for a business needs to be nurtured and nourished so it can grow into a profitable venture. For most of us, a vision that stays on paper or in your mind is not worth much. The path to starting and growing a green business requires addressing issues like:

- What makes your business green?
- How can you secure financing?
- What are your markets and how do you reach them?
- What are the current best practices for greening your business operations?
- How should you communicate your message to investors, consumers, business partners, governments, and other stakeholders?
- What risks and opportunities do government regulations pose?
- How can human resources, IT, and law firms help you succeed?

This book answers these questions and more. Green business leaders have already encountered many of the challenges you will meet, and their advice throughout this book is a ready resource to help you overcome the problems commonly encountered.

Providing the Road Map

What is a green business? There are many ways to answer this question today because there is still no broadly accepted standard

for exactly what being green means. This lack of agreement can be a source of confusion. *Understanding the green business world you're entering* will help you navigate the path to success (Chapter 1).

Having a clear vision for your business is a big step forward, but it's only the first step. *You will need a plan* that lays out what your business will sell, who you will sell to, and how your business will be structured (Chapter 3). In creating your plan, you need to demonstrate how your business will be profitable as well as how it will affect the environment. Creating the plan helps you appreciate right from the start what you need to do to make money *and* make a difference. From there you need to flesh out your vision, breathing life into it to make it real.

All businesses also deal with financing their enterprise. In addition to the resources other entrepreneurs turn to for funding, you will have access to many *unique sources of financing* (Chapter 4). Government assistance, peer-to-peer lending, venture firms, and green angels can all deliver the capital green start-ups need to get off the ground and stimulate the growth of the green economy. But to secure funding from investors, you will have to convince them that you are building a profitable venture.

Green businesses don't just provide green products or services. They are also *greening how they do business* (Chapter 5). Delivering green products with polluting trucks and wasteful buildings will not fly with stakeholders for long, and greening your operations also helps you get leaner and more competitive. Wasted resources are lost money. Increasing energy efficiency of buildings and operations, cutting back on water use, using more efficient transportation, and wasting less material can all help the bottom line and make the difference between profit and loss, between success and failure. Almost any business today deals with IT issues, spending a great deal of time, money, and resources on its computer systems. Greening these systems to reduce power use and reduce waste is an important opportunity for improvement.

Operating a green business is not just about the buildings, factories, and computers, and not just about the planet. It's also about the people. Creating a green work culture is another key step in building a green business. A green focus for a business can energize and focus employees, partners, and consumers and increase the value of companies compared to their less green competitors. Greening the workplace inspires innovation, engages workers, and increases productivity. People connect with their work and give more to it when they believe they are making a meaningful difference in the world. Whatever your industry, getting employees involved in going green helps to make it happen, creates a solid green brand that stands up to close scrutiny, and becomes an important factor in stimulating innovation, attracting talent, and growing your business.

With your plan in place, doors open, and financing secured, you are ready to *reach out to your market* (Chapter 6). Having a great green product or service is not enough if people do not know what it is or why they should buy it. Green consumers are diverse, as are their motivations, and they are increasingly skeptical of businesses claiming to be green. Knowing who your customers are, including how to reach them, what to say, and how to secure their business, is an essential step toward success. One reason businesses are greening their operations is that a wide range of stakeholders are asking or even requiring that they do this, and then reporting on their environmental progress. Finding the best way to talk about sustainability is rapidly becoming essential for businesses in many industries.

Government regulations and legislation can greatly affect how green entrepreneurs start and grow their businesses, and create opportunities (Chapter 7). The government regulates pollution, and is creating incentives to mitigate problems like climate change. With cities and states leading the way on climate change, the U.S. government is moving to take action as well, and a new global agreement on climate change is just around the corner. Governments are encouraging the reduction of landfill waste, take-back programs for electronic waste, water conservation, development of biofuels, production of renewable energy, air pollution reduction, improvements in energy efficiency, and remediation of hazardous waste sites. The more government takes action on green issues, the more opportunities it creates for entrepreneurs who provide solutions. Green businesses are also increasingly getting involved in the legislative process, working together to steer government toward the best green solutions. Chapters 8 to 12 present more in-depth plans for starting a few specific business types. The steps needed to build a business for each of these areas are spelled out by discussing marketing, money, and other challenges.

The types of businesses people start range from innovative technologies, to creating unique green brands, to working with established brands. An increasing number of *green franchises* are available for entrepreneurs to jump-start their own business with proven concepts in green real estate, recycling toner cartridges, and organic pizza, to name just a few (Chapter 8).

For many the opportunity will be building a *business providing energy efficiency*. There is an amazing opportunity in making millions of buildings more energy efficient, addressing climate change, getting the economy moving, and helping people to save money. The opportunity for energy efficiency auditors and contractors is as large as the amount of energy we waste (Chapter 9).

As much as the green economy has grown, most of our economy remains untouched, including most of the vast world of retail businesses. Where pioneers in the *green retail* world have shown the way, there is a fertile field waiting for others to follow, whether online or in a good old-fashioned brick-and-mortar store (Chapter 10).

With increasing pressure to change how we produce energy and with solid government incentives, the opportunity to *start a solar business* has never been greater. The solar industry will experience rapid growth for years to come, creating massive opportunities for installers of solar panels and other solar entrepreneurs (Chapter 11).

Some people need opportunities that provide flexible hours and low startup costs. Green businesses in *direct sales* can be started at home with a very small investment, opening the door to the green revolution to a broader range of people (Chapter 12).

What lies ahead? The economic crisis we are embroiled in has left many uncertain and afraid for their future, but out of this crisis new opportunities are emerging. As consumers slow down spending, they are transforming our consumer economy into a *"conserver economy,"* saving more, spending less, and thinking of the long term. With an emphasis on efficient use of resources as well as on saving money, the conserver economy opens a new range of opportunities for helping people live well in this new world (Conclusion).

One way to improve your chances of success in turning the world green is to reach out for help when you need it. If you have a question, ask—you'll be surprised at how willing and excited people are to help. There are a great variety of resources available to help green entrepreneurs move the economy toward greater sustainability. I founded Starting Up Green (StartingUp Green.com) as one such resource, providing green entrepreneurs with a full range of strategies, resources, and opportunities to start and grow a green business. If you are trying to build your green business and find yourself stuck or confused, I encourage you to reach out to my site or to engage with others who are ready to lend a hand.

Many people wonder if green businesses are another business fad that will fade away, but the evidence says otherwise. The

forces driving the long-term growth of green businesses are not just the residue of momentary sentiment, but solid business fundamentals connected to profound environmental and social value. The imperative to reduce waste, reduce pollution, and use energy more efficiently is strong and lasting. With such powerful forces in their favor, green businesses will not fade; they will continue to grow until all businesses are green.

Sometimes with all of the talk about the problems we face, we lose track of the possibility of the positive world we want to create. Going green is not just about avoiding problems but also about having a vision of a positive future that we want to move toward. What will this world look like in 2030, 2050, and beyond? I believe that in the green world of the future we will see:

- Clean and healthy air, food, and water for all generations to come
- Recycling and reusing of resources in the industrial world without degrading natural systems for resource extraction
- Abundant, inexpensive renewable energy for our homes, cars, and businesses that replaces fossil fuels
- A stable climate not far from the present climate
- No waste or pollution
- Vibrant and diverse ecosystems
- Healthy, rewarding lifestyles
- A strong economy with abundant opportunities for good work and successful businesses around the globe

The more successful your green business is, the more you will be helping us all draw closer to this vision of a greener world. Good luck in your journey. And don't forget to send me a postcard.

1

Welcome to the Revolution

To know where you're going with your business, you need to know where you are and where you've been. This is also true for green businesses, so in this chapter I give a brief history of the green business world and point out the trends that reveal where it's going. Then, after walking through why, what, where green has been, and where it's going, the rest of the book will talk about the how.

Why a Green Business?

The green business world has some big changes in mind, changes so big that many are calling it a revolution. Green businesses want to revolutionize how we power our economy, switching the multitrillion-dollar energy industry from fossil fuels to renewable energy. They are helping homes and businesses waste less energy, save resources, prevent pollution, stimulate economic growth, and fight climate change. The green business revolution is changing how we live and work to strike a balance between living well today and allowing for future generations to live well tomorrow.

Because not everyone has the same motivations, here's a list of the top ten reasons why businesses should go green:

1. Going greener means saving money by wasting less, a strong motivation in the current economy.
2. Shareholders pressure businesses to pay more attention to the environment.
3. Going green attracts and retains top talent, exciting employees about the mission of the company. Reduced turnover means saving money.
4. Going green increases business productivity.
5. Going green drives innovation, setting new challenges for the business to meet and conquer creatively by getting more out of less.
6. Going green reduces risks to a business created by the impact of climate change, legislative changes, increased utility costs, and changing markets.
7. Going green is increasingly where the opportunities are. The more customers and other businesses ask for green products and services, the more businesses move to deliver them.
8. Governments are providing mandates and incentives for consumers and businesses to work and live more sustainably.

Complying with legal requirements created by legislation is another powerful motivation.

9. Going green creates a powerful message to tell about your business, which helps to increase the visibility of your products.

10. Employees, managers, and business owners just plain think it's the right thing to do.

The revolution is not just about changing the buildings, products, and balance sheets of businesses. These are the easy part. The hard part is transforming the thinking that lies behind these. The traditional business world has been focused on a specific definition of profit measured by the flow of money in and out of the business. There's nothing wrong with tracking money or making a profit. The problem with traditional economics is not that it tracks money, but what it doesn't track—the impact of businesses on the world around them. These factors are often called "externalities," since they lie in the terra incognita beyond balance sheets, where few accountants dare to tread, although a few are leading the way.

Traditional economics and business accounting fail to account for many things. When a forest is cleared for lumber and sold, traditional economics measures only the cost of harvesting the wood and the profit from selling it, but there's much more to the story than the wood. Harvesting the wood by clear-cutting may turn a short-term profit for the business but creates a cost by damaging a watershed and destroying biodiversity. These things have value.

> **Defining Moment**
>
> Many green businesses today are tracking the "triple bottom line," looking at business performance in terms of not just profit but also of people and the planet (environmental impact). They measure performance and business success more broadly than the traditional bottom line of money alone.

The so-called externality of watershed loss has a real cost for all of us, often greater than the value of the lumber. In traditional economics, the success of a coal mine is measured by the cost of digging up coal and the profit from selling it, but takes no measure of the cost of pollution from mountaintop removal or climate change from burning coal for power. The indirect but immense cost of changing our atmosphere has for the most part been ignored.

Today these so-called externalities are piling up and coming back to bite us. All of these externalities are not truly external, and they are costing us all a great deal of money.

Around the world governments and businesses are recognizing the true economic cost of externalities, and starting to manage them by creating economic incentives that are reshaping the economy and will continue to do so for decades. Big problems need big solutions, creating massive long-term opportunities. Global agreements on climate change are motivated by the desire to do the right thing for future generations, but enacting such measures also drives investment and creates opportunities. Investing in natural systems today pays off manyfold in the future by protecting resources that will provide much greater economic value if left intact. Pollution legislation, waste-reduction mandates, water conservation, energy efficiency, improved building codes—all of these moves are setting the stage for the solid long-term growth of green businesses. And what's good for green businesses is good for all of us, both economically and environmentally.

Subprime Carbon Assets

Al Gore has called those businesses contributing to climate change "subprime carbon assets" and says they will cause a larger crisis than the current economic crisis (partially the result of subprime mortgages) if left unaddressed. Gore is calling for action to steer the economy toward higher grade investments in a low-carbon economy.

The impact of these environmental externalities are global, but the impact is particularly evident in China. Rapid industrialization has caused China's GDP to grow at a blistering 10 to 12 percent per year, until the present economic crisis. Even in the midst of this crisis, China's government is targeting 7 to 8 percent growth. But such rapid growth has come with a high price. China's big cities like Beijing and Shanghai have sprouted skyscrapers at a dizzying pace, but also often lie shrouded in choking haze. Many of its rivers are terribly polluted with industrial waste, and arable land is being lost at a rapid pace. In his book *Hot, Flat and Crowded*, Thomas Friedman describes the economic toll that this pollution is taking, making the real rate of economic growth smaller than it appears on paper. The economic toll of pollutants dumped into the surroundings will grow if pollution continues worsening along with growth. Friedman describes the potential of "Green GDPism" to take over and transform the Chinese society and economy as the Chinese government sees the limits of externalities and widens the circle to include them.

The revolution is underway. Our paradigms are shifting beneath our feet. In Green 2.0, green consumers and green business leaders began to consider externalities. In Green 4.0, when the entire economy is green, everyone will—the externalities will be everyone's business.

What Green Means

New green products often encounter a great deal of skepticism today. "That's not green," people often argue, listing imperfections that prevent something

Finding Opportunity

While much has been made of China's environmental problems, the very scale of these problems and the need to do something about them make the greening of China an immense opportunity for entrepreneurs. Those who can provide clean energy at "the China price," as Friedman calls it, will be green tycoons.

from meeting their personal understanding of what it means to be green. One person may think that industrialized organic agriculture, in which organic farming methods are applied on large farms, is not very green because it differs from his or her vision of organic farming being small and local. But to another person, the fact that the food is organic is enough to qualify it as green and organic farming on a large scale helps to amplify its environmental benefit. The problem is one of lack of clear definitions and different individual perceptions. The word "green" means different things to different people. With no broad definition that everyone agrees with, green can get confusing.

The same thing goes for green businesses. People often ask, "Is that a green business?" For some people the term is reserved for only the greenest of the green, for the pinnacle of greenness. For others the term is applied more broadly, to any business that is making an effort to improve its environmental impact. I have my own definition, which I hope represents a middle ground:

> *Green Businesses have more sustainable business practices than competitors, benefiting natural systems and helping people live well today and tomorrow while making money and contributing to the economy.*

I think such a broad definition reflects the state of green business today. Green businesses should be a significant and measurable improvement over the current environmental impact of other businesses in the same industry. At the same time, a business needs to be successful and help people as well. Schemes in which people are marginalized are no more sustainable than schemes in which nature is marginalized.

In the absence of broad objective criteria, the green label should be a challenge to achieve and require real environmental progress, but I don't see the benefit of restricting the term to a select few. Nobody is perfectly sustainable yet, not even those who have been working for decades on greening their business. To set the bar at the level of "green businesses have no impact on the environment" is to set a goal that nobody can really achieve today. For me, the key is not to require that a business is perfectly green, but to see if a business is making significant, credible, and honest progress.

Imagine, for example, that your business making widgets uses 500 liters of water for every 100 widgets produced, while everyone else in your industry is using 2,000 liters of water per 100 widgets. You still use water and your business may not be perfect, but at least it is doing better. That can be a noteworthy achievement. Later on you can reclaim and reuse all of your water, and make your widgets from sugarcane waste from organically and sustainably grown cane.

It can be harder to certify a whole business than a specific product. A retail store is much more complex than a shoe, and it's hard to compare a store, factory, hotel, and a restaurant. Programs like The Bay Area Green Business Program in the San Francisco Bay region are working to separate the wheat from the green business chaff. These certification schemes are starting to have an impact, and will increase in importance in the future. If customers can look for a single green logo that holds meaning for everyone who sees it, this decreases confusion and eases green purchasing decisions, helping the market to grow beyond concerns about greenwashing.

It's worth noting that what we call a green business today will probably not be considered very green tomorrow. The definition

> ### Defining Moment
>
> And the meaning of sustainability? Sustainability is about doing business in a way that can be maintained for the long term without degrading the environment and depleting resources. Building sustainable businesses, and a sustainable economy, is the ultimate goal.

Setting the Standard

See more about what is involved in getting certified as a green business at The Bay Area Green Business Program at greenbiz.ca.gov. A growing number of cities and states have their own local certification programs following similar guidelines.

of a green business will change over time as companies innovate to become greener. The greener businesses get, the harder it will be to be considered green compared to everyone else. It is inevitable that the bar will be raised due to growing regulation, more stringent certification, and changing consumer perceptions. The greener everyone else gets, the greener you have to become to stand out. What is a green business today may be considered a gray business tomorrow. Once your business starts going green and gets certified, you should not stop there. You should view the move to green as an ongoing progression, a journey rather than a specific destination.

A Brief History of Green

A brief history of the green business world can help when you are starting your own business. Knowing where things stand today and where the green business community has been, you can better understand where trends are headed in the future.

Green 1.0: The Conservationists (From Prehistory to World War II)

Many cultures value a close connection to nature, but this has not been the case for most of industrialized Western society for the last few hundred years. For most of history, the number of people on the planet and their impact on the environment has been relatively small compared to the vastness of nature. It seemed as if no matter how much garbage we dumped, nature could just soak it up, shrug it off, and wash it away. It seemed that the resources of nature like the fish of the sea and the trees of the forest were so vast that they would last forever. The result of these attitudes is that something which seems unlimited in supply and available to all is perceived to have no real economic value—because it is, in effect, free.

There have been a few outstanding individuals along the way with the foresight to see the limits of this approach, to see that nature has value and is worth saving. John Muir saw Yosemite and the California redwoods and realized that without some protection they would fall prey to development. Teddy Roosevelt was another early conservationist, getting the U.S. National Park System started. These efforts were born out of an almost spiritual regard for natural settings. "In every walk with nature one receives far more than he seeks," wrote Muir.

THE GROWTH OF INDUSTRY AND ENVIRONMENTAL IMPACT IN THE POST–WORLD WAR II WORLD

Despite prevailing attitudes that nature was ours to use as we saw fit, until World War II the impact of industry on the planet was still quite limited and localized compared to today. Except for areas used for agriculture, most of the world's ecosystems remained largely intact.

It's really been since World War II that the world's population and industrial output have kicked into high gear, kicking our environmental impact into high gear as well. The age of the consumer economy changed how we lived and how we made and used things, leaving a much greater footprint on the natural world. By 1960 the world's population was about 3 billion and the level of carbon dioxide in the atmosphere was 317 parts per million (ppm, data from the Mauna Loa observatory in Hawaii), somewhat elevated over preindustrial levels of about 280 ppm. This was when scientists taking readings of carbon dioxide in the

atmosphere first became alarmed. Today the world's population is more than twice this, and the atmospheric carbon dioxide levels are 387 ppm and steadily rising.

These numbers alone may not be that impressive to most people because it's hard to say how the level of greenhouse gases in the atmosphere relates to our daily lives. But this increase in CO_2 is probably connected to the more frequent droughts, wildfires, insect infestations killing huge swaths of forests, and changes in our seasons that we are already seeing. It makes violent hurricanes like Katrina more frequent by warming the oceans. More and more people can see these changes with their own eyes when the spring comes earlier and reservoir levels fall year after year.

It is changes like this that make the externalities impossible to ignore, that have made environmentalism go from an elite concern to everybody's concern. It's not just a matter of preventing roadside litter or preserving scenic wonders and large mammal species. It's a matter of preserving the future for all of us, everywhere.

THE BEGINNING OF THE BEGINNING: RACHEL CARSON AND THE COUNTERCULTURE

The green business movement grew out of the environmental movement, going back to Rachel Carson's 1962 book *Silent Spring* about the impact of the pesticide DDT on the natural world. *Silent Spring* was a lightning rod, drawing fire from many and energizing others to actively protect and protest. People worried about the impact of pesticides and pollution worked through nonprofits, protests, laws, and regulations to ensure that changes were made. Businesses sprang up along the way created by those in the movement, but these small co-ops and businesses were often focused more on the environment than on making a profit.

Organic food has its roots in the green business movement of this era. Organic food may be a big industry today, but it did not start out that way. Some of the big organic food names today like Cascadian Farms started out small. "Today Cascadian Farms is foremost a General Mills brand, but it began as a quasi-communal hippie farm," writes Michael Pollan in *The Omnivore's Dilemma*. Organic food was a move by the counterculture to have different food as part of a different way of living. They were sticking it to the man by growing their own food rather than buying his.

THE BATTLE OF MOUNT REGULATION, PART II

In the 1970s the environmental movement took on big business with new legislation in the United States, including the Endangered Species Act, the Clean Air Act, and the Clean Water Act. Perhaps the icon of this era should be two lawyers squaring off, one for the business world and one for the movement. The good news was real progress has been made as a result of such landmark legislation. The U.S. Clean Air Act of 1970 led to the removal of lead from gasoline and to a dramatic decline in the number of kids with high lead levels in their blood. Los Angeles, renowned for its smog in the 1970s, has much cleaner air today. These advances would not have happened any time soon if left to market forces alone

The bad news is that these environmental gains are not nearly enough,

Finding Opportunity

The electric car is experiencing a rebirth today, with several automakers planning to bring to market electric and plug-in hybrid cars in the next few years. Where GM fits into this remains to be seen, but out of adversity and turmoil will emerge better and cleaner cars, perhaps from companies like Aptera, Better Place, Tesla, or Think. Just as GM's problems ripple outward, so will the opportunities for those providing goods and services related to the changing face of transportation.

and many on both sides believe that continued confrontation may hurt both business and the environment alike. This shift has set the tone for a shift in how many businesses view the environment. While in the age of confrontation action to help the environment was viewed in terms of compliance with regulation and perceived as an expensive liability to be fought against, many businesses have come to perceive environmental action as an opportunity.

The story of General Motors, once the largest automotive company in the world, has an interesting side note. California required the auto producers to come up with electric vehicles in the '80s and early '90s, and they did it. They produced electric vehicles like the EV1 from GM, but only grudgingly, fighting every step of the way, as told in the movie *Who Killed the Electric Car*. Admittedly, technology at the time limited the range of these vehicles, and they were expensive to build. Today GM has a new effort underway to create electrified and hybrid vehicles like the Chevy Volt. But I can't help but wonder: If GM had stayed with the EV1 program rather than crushing the cars, would they be in a better position today?

Green 2.0: Green Leaders Prove that Environmental Action Can Help to Build Businesses

Many businesses have viewed environmental regulations as a hindrance they must comply with or fight—fighting environmental efforts with lawsuits and lobbyists. Today though, many businesses are embracing environmental action. This shift in thinking started with the green business leaders who paved the way for others.

Ray Anderson founded the Interface floor covering company and built it from the ground up, making it a leader in his industry. And yet when he read Paul Hawken's *Ecology of Commerce* in 1994, he suddenly saw that his success came with a heavy price.

In his "spear in the chest moment," Anderson realized that he had to fundamentally transform Interface to do business in a more environmentally sustainable way, as related in his book *Mid-Course Correction*. From there he set out to transform Interface to become a sustainable floor covering business.

Gary Hirshberg, CE-Yo of organic yogurt producer Stonyfield Farm, is another green leader who paved the way for others. In the 1970s he was the executive director of the New Alchemy Institute, developing and educating others about new ways to live and work in an eco-friendly manner by raising their own food organically and producing renewable energy. He describes his own epiphany on visiting the Kraft Pavilion at the Epcot Center that touted the benefits of highly processed and nonorganic foods. He realized that for all of the progress made at the New Alchemy Institute, it would never be able to have the impact he wanted, changing how food is made and consumed by large numbers of people. To do this he would have to develop a business that would successfully compete with the likes of Kraft. "To change anything, we needed the leverage of powerful businesses like Kraft," writes Hirshberg in *Stirring It Up*. "If we had their cash and clout, people would listen and begin to make changes, which led to my key point: To persuade businesses to adopt sustainable practices, I would have to prove they were profitable." From there he went on to grow Stonyfield Farms to be the successful and increasingly sustainable business that he had envisioned, setting the example for others to follow.

Strategies of Green Leaders

The story of Ray Anderson can also be found on the Interface website (interface global.com), which includes information about how the company gathers data on progress, and at mission zero.org, an online community of businesses committed to sustainability.

Green 3.0: Going Mainstream

When the green leaders like Gary Hirshberg and Ray Anderson started their journey, they were trailblazers, trying out a variety of tactics to figure out what works. One of the lessons has been that green businesses are not just about green and not just about business—they're a balance of both. The combination of both is more powerful than either alone, powerful enough to move the world.

Many green businesspeople of Green 2.0 were not in it for the money, and it's still that way for many people today. They were in it for the cause. The commitment to the environment by many of these early green entrepreneurs is unparalleled. When it comes to building a business though, some are uncomfortable with making money, and this discomfort can be a problem. For some, it's about a fear of betraying their environmental commitment and a belief that the evils of money are what got us all into this environmental mess. In fact, if you are starting a business and you don't make money, then you don't have a business. One way or another, your business won't be around long, no matter how well-intentioned you are.

Some go to the other extreme and say that a green business does not really need to be concerned with the environment, as long as the end result is green. If a solar power company produces photovoltaic panels that generate cheap renewable energy and this helps to reduce dependence on coal based on sheer economics, then does it really matter if the solar folks are green at heart or not?

There's some merit to this. What really matters is the CO_2 emitted, not what went on in someone's head, right? I wonder, though, if when the heart and mind of a business and its leaders are not aligned with green goals, sooner or later the business may trip up. A solar company that produces cheap photovoltaic panels but ignores how they are made may end up finding out they were made with a potent greenhouse gas like NF₃, for example, and if left unaddressed while consumers, partners, competitors, and governments advance, this could spell trouble. Businesses will do a better job at staying on the right path if they have a balanced perspective, inside and out.

What we need is a balance. A green business needs to make money, and it needs to consider the environment in all of its actions. I think a green business in Green 3.0 will see its business fundamentals benefit from a sincere and authentic commitment to the environment. And those with a sincere commitment to the environment cannot afford to ignore their business fundamentals.

Preparing for Green 4.0: The Greenest Generation

People are always looking for the next big thing. Nobody can predict the future, particularly in the short term, but there are some green trends that seem almost inevitable in the long run. You don't need a crystal ball to see how these will drive the growth of green businesses in the years and decades to come. Seeing these future trends and acting on them today may provide a leg up down the road. It could provide the difference between being a day trader or being Warren Buffett, between being a follower or a visionary. Knowing these trends and building them into your plan will provide a solid footing to move in the right direction.

Ten Green Trends that Will Change the World
Trend 1. Oil and natural gas get more expensive.

The supply of oil in the ground is finite, particularly the cheap stuff that is easy to pump out. For a long time there has been ardent discussion about how long it will take us to drain this resource, the point at which oil production peaks and then starts to decline, also called "peak oil." Some say peak oil has already

Looking Forward

One of the concerns about the current economic crisis is the price of oil has been suppressed so low that exploration and pumping have been scaled back greatly, reducing the future supply. When the price of oil goes back up it might do so sharply again in a period of months rather than years.

happened, with the moment slipping past unnoticed, while others put the probable date for peak oil 15 or 20 years away. I can't tell you when peak oil will happen, but it will. The surprising thing is that almost everyone agrees with this.

As I write this in early 2009, the price of oil has plunged to around $40 a barrel because of decreased demand during the economic crisis, but the long-term trend toward higher oil prices still holds. The price will go up again as the economy improves and consumption goes back up. At higher oil prices, other alternatives for transportation like electric vehicles become more cost competitive. We will switch from oil before we run out because oil will be the expensive option, as well as the polluting one. Sheikh Zaki Yamani, a former Saudi Arabian oil minister, once said, "The stone age did not end because they ran out of stones." And so it goes with oil.

TAKING ADVANTAGE OF THIS TREND

What will be the impact of expensive fuels? The more expensive oil gets, the more fuel efficiency comes into vogue. Small cars will rule the roads when the economy comes back and oil gets more expensive again. Electric cars will do better when they come to market if gas is more expensive. All of the fuel conservation trends of the summer of 2008 with gas at $4.50 a gallon will happen again, with a big increase in carsharing and ridesharing, and interest in alternative fuels. If you need to buy a corporate car, buy a small car or a hybrid while the economy is down and prices are cheap, if you can. Think about the impact of oil on driving habits and where you locate your business for customers to come to you, or for you to go to them.

Trend 2. Producing greenhouse gases will get more expensive.

Today, dumping carbon dioxide into the atmosphere is free for most businesses in the United States and China, leaving everyone else to pay the price. Climate change is a problem that will require decades of concerted global action, cooperation on a scale never seen before. We can do it, and some of us will spend our lifetime creating megabusinesses solving this problem. Change is already on the way, by putting a price on greenhouse gas emissions. State and regional action on climate change is already underway. The RGGI (Regional Greenhouse Gas Initiative) includes a cap-and-trade system to reduce greenhouse gas emissions by utilities in 10 Northeast and Mid-Atlantic states. In California, the Global Warming Solutions Act of 2006 (also called AB 32) requires that greenhouse gas emissions be reduced to 1990 levels by 2020. Long awaited action by the U.S. government to limit greenhouse gas emissions is looking likely, and global action on climate change by putting a price on carbon will ratchet up in the years ahead.

TAKING ADVANTAGE OF THIS TREND

Businesses that get on board early will have the upper hand in the low-carbon economy of the future. One opportunity is to provide innovative solutions to reduce emissions in carbon-intensive industries like cement, power, and steel. Renewable energy businesses are beneficiaries of the move away from coal, one of the biggest global sources of greenhouse gases. Businesses that provide offsets in areas like methane capture may also do well if offsets are included in the eventual legislation and regulation.

Trend 3. Waste less water.

The world's population is growing steadily, but the supply of fresh water is not. Our economy may run without coal or oil in the future, but we cannot survive without water. Pollution, dwindling groundwater, and climate change will continue to reduce the water supply in many parts of the world, a trend well underway already in places like the U.S. Southwest, Australia, and China. One consequence is that water will either be rationed or its price will rise closer to its true cost, increasing the incentive for businesses and consumers to be more water frugal. The more water a business uses, the more frugality becomes a key factor for success. Industries that are highly water intensive like agriculture, semiconductors, or beverage production will be affected the most.

TAKING ADVANTAGE OF THIS TREND

Water conservation technologies will be hot. The best water source is the water we already have, using and reusing it to get the most out of it. Conserve water in your business from day one to save money and gain a competitive advantage. Create businesses that help others conserve water as well.

Trend 4. Waste less energy.

We waste billions of dollars worth of energy every year. In many cases investments in energy efficiency pay for themselves in two years or less, the equivalent of an investment with a 50 percent annual rate of return. The logic of not wasting all of this energy is overwhelming. In some cases all that is needed are more creative ways of financing energy efficiency. Governments and utilities are doing more to promote energy efficiency, and businesses are realizing that the opportunity to save money helps their bottom line, no matter how they feel about the environment.

TAKING ADVANTAGE OF THIS TREND

Get efficient and start saving right away. Businesses that continue to waste energy are throwing money out the door and will find themselves at a competitive disadvantage. Getting efficient also contributes to your green brand. The opportunity for businesses that help others save money is immense.

Trend 5. Produce clean renewable energy.

Wind and solar power are clean, renewable, and proven technologies. Both have grown rapidly, and with new incentives at the state and federal level in the United States, they should grow even faster. While they produce less than 1 percent of our energy today, President Obama has called for this to double in three years (by 2012), and to provide 20 percent of our electricity by 2020. This trend is global, with countries around the world investing heavily in renewable energy. Many states have renewable energy mandates for utility power production, requiring a growing percentage of energy to be from clean sources like wind and solar. Barack Obama has pledged support for a national renewable energy mandate.

TAKING ADVANTAGE OF THIS TREND

Be a part of the renewable energy industry, with a solar integrator business for example (see Chapter 11). If you don't work in the renewable energy field directly, get involved in a related business (training, parts, maintenance, marketing, sales).

Trend 6. Have stronger green certification.

What is green? It's hard to say sometimes, but various certification schemes are trying to make this clearer by setting clear, open standards that are judged by independent third parties. There is a clear need for certification to avoid the confusion some feel

about the word "green." In the same way that having the FDA provide specific guidelines for the use of the term "organic" helped the organic food industry to grow, defining the word "green" will reduce consumer confusion and encourage the growth of green products. There are still a variety of certification standards for different products and different markets. It's not clear today which certification standards will be around in the long term, but it's likely that we will see one or more of them broadly adopted.

TAKING ADVANTAGE OF THIS TREND

Get certified. It will make you more credible as a green business.

Trend 7. Cleaner food and better health.

OK, this may be optimistic, but so be it—our health is not what it could be, but I think we'll do better in the future. About one in three Americans are obese, which leads to diabetes and other health issues, and has an enormous impact on our health and the health-care system. It is not just an American problem either—the epidemic is spreading worldwide. We can change this, but it may not be fast or easy. We know what the problem is. We have too much cheap, bad food; we don't exercise; and our culture has moved away from healthy habits. There is a strong financial motivation for improving our health. Those paying for our health care have a great incentive to get us back on the right path, since the health-care cost of these issues and their impact on the bottom line are staggering. Look for more money to be spent by insurers, governments, and businesses on preventative medicine, which saves those who pay for health care a great deal of money—and keeps people healthier.

TAKING ADVANTAGE OF THIS TREND

Get involved in the production, distribution, preparation, and provision of healthy, local, whole, organic, and sustainably produced food. Finding ways to make this food fit into people's lives and improve their health as well will be a winning combination. Exercise trends, yoga, boot camps, personal trainers, stress relief, healthy diets, and education all play a role.

Trend 8. The flat world.

In his bestselling books *The World is Flat* and *Hot, Flat and Crowded* and in his columns in *The New York Times*, Thomas Friedman describes the impact of the flattening world economy. Today we are not just competing with other workers and businesses in the United States, but with workers around the world. We find ourselves in early 2009 embroiled in an economic crisis of epic proportions. It's not just Americans losing their jobs, but many businesses are continuing to turn to offshoring as a cost-cutting measure. As our economy restructures itself, the pressure on American workers and businesses to compete in the global marketplace will be intense. The United States can take on this challenge and make the most of this historic opportunity to create millions of high-value jobs here, particularly green jobs, with innovative entrepreneurial ventures leading the way.

TAKING ADVANTAGE OF THIS TREND

Start an innovative green business doing work that cannot be easily outsourced. Don't get complacent, but keep on innovating and working to be better. Businesses tied to the local environment are one niche that resists the tide to move business offshore. You can't send buildings to China for

Strategies of Green Leaders

Green collar jobs are advocated by people like Van Jones as a solution to both our economic and environmental challenges. The author of *The Green Collar Economy* and the founder of Green For All, he was recently appointed Special Advisor for Green Jobs, Enterprise and Innovation on the White House Council on Environmental Quality.

weatherproofing, as Van Jones and author Thomas Friedman have pointed out.

Trend 9. Raising the green bar.

While certification provides standards about what is green and what isn't, these standards will not stand still over time. What people think is green today may not be considered green tomorrow. Today, the bar is relatively low as businesses start to consider sustainability. With time, as they progress, the standards for being green will progress as well. Green businesses will need to keep innovating because of competition, changing attitudes, and certification.

TAKING ADVANTAGE OF THIS TREND

Start the journey today, getting ahead of the pack, and keep on looking for ways to be better and greener to stay ahead of the pack.

Trend 10. The conserver economy.

In early 2009 the consumer economy slowed to a crawl amid the credit crunch, millions of lost jobs, rising fear, and plummeting home values, but as the consumer economy shrinks the conserver economy is growing. The current economic crisis won't last forever, but the impact of this crisis won't pass quickly. Like the green economy, the conserver economy emphasizes being efficient with resources, but it is more closely connected to pocketbooks than to polar bears. In the conserver economy people are wasting less, saving more, and thinking of the long term.

TAKING ADVANTAGE OF THIS TREND

We are seeing the economy shift in a new direction, a shift with long-term implications. The shift from consumer to conserver holds a wealth of opportunities for businesses that share, repair, reuse, rent, rethink, and rebuild. Start a business in one of these niches in the new conserver economy.

Going Green Is Not a Fad but a Long-Term Reality

Our attention is usually absorbed by what is going on right now, at this moment—the ups and downs of the market are reported minute by minute. The success of a business, however, is not built on what happens in one day though; success stems from the long-term trends described above. It is the difference between a rainstorm and climate change. The rainstorm gets our attention, but the slow steady advance of climate change will be far more important in the long run. We can do little to change or predict the daily ups and downs of business world, any more than we can stop the rain, but we have a great deal of power to determine what happens with our businesses by connecting to bigger trends in the years ahead.

Some have wondered if the green trend would die in the down economy. The unspoken assumption is that green is an expensive luxury, one that nobody can afford when things are lean. On to the next fad, maybe "orange businesses," I suppose.

I've got news for them—reports of the death of green business are greatly exaggerated. Green business is, in fact, alive and kicking, and has immense growth ahead still. Why? Because it makes sense. For many people it calls to their basic sense of *rightness*, the way they think things should be. For others, it's all about making money. In addition, the large incentives being put in place by governments to support green behavior and green businesses are likely to continue. No matter what the latest issue of *Vanity Fair* holds, green or not, these fundamental forces will continue supporting the ongoing growth of green businesses.

Green Leader
GARY HIRSHBERG

The CE-Yo of Stonyfield Farm, Gary Hirshberg has a long history of working to change not just yogurt but the food business in general to make products that are healthy for both people and the planet. Hirshberg helped Stonyfield become a successful producer of organic yogurt with sales greater than $300 million a year and growing. In addition to building Stonyfield Farm, he encourages other businesses to go green as well, proving that going green is not just the right thing to do but the path toward building a successful business.

The green economy has just begun. For all of their growth so far, green businesses have just scratched the surface. The huge upside, combined with the factors driving it forward, make green businesses the opportunities of our lifetime.

One benefit of going green is the loyalty of customers that Hirshberg describes in his book *Stirring It Up: How to Make Money and Save the World*. By sticking to high-quality organic products and producing them in an eco-friendly manner, Stonyfield has built a loyal base of customers. Stonyfield was measuring its carbon footprint long before most companies knew what that was, and striving to reduce it. It has aggressively reduced its waste and increased its efficiency, increasing profits even as it has grown immensely. By helping organic farmers, it has had a positive impact on its suppliers as well as its customers, providing a model for other green companies to follow.

When I talked with Hirshberg at the Fortune Brainstorm Green Conference in 2008, he shared his thoughts about the environmental business issues facing the food industry, including his own company.

As the CE-Yo of Stonyfield Farm, Hirshberg is a highly visible business figure who has led the way in the growing market for organic food products. The impact of organic foods extends all the way into the fields where it all starts, with the plants and livestock that are grown without synthetic hormones, pesticides, or antibiotics. The soil in organic agriculture is replenished with manure, compost, or crop rotation rather than synthetic fertilizers, helping to restore soils and build them for the future, rather than deplete and erode soils as happens in modern agricultural practices. Preserving and building soils for the future is a solid investment in our future. "As a species we have been slow to understand how linear thinking doesn't work in a cyclic world," says Hirshberg. "We have a tendency to bring same mistaken thinking to the problems that created the problem in the first place. For example, harvesting bio-material and not putting anything back into the soil doesn't work. Soil is the only true equity that we can build."

Another trend in the food movement is to buy food from local sources, often within a radius of a hundred miles. In the modern food distribution system, food often travels 1,500 miles or farther from farm to store to your home. Among the benefits of buying local food is the reduced impact on climate change because it travels less, requiring fewer transportation resources, generating fewer greenhouse gases as a result.

In Hirshberg's experience this issue is not always so simple. "When you take a factual look as opposed to assumptions, the

> ## Strategies of Green Leaders
>
> See more about Gary Hirshberg and the latest products and environmental efforts at Stonyfield at its website: stonyfield.com. When you are done licking one of their yogurt lids, take a look at the lid—it provides interesting information tidbits as well and an example of creative outreach to customers.

answer can be surprising," says Hirshberg. Stonyfield has often sourced the milk used to make its yogurt from local sources, but when it reexamined its options it found that local was not always superior in terms of its impact on climate change. "We [Stonyfield Farm] looked at organic dried milk powder from New Zealand, which was in surplus there, and found it has 60 percent of the carbon footprint of fluid milk from closer to home. Every farm was organic, so much of the energy expended in the fluid milk system is absent. Organic local farms are great, but the short version of a long story is that we can't make the perfect the enemy of the good."

And looking at only one factor like climate impact can ignore other important issues affecting product quality and its impact on health and the environment. "Carbon is not the whole story," says Hirshberg. "If you focus just on carbon, you might miss toxicity found in some foods that are not organic. Large companies that are shrinking their carbon footprint using plastic might be missing toxicity problems. It's hard to find simple answers because we live in a multivariate world. For every problem there is a solution that is obvious, and wrong."

Based on his many years of experience at Stonyfield, Hirshberg has learned a great deal about what works for green businesses, helping them to grow and succeed, and also learned a great deal about what doesn't work for green entrepreneurs. "There are a couple of keys to be sure," shared Hirshberg. "One is to resist the temptation to compete on price. If you do, you're screwed. You are selling authenticity. When you reduce quality, you have breached the relationship with the consumer. Providing higher quality is the key to differentiate yourself. Most commerce is done on cost reduction."

Rather than competing on cost, Hirshberg advises green businesses to offer high-quality products as he has done with the yogurt from Stonyfield. "What works with green though is to improve quality, to build demand," he says. "Building a green business is never going to work by competing on cost alone, although net margins are the same or better than competitors. The difference is that green businesses spend less on A & P [advertising and promotion] by creating loyalty."

Going this route may not always be easy because there are many pressures on businesses to move in the other direction. "Building a green business is not for the meek; you need to have strong vertebrae," Hirshberg says. "Organic food as an industry is only 3.5 percent of total food. If you are not increasing growth and velocity, take slotting fees. Find a way to grow your supply chain. The only way that you can do that is by maintaining reputation and quality."

Some businesses green entrepreneurs deal with will push in the other direction, pressuring them to lower prices, cutting into profits and forcing compromises on quality. But staying true to your vision will pay off in the long run. "Retailers say 'Give me a deal, give me a promotion.' Wal-Mart never pressures us on price," says Hirshberg. "They have been as honorable as anyone, maybe because they know that if my offering is not as good then it will reflect on them. And always believe in your mission, believe in your ethic, and don't compromise it. If you do, you lose your advantage."

One factor in maintaining quality is to work in concert with your suppliers. Stonyfield has worked to provide a guaranteed price for the organic milk it uses, rather than buying it on the market at the lowest possible price. The result has been to increase the organic milk supply that is available, ensuring sufficient supply to drive the steady growth of its products. "Reward your supply chain, make sure they are partners," advises Hirshberg. "Don't let them become adversaries."

Getting employees on board with producing high-quality green products is another important factor that cannot be

ignored. Communicating goals and getting buy-in from employees makes them a part of your efforts, transforming employees into partners in the success of the business. "Keep your books open to make sure employees see what is going on," says Hirshberg. "Help them understand why we do the things we do. They have to get why we have a zero tolerance on sacrificing quality. My cost of goods are so high, I have to get to a different place. I have to get below the line."

Some of the benefits of greening your business, and the value of communicating, are through the impact on employees, attracting the best talent to work in a business engaged in a purpose that they can share and believe in. "Going green improves retention, employee loyalty, and pride," says Hirshberg. "What do employees want? They want wages, and meaningful work. To find the right chemistry, and get up to speed, it takes new employees six months to contribute. Employers understand that the cost of losing a good person is incalculable, and see the value in making the change. Everybody wants to do the right thing, if they can find a way to do it."

Although organic food and organic farming are a small percentage of our food today, they may grow in the future to become the predominant way of producing food. "It's easy to predict that organic food will grow and become predominant," says Hirshberg. "Conventional food depletes the soil and resources, and organics are the opposite, putting carbon in soil. And the price of oil will drive this, raising the price of food grown with conventional methods. It's hard to say when it will happen, when organic will become the standard way of growing our food, but it will."

CHAPTER

 2

Finding the Right Opportunity:

RISE

So you want to start a green business. What kind of business will it be? Every business starts with the vision of an entrepreneur. What business do you envision and how will it make money? You need a plan to realize success. You may not have all the answers upfront. The plan may change over time, but as Steven Covey counsels in his book *The 7 Habits of Highly Successful People*, "Begin with the end in mind."

Not every opportunity or business structure is right for every person. This chapter will guide you through finding the business that is right for you.

What Are the Opportunities for Green Businesses?

In my book *75 Green Businesses You Can Start to Make Money and Make a Difference,* I describe businesses providing clean energy, water, food, buildings, and many other products and services. I might be biased, but I think *75 Green Businesses* is a good place to start if you're looking for business opportunities that a wide range of people can pursue. Every day I hear about creative new ventures that green entrepreneurs are building. Of course there are more than 75 green business opportunities in the world—the possibilities are endless and the ingenuity of entrepreneurs never ceases to surprise me.

Where else to find opportunities? By being a sponge when it comes to current events and ideas. Read a great deal: books, magazines, newspapers, and blogs. There will be a huge need for solar installers, organic farmers, and producers of organic T-shirts in the green economy, but the opportunities

Resource Guide

Another great resource is Scott Cooney's book *Build a Green Small Business*, which describes green business opportunities and strategies for a broad range of green-thinking entrepreneurs. Cooney and I think alike in many ways; both of us focusing on solutions entrepreneurs can provide to make a profit and help the environment.

do not end there. Keep your eyes and ears open. Ideas can come from anywhere. Talk to people, including the green and the not-so-green people. Often businesses get started as a result of everyday events. You'll be talking to someone in line at the grocery store, and suddenly it will hit you, "Why don't they ____?" And importantly, listen to yourself in addition to listening to others. Not your doubts and fears, but the creative place deep inside. If you have a hunch, don't dismiss it. Don't bet the bank on it right off, but at least write it down and look into it.

If you open your mind, the next great green opportunity will be there for you. You have to find what works for you, but the opportunity is out there waiting for you to find it. It might be right in front of you already.

The Right Opportunity

What kind of business opportunity will you pursue? While there are a great variety of opportunities, I believe there is no one-size-fits-all green business opportunity. Learn from others and adapt it to work for you.

Finding Opportunity

There is a mind trap that people often get into that prevents them from pursuing their ideas. They have an idea and then think "If it's such a good idea, I'm sure someone's doing it already." And so they look around and don't see it happening, but then someone says, "Well, if nobody else is doing it, that there's something wrong with the idea." It's a trap. Don't get stuck in it.

I also believe that pursuing the path of least resistance can be a great way to go. Before leaping into the unknown, think about taking advantage of opportunities that are close to your existing skills, knowledge, and resources. There is a place for leaping, but if an opportunity is knocking right on your door, check it out first before you leap in some other direction. Why make things harder than they have to be?

The place to start is by taking stock of your personal inventory, the resources you already have today. Clear your mind and take a fresh look at you, thinking about who you are and what you have to offer. Think about it honestly—for you, and not for anyone else—allowing a bit of positive spin to silence your doubts for the moment. You have more going for you than you imagine.

Figure 2.1—**The Resource Inventory Self-Evaluation (RISE)**

The questions to ask yourself in the self-inventory are:

· What professional experience do you have?_____

_____

· What internal resources do you have to offer (skills, knowledge, talents, and personality)? _____

_____

· What external resources do you have to work with (time, money, equipment, office space, car)? _____

_____

· Where are you geographically and what kind of opportunities are there in your region? _____

_____

· What excites you? _____

_____

Be honest when answering these questions.

Questions like those listed in Figure 2.1 can help focus your thinking. By writing down answers to these questions, you can evaluate where you are today. One rule as you write down your assets: Don't list your limitations, only your assets. If you don't have much time, don't write: "I have no time to start anything." Same goes for money. Instead you can say "I have time at night, for two hours every day" or maybe even once a week. This approach helps keep things productive and positive, rather than grinding to a halt before you even start.

Starting Green

Assessing Your Professional Experience

Many green businesses are greener versions of existing businesses. Look at the industries you have worked in, the types of businesses where you have experience. Is there a green business opportunity waiting for you based on one of these? You've probably invested years of time and effort getting to where you are in your professional life, so it's worth thinking through the opportunities that lie closest to where you stand. If there isn't a green version of your business yet, that's an opportunity to be the one who creates it. Even if you hope to jump to an entirely new industry, your training, network, and other transferable skills should not be discounted. A few examples:

- *Are you a plumber?* What about starting a business as a green plumber, specializing in water conservation and recycled plumbing fixtures (sinks, tubs, faucets)?
- *Are you an electrician?* You could start a business as a green electrician, emphasizing energy-efficient lighting, solar power, and home automation.
- *Are you a landscaper?* You could open a green landscaping business, providing low-water-use plants, electric mowers, and organic gardening (see Clean Air Lawn Care in Chapter 8).
- *Do you work in construction?* You can study up on green building methods, building on what you already know, and get involved in the green building field as an energy efficiency auditor or contractor (see Chapter 9).
- *Do you have a retail clothing store?* It's not a leap then to create a green clothing store, changing what you sell and revamping your retail space to be greener.
- *Do you have a stationery or office supply store?* How about changing over to a green office supply store, selling recycled and eco-friendly products?

🍃 *Are you a printer?* You can open a green printing business, using recycled paper products and eco-friendly dyes (see Chapter 5).

🍃 *You're a real estate agent?* Guess what, you could be a green real estate agent, focusing on green homes, and greening homes (see Chapter 8).

🍃 *You own a restaurant?* You're in luck! You can change over to a green restaurant format, serving local, organic, vegetarian, and healthy food in a green building (see Pizza Fusion, Chapter 8).

And so on—you get the idea.

Do you have any professional certifications or permits? Are you a licensed contractor? Have you been to professional training courses? These could be important assets, no matter what you do. See what you can do with them before you walk away from the time you've invested here.

Your resume is a good place to start. Is your resume up to date and complete? Even if you are thinking of a new business and not a new job, your resume can help to remind you of the experience you have in your asset column. You probably have more experience going for you than you realize. What have you left off of your resume? It's probably more important to think about the professional skills and experience you have than the positions you have held. Be specific, brief, and honest. Don't edit yourself the first time around—just let it flow and come back to edit later. This is for you, not for anyone else.

Assessing Your Internal Resources

Your resume is your history, but it does not tell the whole story. Your assets go far beyond what you done in your professional life and also include what you hold inside, a wealth of skills, knowledge, talents, and unique personality traits that all add up to make you who you are. These may not be on your resume. What classes and training courses have you taken? What languages do you know? Do you like working with your hands? Do you love organizing things? Are you good with numbers? Are you an extrovert or an introvert?

Think about your hobbies, things you like to do outside of work, or things you once did in the past. In his best-selling book *Start Late and Finish Rich*, David Bach tells the story of a man who comes to him and says he has no skills other than putting rear axles on cars, which he had been doing for decades in an auto assembly plant. After some discussion it turned out that the man had been doing the books for the Boy Scouts and picked up some accounting skills at home as a result, something he could build on for a new career direction.

Perhaps you are an accountant by day, but an avid organic gardener on weekends, organizing a community garden. Maybe it comes to you in a flash that you don't really like accounting, but you love working in the garden. You think you could make a living of landscaping. Maybe there is a huge need in your area for landscaping that is more drought-tolerant, and uses organic methods. Next thing you know, you're on your way. See Figure 2.2, Internal Resource Evaluation, for help here.

Going green at home is a hobby for many. Do you have a compost heap in your backyard? Have you read up on the health hazards of indoor air and started looking for no VOC paint at your hardware store? Are you tinkering to fix your old appliances and

Resource Guide

There are a variety of self-assessment tools available to illuminate what might work best for you, tools like the Myers-Briggs Type Indicator® (MBTI), which sorts personality traits on four different axes. If you are honest with such tests, they can tell you a lot about yourself. There are many variations on this, like the Kingdomality test (Kingdomality.com). Send me an e-mail to tell me how the test came out for you, and I'll tell you what I got when I took the test.

*Figure 2.2—***Internal Resource Evaluation**

Consider these questions when assessing your skills, knowledge, and talent.

· *What type of computer skills do you have?* Maybe an online business would work for you if you are a techno-savvy person. _____

_____

· *Do you like selling things?* Every green business needs someone selling it. You might use low-cost, word of mouth, but this still involves old fashioned marketing, getting out and talking to people one on one._____

_____

· *How do you feel about teaching?* Education and training are important themes running through the green business world and this book. Could your business be teaching, training, or coaching?

_____

· *Are you good with mechanical objects and electrical work?* Are you a contractor? There could be a powerful opportunity waiting for you in renewable energy, such as starting a solar installation business or doing energy efficiency retrofits. Maybe your business could be repairing appliances, saving resources by bringing back to life objects that would otherwise be thrown away.

_____

· *How about craft work?* Have you thought about making something from recycled material, like clothing, bags, or furniture?_____

_____

· *Do you like the outdoors?* Maybe you can work in organic lawn care, farming, or environmental monitoring._____

_____

save resources rather than throwing them away? Do you pester your friends and neighbors to change their old light bulbs to compact fluorescent bulbs? Maybe you can use this experience to fashion a new business.

It always helps to have a good grasp of all of the resources you have, including your own past history, but you don't have to feel restricted to what your resume has on it already. You may decide to set out in a new direction, away from the beaten path, because you are dissatisfied with what you've been doing and ready for a new challenge, a leap into new territory. People often make big changes in their work lives, and while change can be frightening, it can also be very rewarding. One of the silver linings I've heard about times of economic turmoil is that people who lost their jobs and were initially in terror eventually found new opportunities that were even better than what they were doing before, often by taking the leap and following their dream. Necessity has been the mother of some great new businesses. When you are cut loose from your job, there can be some real freedom in having nothing to lose.

Look before you leap, and sketch out the skills sets you might need in the new field. Don't quit your day job yet if you can't afford to and need to fill in some gaps before getting started. Talk

Finding Opportunity

The deep economic crisis of late has caused great difficulty for millions of people, but there is something larger occurring here than just a downturn—it is a shift in a new direction that is creating new opportunities. See *The New York Times* article "Job Losses Hint at Vast Remaking of Economy" (March 7, 2009), and another from the Associated Press: "Obama: Time of crisis can be 'great opportunity.'" The economy is changing in a big way, shifting beneath our feet. Try to stay on your feet and see where things are going, then get ahead of the curve. See also the conclusion of this book about the emergence of the Conserver Economy.

to people who work in the field you are interested in to get the real story from people with real world experience. The internet can be a great resource, but it's no substitute for talking to real people. You read some crazy things on the internet, let me tell you.

Assessing Your External Resources

Starting a business is not always quick or easy. It can take money, time, and other resources. What kind of money can you bring to the table? This might flavor the type of opportunity that you pursue. You might have only a small amount of money to commit to your business, a few hundred or a few thousand dollars, but if you have a great idea that drives you, that ignites you, that keeps you up at night, then you can decide to get going with what you have and bootstrap your way forward.

Thinking about money should not keep you from getting started, but it should at least be considered and solutions developed to deal realistically with where you stand today. Knowing your financial status can help you decide what kind of opportunity to take on and when. For some, it's surprisingly difficult to determine their precise financial situation because they're really not sure what is going on with their money. Getting a firm grasp of your personal finances is an important step leading up to developing your business. Running your credit report and seeing where you stand with your assets and debts will prepare you for when others, such as a bank, are asking you these same questions.

Time is another key resource. Starting a business is almost never easy; it takes time and dedication to make most things work. How much time can

Resource Guide

One note about the money—it does not all have to come from you. Starting a business with your savings is a great option, but not everyone can do it that way. There are other ways to get your business started (see Chapter 4).

you bring to the business you want to start? Busy moms often seek businesses they can start at home, allowing them to work flexible hours, and with low upfront costs. Luckily, there are some green options that meet this need (see Chapter 12).

On the other hand, if you have money now, and want to get up to speed quickly in a business, a franchise is an option to consider, perhaps one of the green franchise options discussed in Chapter 8.

If you're not employed currently, look on the bright side—you've got the time on your hands to start something new. Turn this into one of your strengths, using sweat equity (hard work) and your time to get a start on that business you were always thinking of. Difficult economic times are an engine of entrepreneurial creativity, with people starting new ventures left and right because they suddenly find themselves with abundant time and even more abundant motivation. Necessity really is the mother of invention, and It can be one mean mother at that. See Figure 2.3, Practical Resource Evaluation, for help here.

---

*Figure 2.3—***Practical Resource Evaluation**

There are other practical resources that you should list as assets on your blank sheet of paper: Answer the following questions as fully as possible.

· Do you have a car? Does it have room to carry stuff? Is it an eco-friendly car you can use to deliver eco-friendly goods? _____

_____

· Do you have space at home you can use for your business? Can you use it as an office? Are you a tinkerer, with room in your garage to work on assembling your prototype? _____

_____

*Figure 2.3—***Practical Resource Evaluation,** continued

- Do you have a phone, internet access, and computer? _____

  _____

- Do you have tools? Are they tools of a specialized trade, like an electrician's gear or a carpenter? _____

  _____

- Do you have an extensive list of contacts and business acquaintances? If so, in what types of industries? _____

  _____

Your Location and Regional Opportunities

Where do you live? Geography can have clear implications for business opportunities. While there are certainly green business opportunities in San Francisco, London, and Boise, the opportunities in each of these places may be distinct in many ways. Wherever you are, what's going on there in your local community? Most businesses start locally, even if their owners have global dreams. Relating closely to your local community gives you strong roots to grow.

The local weather affects the business opportunities that can be found there. Cool reflective roofing is of greater interest in Arizona than Maine. Growing sugarcane is great in Brazil, but not so great in most of the United States.

One aspect of geography is the unique incentives and regulations provided by the governments that have an impact on opportunity (see Chapter 7). The development of the green scene in Copenhagen is quite distinct from the United States, in part because of strong incentives and regulations supporting green habits, such as the huge gas tax that has been in place there for many years. Looking to Europe or Japan may reveal opportunities as efforts on energy efficiency, waste reduction, and climate change exert more pressure on the U.S. market.

> ### Tip for Success
> Your local business network is an essential component of your local geography. Green businesses you can network with in your region are one resource, but the broader business community is another valuable resource that you should plug into to reach a broader market.

Your locality also influences available resources. Green businesses often emphasize local sourcing of materials when possible. What is produced where you live? Are there factories in your town producing waste that you might turn into products? If you have access to a wealth of corncobs or wood dust from a factory nearby, what can you do with these?

Geography can affect demand for products. The green building market or the demand for solar power systems are not evenly distributed across the United States. What are people looking for where you live? Is there a new more stringent building code that has just been implemented, leading more homeowners to invest in insulation or water conservation hardware? The trends in green building, solar, and organic food often tend to take hold on the east and west coasts of the United States and move out from there. If you are in one of the states without a great deal of green business activity today, this is not cause for despair; it might just mean that there is lots of room for green business to grow there in the future, to catch the wave as it sweeps your way.

Choose Excitement

Let's assume that your business is going to succeed. Close your eyes and imagine how it will look once it is up and running. Is it

a store? How will it look, and how will the customers be interacting with you? How do you feel about it?

Over and over again, people advise us to pursue something that excites us, something we really care about. "Follow your bliss," Joseph Campbell says. I think this is good advice. Perhaps you know someone who has labored dutifully for years to pay the bills, and done OK, but secretly hated it. Maybe it's you. Life is short. If you are going to pour your time, money, and energy into starting a new business, you will be happier and more likely to succeed if you find something that really turns you on and keeps you going through the rough spots. What gets you so excited when you think about it that you can't wait to start? The answer to this could decide what business direction you want to take. If you are really on fire about an idea, you will work to overcome all obstacles to get where you want to be.

Luckily green businesses are easy to believe in and get excited about. People are drawn to green businesses because of their connection to helping the environment, helping people, and to building a better world for all of us to share. Connecting to this kind of deep purpose unleashes your energy as well as that of your employees, your suppliers, and your customers. If you are making a good living in your current career or business but are still dissatisfied, then this sort of purpose and meaning may be what you are missing.

Whatever business you start, if you are not excited about it, then it's going to be a long hard slog after the initial enthusiasm wears off. In exploring what excites you, you may realize that your true bliss is helping people learn to read or devoting yourself to wildlife preservation, and not really starting a business at all. It's best to know this before you start. Working through an environmental nonprofit or becoming a social entrepreneur might be the answer for you.

3

From Green Dreams to Open Doors

Having taken stock of your inventory, it's time to get down to the nuts and bolts. What is your plan to breathe life into your business? What product or service will you sell and to whom? How will the business help the environment? How will the business be structured? However well-intentioned, green businesses will only survive and help the planet if they have clear answers to these questions, laying out a plan.

Your Plan

Once you have a vision of the business you want to create, how will you get there? Your plan is your map to find your way. While green businesses are often rich in passion about the environment, they sometimes fall down on business basics like having a plan. The further you go with your business, the more of a problem this will become. A full-blown formal business plan may not be necessary to get started, but you owe it to yourself, your investors, and your partners to at least flesh out the basics of how, where, and when you plan to make money. Writing a full business plan is so imposing that it can stop some people in their tracks, but a full-blown plan is often not necessary. You might need a formal business plan for raising money from some investors, but a simpler, shorter plan can often be just as good to start, if not better in some ways.

I recommend *The One Page Business Plan* by Jim Horan. It's a book that is not just for passively reading, but for active participation. It asks questions and leads you through exercises to help you to refine your ideas for your business. Part of its power is its simplicity. For whatever business you envision, the book walks you through the process of creating a simple one-page plan that includes:

- 🍃 your vision,
- 🍃 the mission,
- 🍃 objectives,
- 🍃 strategies, and
- 🍃 plans.

The business plan is not something you produce just to satisfy the requirements of others. One of the benefits of writing

Resource Guide

Throughout the book I shall sketch out one-page plans for a few green businesses as examples using the layout provided by *The One Page Business Plan*. Of course, these are only examples. Your plan will ultimately be one that only you can create.

down the plan is to help you better understand your own business. "The most important reason to have a business plan is to clarify your thinking, regardless of the size of your company," writes Horan. By keeping it short, the plan is simple, concrete, and meaningful to the person writing it out.

Business plan consultants can add the extra polish that your plan needs for your business expansion or startup. A few things to keep in mind when finding a consultant to help with your plan:

Resource Guide

Mia Moore and her associate MBAs have experience writing plans since 2001. They can provide a professionally written business plan at a price that you name. Find out more at Nameyourpricebiz plans.com.

1. Business plan consultants should be available for you and should have great communication skills. They should have working hours where you can reach them and have questions answered.
2. They need to have experience to assist you. You can ask to see a sample of their work, ask for testimonials, and look at a resume of their past accomplishments.
3. Whoever you work with needs to be available at a price that makes sense for both of you.

As the founder of Nameyourpricebizplans, Mia Moore helps entrepreneurs get started with business planning. She suggests that entrepreneurs start with answers to essential questions: "What resources will you need? Who is your market? What will you do? I suggest developing a basic Who, What, When, Why, Where, and How plan," says Moore.

The questions she suggests addressing are:

🍃 Who will you serve?
🍃 What will you do for them?

🍃 When will your business get started?

🍃 Where will you serve or sell? Will you be online? Local? National? At home? In a store? In an office?

🍃 Why do people need your services or products? Why would they buy from you?

🍃 How will you provide your services?

🍃 What resources do you need to get started and to operate (time, money, contacts, inventory, supplies, other human resources, etc)?

🍃 How will you function every day? How will your ideal and not-so-ideal day go?

"Once you have developed your Who, What, When, Why, and Where plan, then use the How part of your plan to figure out how to implement the process of making money from your talents," says Moore. "Make to-do lists that can be carried out on a quarterly, monthly, weekly, and daily basis."

Your Product

There are some fundamental questions you need to ask yourself when planning your business. One essential question you need to have crystalline clarity about is "What is your product?" This might seem obvious, but the answer is not always as simple as you think. For example, if you are planning to sell organic cotton T-shirts, then the answer seems obvious. But is it? Are you going to open a store selling the shirts, or are you selling designs for shirts that someone else uses to produce them? Are you going to buy blank tees and do silk screening yourself, or have someone else do it? Are you selling them on the internet, at the beach, or in a retail space at the mall?

If you have an idea for an innovative home design, do you want to build homes and sell them, do you want to license your technology to someone else, or do you want to have a design studio selling your services and leave all of the actual construction and selling of buildings to someone else?

You might feel you already have a clear vision in your mind, but putting it on paper can reveal the holes in your ideas that you weren't aware of. If you have an idea for something you can make, think through what you are actually going to sell. Another helpful step is having someone else read your plan early on. The right person will see gaps and ask good questions, without just shooting you down. Hopefully this person can provide constructive alternatives if needed, joining in the creative process with you. Early feedback can save a lot of time in the long run, and saved time is saved money.

If your product is innovative, do you need to patent it? A patent can be a valuable demonstration and add value for technical products. Investors like the idea of investing in a patented product or process because this is a solid asset that can be bought, sold, or licensed. Trade secrets are another form of protection for products that might be worth considering in some cases.

Tip for Success

A word of advice, don't rely solely on family members for your constructive criticism. Family is golden, but they may not be entirely objective. You want honesty, but it may work out better if criticism comes from someone you are not too closely involved with and who can keep some perspective on your ideas.

The product development process has a big influence on your final product. Being able to produce a prototype goes a long way in convincing people that you are the real deal, that you have "traction," as they say. When it comes time to produce a prototype, the rubber starts to hit the road. Any problems with your initial vision will be revealed. If the materials do not perform the way you hoped or are too expensive, you may need to go back to the drawing board, while staying true to your vision.

Customers

When you have a clear vision of your product or service, you'll be excited about getting started. Maybe you even have a prototype or some samples ready to go. Time to get started, right? But there are still more questions, including questions about your market. Who are you selling to?

If you say "everyone," you need to clarify your vision before you go any further. There are not many things that appeal to everyone on the planet. Maybe breathing. Who your market is says a great deal about what your product is, how it works, and how you can sell it. What is your target age group? Men or women? Income level? What benefits of your products are you selling? Do you sell online or retail? How can you market your product to reach your target market? It's hard to have all the answers when you start, but the more you know the better. Chapter 6 is all about marketing.

One quick comment. There is not just one green market. There are a diverse group of people who buy green products for many different reasons. All the more reason to give your markets careful consideration. Tools like demographics can help to describe the people you need to communicate with, those who are most likely to be interested in what you have to offer.

Starting to sell some of your early product and produce revenue is another important demonstration of traction for your budding business. Then not only do you have a real product, but it has a real market.

Your Environmental Credentials

A green business is a unique creature—a business that is about more than making money. Not every startup worries if it's doing the right thing for the environment. For some green businesses their contribution to the environment is so fundamental to the business, so central to their purpose, that they write this goal of the business right into their by-laws.

The details are up to you. You might demonstrate an environmental benefit in a different way than others have, and the impact may be direct or indirect. The environmental aspects of your business and products are among the benefits of the products you sell.

Environmental or other green benefits can include:

- Reducing pollution
- Saving energy and money
- Reducing exposure to potentially hazardous chemicals
- Switching from oil-based to renewable products
- Stimulating local economies
- Ensuring fair wages, fair trade, and fair labor practices
- Designing products that can be reused as new products
- Saving water and reducing consumption of other resources
- Preserving biodiversity and habitats
- Avoiding depletion of fisheries, forests, and other natural resources
- Preserving ecosystems that perform essential services we depend on and that generate economic activity
- Reducing greenhouse gas emissions
- Helping people live better, healthier, and more meaningful lives

In addition to having these environmental benefits embedded in your products and services, you need a way to communicate this information to consumers for it to influence their buying decisions. Timberland is working to label its shoes with tags describing their environmental benefits such as climate impact, what kind of chemicals they use, and how much energy or other resources were used. Other businesses are exploring ways to communicate the climate impact of their products, making it a key part of the brand.

Making Money

Last but not least, how will your business make money? This is a biggie. You might think this part goes without saying, but surprisingly, this is not always true. Very often people focus first on the ideas for what they can do, for an interesting product or service they could deliver, but become so close to their idea, so wrapped up in it, that they lose track of how it will make money, how it will actually be a business.

An example of this problem is an entrepreneur with an idea for a product that is an impressive technical feat but not necessarily a viable business: "I can produce a piano made entirely of FSC-certified hardwood and reclaimed metals, making it the first completely eco-friendly piano." Now, I've never built a piano, but I'm pretty sure that would be quite a feat. Still, is there a market for an eco-friendly piano? Is this something that piano purchasers are looking for? How much will the eco-friendly piano cost to build and how much are consumers willing to pay? How big is the market for eco-friendly pianos? No matter how impressive a feat producing an eco-friendly piano is, it's not a business if nobody buys it for more than it costs you to produce it.

> ### Send Your Stories
>
> I hope I'm not talking about your business here. Let me know if your business is eco-friendly pianos. I'm sure it's a great business, right?

Another category of entrepreneur is focused on solving an environmental problem and has an idea for a way to do this, but upon closer inspection there is no obvious form of revenue. No money means no business. For example, you want to plant trees to prevent watershed degradation. That's a worthy goal. But who are you selling trees to? Who is paying you to plant them? Planting the trees alone is not a business if it does not produce revenue.

Often assumptions built into your business plan affect your prospects for making money. Does the price of oil need to be higher than $100 per barrel before you make money? It's OK to have assumptions, as long as you know what they are and how they affect your plan. If oil needs to be $100 a barrel for your business to make money and you figure this out beforehand, at least you know where you stand when oil sinks to $40 a barrel and stays there. Bigger problems come from hidden assumptions, the things that you assumed from the start without even thinking about them.

Making a Business Out of It

Saving the rain forest alone may not be a business. If you are acquiring land to preserve a forest that would otherwise have been cleared and can sell offsets for the net reduction in greenhouse gas emissions by keeping carbon locked inside trees rather than being released into the atmosphere, then you're talking business.

It's Still a Business, Silly
(ISABS, or "It's OK to Make Money")

Including consideration of the environment can help any business I believe, and is essential for green businesses. The world needs more of this. But (and this is a big but) businesses need to make a profit, including the old-fashioned financial kind, or they won't survive.

It's good to be aware of your attitudes about money and how they are shaping your thinking as you plan and develop your business. If you are committed to making the greatest possible profit at any costs, environmental or otherwise, a green business is probably not the way for you to go. Similarly, if you don't care a whit about making money and feel making money means that you have sold out and turned your back on the environment, you might not be ready for running a business, green or otherwise. A pitfall some green entrepreneurs run into is that

they are uncomfortable making money, and this pervades what they do. Use Figure 3.1 to help you arrive at your attitude about making money.

When speaking with a green entrepreneur several months ago, I asked him how business was. "Bad, really slow," he said, complaining that people did not see the necessity of buying his product, and how the world of business had driven our world into the ground because capitalism doesn't work. It was all going to collapse in about six months, he predicted, not just a crisis but THE END. I was shocked, but it made sense of things. If you are convinced that business is wrong and the end is near, you will probably not do a great job at working toward a positive future.

It comes out when I talk to people about the efforts of some larger businesses to green what they do. "Sure, but they're just doing it for the money" is a common objection. Another version is "All businesses care about is making money."

These statements also reveal the internal conflict these people are struggling with. The difficulties that some green entrepreneurs encounter may not be the result of external forces such as the market, the economy, and the competition. They may reflect what is going on in their mind. Some green entrepreneurs run into a basic conflict: Doing the right thing seems to run counter to making money for them. It's funny, but they are the mirror image of folks who believe that if you do the right thing for the environment you can't make money. Both sides hold the fundamental belief that making money and helping the environment are opposites that cannot coexist.

If you make money, then you're just part of the problem, right? If you have this inner conflict about making money, it will color and shape the decisions you make, holding you back.

It's OK for a green business to make money. In fact, it's more than OK—it's essential. Your business will disappear if you fail to

Figure 3.1—**Evaluating Your Attitudes about Money**

Here's a quick quiz for you to probe your attitudes about money. Look at each of the following statements and answer yes or no:

1. I'd like to make more money, but I'm not sure how. _____

2. I think businesses can make money and still do the right thing for the environment. _____

3. I would make more money but people just don't understand what I'm trying to do. _____

4. Making money causes all of the problems we face. _____

5. I'm not interested in making money—it's not what I'm in business for. _____

6. If money got us into this problem, it will only get us in deeper. _____

7. Capitalism is wrong. _____

🍃 🍃 🍃

How many statements did you agree with? _____

If you agree with the first statement, you have a pretty normal level of uncertainty that needs to be clarified.

If you agree with the second statement, I think you are right on track.

If you said yes for question 3, your lack of external clarity may reflect a lack of clarity in your own thinking.

If you answered yes to questions 4 through 7, you might want to think a little about how your money attitudes might impact your business.

make money. Failure to make money means failure to have an impact on the world, no matter how well-intentioned your goals are. I'm not saying to do anything wrong or immoral and I'm not being the Green Gordon Gekko. It's not that Green Greed is Good. But properly regulated, morally and environmentally sound capitalism is not just OK, it could be the thing that saves both the economy and the environment. Capitalism funnels capital to fuel innovation. Do the right thing, and make money while you're doing it, that's all I'm saying.

Think about your motivations. Examine your feelings about making money. If you really want to help the environment, and are not very interested in making money, maybe what you really want is to pursue a different course. Working through some of these questions before you start might avoid heartache and headaches later on.

Green Nonprofits

Starting a green nonprofit is another great option, of course. Focus on a cause if this is your passion. Some organizations create both a for-profit and a nonprofit that can play off of each other's strengths. See GreenNonProfits and CEO Ted Hart at greennon profits.org, to start earning points to get certified as a green nonprofit.

Your Business Structure

There are many books and resources about working with different types of business structures. The options available are not fundamentally different for green businesses than for anyone else. I'll mention them quickly, and let you peruse the wealth of other resources to dig into more depth about your choices.

Getting started even with an LLC can still take a little time, and there's paperwork to sort through. You can probably do this yourself, without a lawyer, but there are other options. If you'd like a little help, there are businesses that will take care of filing paperwork for you. BizFilings.com is one, and there are others. It costs a little more than doing it yourself, but still I'm talking a few hundred dollars. For more complex situations, you might want a lawyer to help you and to make sure everything is on the up and up. A little money spent on a lawyer upfront could avoid a lot of money and headaches later.

A quick note. Whatever business structure you set up, you will need to take a few steps to keep it legal. Make sure whatever business licenses you need are in order. You will probably require a local business license, and for some particular types of businesses such as those for serving or preparing food other licenses and permits may be required. You need to comply with accounting requirements, tax payments, payroll issues, labor laws, and industry-specific regulations. If you are selling retail, you will need a seller's permit, or merchant's license. The requirements vary from place to place, and while much of this can be done by you, having assistance can help you to sort through it all and get it done more rapidly.

Resource Guide

The work done by Bizfilings.com is not limited to green businesses, but it can whiz you through the paperwork to start a business. For LLCs, you can also go to sites like myllc.com, which features Jennifer Reuting, the author of *Limited Liability Companies for Dummies* (For Dummies, 2007).

The Not-So-Fine Print

Disclaimer here, I'm not a lawyer, nor do I play one on TV. Consult a lawyer if you have any questions of a legal nature. It will probably cost you some money, but will be worth it in the long run.

Sole Proprietorship

The simplest type of business is a sole proprietorship. Whenever

someone operates a business alone, he or she by default is a sole proprietor. A business license alone is just about all you need in many cases (unless the type of business has a statutory requirement for permits or licenses, such as for medicine, providing food, being a lawyer, investment advisor, etc.). Simplicity is a big part of the upside of doing business this way, and millions of people do.

For a sole proprietorship, the taxes flow through to the individual running the business because basically the individual is the business—in the eyes of the IRS they are the same. This is in general viewed positively because of its simplicity, again.

The downside is that a sole proprietorship offers no liability protection. Liability protection of your personal assets requires that you and your business are distinct entities. If you are a sole proprietor, there is no distinction between you and your business, and your personal assets are completely on the line in the event of a lawsuit, whether the asset is involved in the business or not. This is a pretty big downside that drives many entrepreneurs to seek other options.

Also, if you want to sell equity in the company, there is no means to do it with a sole proprietorship. You can't really sell a piece of yourself.

Partnership

A partnership is an arrangement in which two or more people join together and share assets as well as debts, but without a corporate structure. According to Jennifer Reuting, author of *Limited Liability Companies for Dummies*, a general partnership often can be formed without any paperwork or filings, with two or more people. While partners can share in the profits from a business, they also share in any and all liability. And because a partnership is not a corporation and is the sum of the people in it, it provides no liability protection. If one of the partners runs afoul of a client, all of the partners can be wiped out in a lawsuit.

Limited Liability Partnership (LLP)

Don't let the name fool you—there is plenty of liability to go around for all of the general partners who are involved in running the business, and that means you, if you're reading this book. Investors and the like who can share the profits but don't run the business are called limited partners. In the event of a problem with the business, the limited partners can avoid personal liability, but the general partners are still on the hook for everything.

Arthur Andersen, the once mighty consulting giant, was organized in LLPs. When Andersen was sued over dealings with Enron, the damage was not limited to those who had done work with Enron. It affected all of the general partners, and the business was decimated.

Limited Liability Corporation (LLC)

For many people LLCs offer the best of both worlds. They are still quite simple to set up, although there is a little more work than with sole proprietorships, and the taxation is simple, flowing through to the LLC members. LLCs , however, can provide effective liability protection for you and your personal assets. The key is to create and maintain the LLC as a distinct entity from your personal affairs. If you want it to be treated as a business by others, you need to treat it as a business yourself, keeping the money distinct and keeping your paperwork in order.

The rules for LLCs vary from state to state. Many people favor Delaware and Nevada as places to form LLCs because of the low taxes, simple procedures, and strong case law (particularly in Delaware).

S Corporation

S corps were once the business structure of choice, but LLCs are becoming more popular for many businesses. Like an LLC, owners

Starting Green

in an S corp are protected from liability but can have flow-through of profits to their own personal taxes, preventing the business income from getting taxed twice. There are also some key differences that can become important along the way. S corporations have a limit on the number of shareholders, while LLCs can have an unlimited number of shareholders. LLCs also have greater flexibility in their management structure, including who does the management and how they do it.

There are also advantages of S corporations compared to LLCs. The stock of S corps can be readily sold to other people, while owners of an LLC must get permission from the other members before selling their interest.

Employee Participation in Equity

One way to get employees engaged in the business is to make them part owners, giving them equity. In a small business, everybody can have a big impact on the performance of the business, and providing equity quickly can get people excited about the prospects of growing the business. Profit sharing can do the same thing.

Green Leaders
RAY ANDERSON AND JIM HARTZFELD OF INTERFACE

(adapted from *PRNews*, Case Studies in Outstanding Green Business Practices)

As you work to start your business, there will be a hundred voices along the way saying it cannot be done or that you must water down, redirect, or rework your idea beyond recognition. Some of these voices will come

ANDERSON AND HARTZFELD, CONTINUED

from within, from your own inner doubts. Sometimes your advisors will have wise thoughts and concerns that it's important to listen to, but staying true to your vision is important. As Polonius says in *Hamlet*, "To thine own self be true."

Ray Anderson is widely recognized today as a successful green business leader, someone who has paved the way for others. His company, Interface Inc., is a leader in floor coverings, specializing in floor tiles for commercial space. Although he is a green leader today, his story may not be what you expect. The carpet and floor covering business has historically been one with a heavy environmental toll. Interface was already a rapidly growing business that was a success by most standards in 1994 when someone asked Anderson about his environmental policy and he realized that he did not really have one beyond environmental compliance and had not given it much thought. When reading Paul Hawken's book *The Ecology of Commerce*, he experienced a sudden change of heart, a "spear in the chest moment," and embarked on a mission for Interface to become a sustainable floor-covering business.

Anderson's story is related in his book *Mid-Course Correction* (Peregrinzilla Press, 1999), essential reading for green entrepreneurs. Working with an Interface team that included Jim Hartzfeld and others, he has steadily reduced Interface's environmental impact to be more sustainable. Learning what works, the team now has a great deal to teach others—and it does.

Often people assume that making money runs counter to doing the right thing for the environment. We've often heard this, that environmental action will greatly increase the price of everything. The work of

ANDERSON AND HARTZFELD, CONTINUED

green pioneers like Interface has demonstrated though that it can be done, that a business can reduce its environmental impact while becoming more successful than ever. "There is no choice to be made between the environment and the economy," Anderson observes. Interface has reduced its greenhouse gas emissions 90 percent since 1994 through a combination of renewable energy, energy efficiency, and carbon offsets. The incorporation of renewable resources in products has increased to 19 percent and water consumption is down by 79 percent relative to production. Anderson estimated in 2007 the company is about 45 to 50 percent of the way toward sustainability, all while growing a successful business.

Jim Hartzfeld is the founder and managing director of InterfaceRAISE, the consulting group at Interface that advises others on how to green their businesses. When he investigated how Interface succeeded in being more sustainable, he found that the lessons were not just about floor covering or environmental issues, but about business fundamentals that every company faces, including reducing costs, increasing productivity, building a brand, and accessing talent. Advising diverse businesses in fields such as aviation, foods, and textiles, he has found that many of the same principles apply, no matter what industry is involved.

Wasting energy, materials, and water also wastes money. One of the benefits to going green and reducing waste is the money it can save a business, money that goes right to the bottom line. Interface has avoided over $350 million in costs through its environmental efforts over a period of 12 years, making money by saving money.

ANDERSON AND HARTZFELD, CONTINUED

One of the biggest obstacles Hartzfeld has encountered in working with businesses is the common management mindset that going green is too expensive. To get around this, he helps clients create a plan to start small with low-cost measures in areas like energy efficiency that can pay for themselves quickly. InterfaceRAISE has worked with companies as large as Wal-Mart, helping them save money with efficiency measures such as using LED lighting in refrigerator cases, increasing efficiency of stores, encouraging more efficient transportation in their supply chain, and working with suppliers to reduce packaging.

Anderson describes the steps needed to move a business toward environmental sustainability as the seven faces of Mt Sustainability:

1. Eliminate waste.
2. Reduce emissions by reshaping the supply stream upstream and downstream.
3. Use renewable energy and energy efficiency to reduce fossil fuel consumption.
4. Reduce virgin material flows, creating cyclical material flows.
5. Reduce oil-based transportation.
6. Create a culture shift, changing the mindset of employees, suppliers, customers, and communities to embrace environmental issues.
7. Redesign commerce itself to deliver not only products, but services that products provide.

One of the biggest impacts that going green has on a business is not just the money it saves but also the value it creates by giving employees a

ANDERSON AND HARTZFELD, CONTINUED

greater sense of purpose in their work and engagement in the company. "Have a big vision," Hartzfeld advises, "but take the first step and get started, engaging all employees." Going green gets workers "organized and energized around your goals," says Hartzfeld, adding that "higher purpose improves productivity." Employees care more about their work when they believe in what the company is doing and start finding solutions where before they only saw problems. "People start seeing the world in a different way and start cracking old problems," says Hartzfeld.

Greening your business also builds brand and reputation, valuable commodities. Part of Interface's success is due to the reputation it has built by leading the green business movement. Green brands attract talent, a valuable commodity. Intense business competition requires innovation and excellent execution, making the ability to attract the best talent an important business success factor.

Accurate and transparent reporting of environmental efforts is a part of the effort. Once data on environmental performance is collected, Hartzfeld and Anderson suggest laying it out for all to see and seeking solutions. Hartzfeld found that one of the best things the team did in its sustainability report was being completely open, listing all of its work with full transparency in an honest and authentic way. No business is perfectly sustainable yet, but providing transparency allows all stakeholders to take appropriate action. "Be willing to look at the shadows," Hartzfeld suggests, reporting beyond what is required to provide the full picture.

ANDERSON AND HARTZFELD, CONTINUED

Interface is continuing to work to achieve Mission Zero, eliminating any negative impact on the environment by the year 2020, and helping others do well by adopting best practices like these. They are not done yet, but continue to make great progress in the climb up Mt. Sustainability, helping others up to the top along with them.

4

Finding Money to Start and Grow Your Business

The vision entrepreneurs have for their business can run up against the reality of finding enough capital to make it happen. No matter what type of business you have, you're going to need money to start and grow it.

Many of the sources of money for green businesses are the same as for other businesses: savings, friends and family, business loans, angel investors, private equity, and venture capital. There are also unique funding opportunities to support green businesses, with many investors seeking cleantech businesses they believe hold huge promise for the future. Governments at all levels provide another resource as they spend billions of dollars on transportation, energy efficiency, and renewable energy to stimulate the economy and make a down payment on environmental progress.

Like entrepreneurs, those who help fund green businesses have varied motivations. Those who believe that green is the way of the future see green businesses as a good investment for the long term, likely to grow as the green economy grows. Many people see green businesses as having a lower risk than competitors, particularly with government support. The large potential upside and lowered risk make for an attractive combination. Socially responsible investing (SRI), or sustainable investing, is a growing trend in which investors seek to invest in businesses following green, sustainable practices. These investors are both pursuing the solid investment opportunity they believe green businesses provide and working to drive change by supporting green innovation.

Being green is no guarantee that investors will fund your business however. You still need to convince those providing financing that your business will be viable. Each company will be judged on its own merits.

Using Your Own Savings

Starting your business with your own money is a great option, if you have enough. If you do—congratulations! Starting with your own money provides you freedom from investors to satisfy, from spending time raising money, and from debt obligations.

If you are not yet in this position, if you need more money than you currently have on hand to get started, and you don't want to wait, don't give up—read on.

Bootstrapping

When it comes to raising money, one option is to not do it. Many businesses start this way, with almost no money, raising themselves up by their own bootstraps. Bootstrapping is the classic rags to riches story, the dream of starting from nothing and working your way up. I've got a feeling this is going to be a very common theme at present, when some of the traditional funding channels are not available.

Being resourceful is the key to bootstrapping—getting as lean as is humanly possible. How can you do more with less? Can you barter to get what you need? Can you work at home and start in your garage or office while you keep your day job? It turns the

THE EIGHT ADVANTAGES OF BOOTSTRAPPING

Not having cash can make life difficult, but having limits like this to work within can also unleash creativity. Having a lot of cash on hand seems great, but that can lead to waste and misdirection. Not having cash on hand creates the necessity of generating immediate business and cash flow. While some might view bootstrapping as a limitation, authors Greg Gianforte and Marcus Gibson in *Bootstrapping Your Business* point out eight advantages of bootstrapping:

1. You are forced to build a real business, one with paying customers. In the absence of testing ideas in the real world, vague assumptions can stick around longer.

2, You start selling early, if not sooner, and learn quickly what selling strategies work.

THE EIGHT ADVANTAGES OF BOOTSTRAPPING, CONTINUED

3. You don't waste money since you have none to waste.

4. You can start the business immediately, without waiting for money from investors.

5. You don't make huge financial mistakes.

6. You are forced to innovate, to think out of the box, compensating for your lack of financial resources with good old-fashioned necessity-driven creativity.

7. You don't have investors to answer to, so you can do whatever you want.

8. You end up owning more of your business because you have not sold off equity.

question around from "What do I need to get started" to "What can I do with what I have today?" Then, as the business grows and starts to make some money, you can use that money to steadily expand.

Tight management of money is a key to bootstrapping. You need to pay close attention to accounts receivables, keep inventory low, and work with your vendors to see if they will extend credit. If they do, you can come back later and ask for a little more.

The great thing about bootstrapping is that you don't let money, or a lack of it, keep you from getting started. The determined person finds a way to see how much they can do with whatever they have today. Some businesses, however, simply can't be bootstrapped, I'm afraid. If you want to start a franchise, you'll need some money to buy it. If you want to open a restaurant, you can't run it out of your garage first.

Debt versus Equity Financing

There are basically two ways you can raise money. One is with debt, and the other is by selling a piece of your business, the equity. They both have their pros and cons. Debt is money that you borrow, generally at a predetermined interest rate, repaying the loan over time. The upside of debt is that it generally comes with few strings attached, other than the obligation to repay the borrowed money according to the terms of the agreement. The downside is that you have to make payments and keep these up. Also, the debt can drag down your credit score, particularly if something goes wrong like missing a payment.

The upside of equity is that by selling a piece of your business to raise money you don't have to make payments. The downside of an equity investment is that you have investors to answer to. It can be a fantastic feeling at first to get the cash needed to move forward, but depending on who the equity investors are and what kind of terms you give them, you might not be as excited later on. The investors may exact terms that can reduce your control over the business or create a great deal of pressure to achieve specific milestones.

There is a relationship between the size of equity investment, the stage of business development, and the risk involved. The farther along a company is in its development, the lower the risk for investors, and the larger the investment, generally. The earlier the business stage, the lower its valuation and the more equity you need to sell to raise money. Seed stage money for the earliest startups usually comes from your savings and people you know.

This is the earliest stage and the riskiest for investors because you don't have products yet and it's far from clear how things will go. Angels and venture capitalists can move product development forward for a business developing an innovative technology or help fund production. The risk is lower at this stage, though still significant, but the investments are larger. These investors are looking for a big upside and a way to cash out their investment by selling their equity when possible. If there is no market for public offerings, thus blocking their exit, investor enthusiasm is dampened.

Personal Loans: Friends and Family

Borrowing from friends and family is another common option for acquiring money to start a business. People often think that borrowing money from family is easy, and in a way it is, relatively speaking (no pun intended). Family members seldom run your credit report or report a late payment to the credit agencies. It can also be hard for them to say no, in some families at least. But while borrowing money from friends and family is common, it can still be fraught with potential difficulty.

If all goes well with the business and the terms of the agreement are clear and well-written, then everything should be OK. If getting the business going takes longer than you thought or does not go at all, then things could get ugly. What is your uncle going to say when you start stalling on paying him back? Are you going to start avoiding your family members and stop answering the phone?

If you want to go the family route, it's best to do it right. Talk to people honestly about your plans and the potential risks. A good strategy would be to treat family members like you would other investors. You believe you will make money, but there is some risk that you will not. I would suggest avoiding the words "sure thing" when describing the business, to family members or any other investor. Everything has a risk. It's probably best to only accept the investment people can afford to lose. It's bad enough if you lose some of the family's money (not that you will), but losing *all* of its money could be downright awful.

Have your business structure in place, and have the terms of the deal explicitly and clearly written up and signed. Getting a lawyer involved in these transactions is a good idea, as it is with investments from other sources. Yes, the lawyer may cost some money (see Chapter 7), but it's money well spent. The more money involved, the more important a lawyer becomes. Is the money a loan or are shares being purchased? If it's a loan, what are the terms for repayment? What interest will be paid on the loan and what will the payments be? What will happen to the loan if the business can't pay it back? When you draw up documents, think about contingencies. They say that whatever you think won't happen, probably will happen. It's best to be ready for anything.

Credit Cards

OK, let me say right upfront that I'm not advising anyone to go out and max out all of their credit cards. It's probably not a good idea. The exorbitant interest on credit cards can eat you alive, and the credit card companies are not in a freewheeling credit-happy mood presently. Many companies are cutting credit limits and raising rates for a wide range of customers. Those credit card fliers are getting a lot less common in the mail for most of us.

But still, there are stories of successful businesses that have been started on credit cards. They are legend. I suppose we don't hear much about the businesses started this way that did not make it. Credit cards do avoid the friends-and-family problems of getting your personal life embroiled in the business. The credit

card companies do not bother to ask for one of those pesky business plans. They do not require milestones to be met every step of the way. Once you have the card in your hand, its pretty much for you to worry about what happens after that.

Method, the producer of green home products, provides one story of a green business started in part on credit cards, in this case by founders Adam Lowry and Eric Ryan (as related in *Inc.* magazine, May 2008). Founding Method amidst the dotcom bust of 2000, they found capital hard to raise and ended up running the business on their credit cards, racking up $300,000 in debt among three men, including their new CEO. They managed to get funding, pay off the debt, and get the business on more solid ground by the skin of their teeth. Today, just a few years later, Method is one of the best known brands of green cleaning products.

But like I said, I don't advise people to start their business on credit cards.

Bank Loans

Maybe you've heard this one or experienced it—banks are only willing to lend your business money if you don't need it. This seems particularly true today, when some banks have stopped lending even to creditworthy business clients. According to *Start, Run and Grow a Successful Business* (Toolkit Media Group, 2008), banks are generally looking for four things:

1. the credit history of the borrower,
2. collateral to secure the loan,
3. cash flow, past and future, and
4. character of the borrower.

The largest banks have run into severe trouble of late (as of late 2008), sitting on murky pools of toxic assets. The banks with the biggest trouble have been those with the greatest exposure to a variety of risky investments, such as mortgage-backed securities, that did not seem so risky at the time. But the problem is not universal. Smaller banks—like community banks and credit unions—have in many cases steadily pursued conservative policies and are still plugging along. There are still options in the world of banks.

If your business has a good plan, has revenue coming in and makes a profit, and can demonstrate how the loan will be repaid, the right bank is likely to listen. Banks are just not likely to front unsecured money for a risky seed venture. And about any startup business is considered risky. Startups are just not their business. Arguing with them about it probably won't help. If the bank says no and you have a good plan, try another bank. Or try another option.

Green Banks

Most banks today are not too interested in the details of what your business does. If they are making a loan, they want to know the financial status of the business and how they will get their money back. There are not generally any bonus points for being a sustainable business when going to a big bank for a loan.

While most banks are not going to care too much if your business is green or not, there are a few banks that are different—green banks that are specifically targeting the green business world for their business. These banks seek out green entrepreneurs as clients, helping to build the close-knit network of interacting business partners in their communities. They also accept deposits from a wide range of clients who are attracted by the knowledge that their deposits in a green bank are making a positive difference by supporting the efforts of green entrepreneurs. They are still banks, and will not generally provide seed money for newly minted businesses. They can, however, help startups by taking care of their banking needs and by connecting them to

others in their network who can provide the capital, business services, and experience they need to advance their business.

Green Bank Case Study
SHOREBANK PACIFIC

Headquartered in Ilwaco, Washington, with additional offices in Seattle and Portland, Oregon, ShoreBank Pacific is a sustainable community development bank focused on small and midsize businesses. While the businesses it lends to are located primarily in the Pacific Northwest, its depositors are located everywhere. "They are attracted to us because their deposits go to a good cause, to support lending to sustainable businesses," says David Williams, CEO of Shore-Bank Pacific. ShoreBank Pacific helps not just individual businesses, but the whole community that it is a part of. Working with sustainable businesses in communities, nothing happens in isolation. All of the businesses connect in a network of interactions like a spiderweb, reinforcing and helping each other to make the whole network stronger.

"Sustainability drives you to think about communities differently," says Williams. "The question you are driven to ask is 'How do I operate within the community in which I live? How do I find and use local products?' Strong sustainable businesses help the community and a strong community helps build strong businesses. Once you get the ball spinning then it keeps spinning on its own."

In the midst of our current banking crisis, many people are rethinking how banks function and how they interact with customers and communities. Many community banks are faring relatively well in the current economic crisis, in part because their practices are distinct from those

SHOREBANK PACIFIC, CONTINUED

of the large banks. Still, perhaps the difference is not that community banks are doing something new, but that everyone else changed and they stayed the same. "What we do is not really new, but the way it used to be done by all banks," says Williams. "We build close relationships with our customers, getting to know them and working with them closely. Because of our focus on sustainable businesses we expect to have long-lasting and stable relationships with our customers. We need to know their business as well as they do. This used to be the way banks did business, however, this is not the way large banks have been run for the last 20 years."

One way that ShoreBank Pacific connects with clients is by not just dealing with their money, but by really getting out into the community to know the business of their clients, and using this information to help them out. "We have people working at our bank who specialize in each of the industries on which we focus, getting to know the underlying industries in the communities where we are working," says Williams. "In a coastal community, we have someone who knows the fishing industry. In a rural or farming area, we have someone who can provide alternative energy support for wind farms in wheat fields, or methane digesters on dairy farms. We expect these guys to be engaged in support of the community and groups that support important industries in that area. If there is an alliance to support sustainable agriculture, we get to know them and have them as a customer. We pursued the regional chapter of the U.S. Green Building Council as a customer because they are involved in green building, which is important for our customers."

SHOREBANK PACIFIC, CONTINUED

Since the bank is involved in the local community, it can also get more involved in helping out its clients. "We have a network of business connections in our community," says Williams. We get to know them, see what they need, and help them make the right connections to people who can help them with all of the steps they need to take."

While the bank won't probably be able to lend money to startups, it might still be able to help them by connecting them to lenders and investors who do invest in startups. "When businesses are getting started, we help them by taking their deposits, not lending," says Williams. "If we know their industry well, we often know equity players who are interested in investments. We can connect them with groups that lend and invest in startups, people who come in and provide funding for early stage companies. If it is a strong business plan with the right kind of people who need extra support to get going, we can help them get that extra boost."

Like many banks, it often lends money for building projects, but with a green twist. "If they want to build green, we can help them," says Williams. In some cases we can put together a program in conjunction with our nonprofit, ShoreBank Enterprise Cascadia, for higher than normal loan to value. If a business wants to renovate and add features for energy efficiency or renewable energy that will raise the cost beyond what the appraiser says, we can arrange this through our nonprofit. We can also sit down and talk not just about a greener building, but help our customers to invest in reducing costs of their building over time through energy efficiency. We help them to reduce their operating costs through our expertise in areas like green building."

SHOREBANK PACIFIC, CONTINUED

One of the challenges ShoreBank Pacific encounters is common to many in the green business world, that there is overall not a clear definition of what being green means. "Businesses still often don't have a standard about what is sustainable and what isn't," says Williams. There is a risk as sustainability becomes a big deal that banks will claim to be sustainable without the support staff to validate that position. They are selling green without being green."

To overcome this, ShoreBank Pacific put together its own program where it analyzed what it means to be sustainable, including not just environmental issues but also business and community-related issues. To help its clients see where they stand, it created a scorecard rating sustainable business practices. "For environmental issues, we look at how you use water, how you recover water and clean it, how you use energy, if you produce clean energy, how you manage CO_2, whether you are you offsetting CO_2 that your product produces, if you are using sustainably produced materials," explains Williams. All of this goes on the scorecard which we use to determine how they are doing. We find some things upon which they can improve, and make those suggestions. In addition, we talk to them annually to see how they are becoming a more sustainable business."

The way a business is planning on getting access to capital can have a big impact on how sustainably they are being managed. "We like to work with businesses we think are going to be around for 100 years, like the community in which the business is located. A mill town is there because there were a lot of trees; if they cut all the trees down, then there is no town."

SHOREBANK PACIFIC, CONTINUED

While many of the green businesses they work with are in fairly good shape regarding questions about their impact on the environment, they are often less on top of questions about how they deal with employees, observes Williams. "Depending on the business, they may understand nothing or everything about the community. Often though they are not thinking about their employees in a long-term strategic fashion."

Like many others, Williams emphasizes the importance of treating employees well for the health of the business and the community. "We need to be committed to long-term success of the business and the employees as members of the community. The best businesses provide health benefits, pay fairly, support education, and provide training. We need to educate young people who are the workers of tomorrow, reaching out to get involved with the school system and community."

Thinking of the long term. That sounds like a sustainable concept.

New Resource Bank

New Resource Bank in San Francisco was founded in 2005 as a community bank, working closely with the innovative green business community there. Going green is not an extra layer it's added on top, but a core part of its business of helping green entrepreneurs succeed. It helped a wide variety of businesses like local cheese maker Cowgirl Creamery, recycled paper producer New Leaf Paper, and green architect Michelle Kaufman Designs. New Resource has grown immensely since opening its doors. It raised an additional $14 million in September 2008, in the midst of the credit crisis, demonstrating the confidence investors have in the bank and in its green business clients. Working with a community bank like New Resource, one connected so closely to the local green community, can help green entrepreneurs make new connections for more business of their own.

More Options

You can find New Resource at newresourcebank.com. Green banks can also be found at various stages of development in other cities, such as Green Bank Inc. (greenbank.com), based in Texas, or Wainright Bank in Boston.

Person-to-Person Lending

When it comes to lending money, you would think there's nothing new under the sun, but you would be wrong. A new phenomenon called person-to-person lending (also called social lending or peer-to-peer lending) has emerged in the last few years, providing an alternative to banks and other traditional financial institutions. When you borrow money from a bank, the bank does the work of judging the risk of each borrower, and the bank assumes the risk of default. Those who provide money (those making deposits or investments in the bank) generally do not have a direct connection to those who borrow the money. Person-to-person lending removes the bank from the relationship, helping borrowers and lenders

Putting Things in Perspective

The funny thing about social lending is that it's not actually all that new. Before there were banks or credit reporting agencies, all lending was social lending, arranged between borrowers and wealthy lenders they knew, based on reputation. As is often the case, there are opportunities to rediscover the value in old ways of doing things, but with a new twist.

Person-to-Person Case Study
PROSPER

Prosper is the largest person-to-person lending marketplace in the United States, allowing borrowers to post information about themselves and allowing lenders to bid on loans. Launched in early 2006, Prosper has already helped mediate over $100 million in loans. Borrowers get an alternative source for loans, and a lending source that sees them as more than just a credit score. Lenders get the opportunity to invest and earn a high rate of return, as well as the opportunity to help borrowers working on causes they believe in, such as going green.

Green entrepreneurs looking for money for their business might find peer-to-peer lending systems like Prosper a valuable resource. A survey of Prosper lenders found that 25 percent have bid on loans for green projects and 93 percent of lenders are interested in lending for such projects. This can include green projects for homes or loans for green businesses. A Prosper survey of consumers found that the majority of people are interested in energy efficiency and other green projects, but 71 percent are held back by the cost. Having a financial resource like Prosper available can help businesses working in energy efficiency or other green business areas move projects forward with their customers.

When I spoke with Prosper co-founder Chris Larsen in August 2008, he described Prosper as a "person-to-person lending marketplace, an eBay for lending." Those seeking to borrow money make a loan listing on the Prosper website, revealing as much or as little as they want, and

PROSPER, CONTINUED

lenders bid for loans. When a listing goes up, anyone can bid to lend money.

Bids with the lowest rates are combined into one simple loan. Their loans are all for three years, fully amortizing, and borrowers can have two active loans at one time. Loans can be as large as $25,000. "Right now we have over 2,000 active loans," says Larsen, "which is pretty typical."

connect more directly. The internet helps people make this connection, either through a marketplace where lenders bid to provide pieces of loans (like Prosper) or by lenders taking part of pools of loans at predetermined rates (like Lending Club). While there is nothing specifically green about this development, green projects have proven particularly successful at raising smaller amounts of money (less than $25,000) this way, making them of particular interest at present when other funding venues are closed off.

About 25 percent of loans are small-business-oriented, and these involve the personal credit rating of the person who runs the business, not a business credit score. "The listing

Late-Breaking Update

The SEC is now requiring that peer-to-peer lending sites register their notes on loans as securities (see *BusinessWeek*, April 6, 2009). As of this writing, Prosper is not accepting new loans, pending SEC review of its paperwork. Registering with the SEC could make business more difficult for sites like Prosper, but could also help increase credibility of the field.

More Options

Other peer-to-peer lending groups display variations on this theme, including Kiva, which is a microfinance-oriented peer-to-peer lending system. Another relatively new entrant in peer-to-peer lending is Pertuity Direct, which has investors pool money in a mutual fund that is used as the source of all loans, rather than having investors invest in specific loans.

includes more than just the credit score though," says Prosper's Chris Larsen. "When a listing gets made, most small businesspeople will add links, maybe a simple business plan, and they will show off with pictures to try to engage people. Engaging lenders is important for the borrowers because it helps get a better rate, improving your economics."

Larsen confirmed the unique appeal of green businesses for lenders in the Prosper system. With a green business, the interest of lenders is both economically based and also based on interest in what the green business does, which makes the loan more interesting, says Larsen. "Green listings have been pretty popular, and our survey of lenders found that an extremely high percentage of people would consider the green aspect a big plus, and bid more attractively."

They go to great lengths to eliminate the potential for fraud in their system and make sure it's a safe marketplace. "One of our biggest jobs is making sure it's a safe marketplace," says Larsen. We have state-of-the-art technology to see if borrowers are who they say they are, including ID checking, credit checks, and strong procedures to prevent ID theft. We have a 100 percent guarantee against losing money through identity theft, and if anyone loses money because of this, we would make it right."

Government Funding Programs

Recognizing the importance of small businesses for economic growth, the government provides support for them in several

Case Study
THE LENDING CLUB

The Lending Club is another internet-based social lending business. A little money can go a long way for many small businesses, but in the midst of the current credit crunch, money is not always easy to come by. Traditional credit channels like credit lines from banks have become suddenly much tighter, and many businesses have found their credit lines suddenly lowered in amount or their rates increased as banks become reluctant to lend. There are other options though, including peer-to-peer lending with Lending Club. To find out more about Lending Club, I spoke with Rob Garcia, its director of product strategy.

When a borrower seeks money with Lending Club, he or she can request the amount, between $1,000 and $25,000, as unsecured loans that are repaid over a three-year period. The low operating costs of Lending Club helps it keep rates lower than borrowers would generally pay to borrow money from banks or credit cards.

Loans can be made for almost any purpose, including use for a small business. Garcia confirmed that loans for a green purpose generally are well received, attracting funding from lenders. Small businesses often turn to Lending Club for loans because of its many advantages—ease of application, rapid process, and low interest rates, particularly in today's financial climate.

The online application process is easy and fast; it can be completed in minutes. A credit check is performed. Borrowers must have good credit, with a FICO score higher than 660, and without excessive revolving debt or other indicators of credit problems. Once the application is

THE LENDING CLUB, CONTINUED

completed, the loan is priced according to the risk calculated for each borrower and assigned an interest rate. Lenders in its system can then fund a portion of the desired loan. Verification of identities, making sure people are who they say they are, is also an important step. The calculation of the interest rate uses an advanced automated system, finding the right price for the risk. If the full loan is funded, then the loan is initiated at the interest rate indicated.

"It can be hard for lenders to know themselves how much risk each borrower is or the right interest rate to charge," says Garcia. By having its system score the risk and find the right interest rate, it removes the guesswork for lenders. Because Lending Club has a strict credit policy, not every loan request will be put in front of lenders. Those that are, however, have relatively low risk and a predetermined interest rate. "We are like the Amazon of peer-to-peer lending," says Garcia, with set pricing and no bidding over rates involved. As you start and grow your own green business, getting a loan from Lending Club may provide the extra boost you need to be successful.

ways. The most obvious form is with the U.S. Small Business Administration (SBA). The SBA does not itself make loans, but guarantees loans to small businesses that banks or other lenders provide. If you go to a bank for a loan, it might turn you down, but you could still have a shot at an SBA loan. There is an application process like that at a bank, and you need to qualify. SBA loans guarantees are for established businesses, not really for startups. The SBA wants to see cash flow.

To qualify, the SBA looks for:

- *Collateral.* The SBA and the bank are going to want to see collateral, including personal assets.
- *Equity participation by the business owner.* It wants you to have some skin in the game, to ensure that you are not going to walk away from the business and the loan if things get rough.
- *Reliability.* Like the banks, it wants to know that you, the business owner, are reliable.
- *Small businesses.* The definition can vary for different loan programs and different types of businesses, but in general according to the SBA, a small business has fewer than 500 employees and annual revenues below several million dollars.
- *Loan denial.* You typically need to show that you have been denied a loan after trying the normal lending routes from banks.

There are a variety of SBA loan programs. The SBA website has all the information, and many other websites talk about the merits of various SBA programs. Some of the programs are targeted to provide funding to women, minorities, and veterans. In the recent credit crisis, the rate of small-business loans has declined, and the government has increased the loan guarantee percentage to encourage greater SBA

> ### More Options
>
> If you are engaged in a business that does research and development, look into research grants that might be available from SBIR (Small Business Innovation Research) grants from the Department of Energy or the EPA. Grants are not free money though. You need to invest a great deal of time and energy in writing the grant proposal, and if you win the grant, you will need to invest more time and energy in doing the proposed work.

lending. The SBA provides help for small businesses in a variety of other ways as well. Its website has a wealth of information about planning, grants, marketing, and through local offices around the country, you can connect to resources like SCORE for guidance and mentoring.

Other measures to support renewable energy and energy efficiency are also being developed, like on-bill financing getting started in California. With on-bill financing of energy efficiency projects, utilities help businesses fund energy efficiency improvements that are paid back through their utility bill, helping them save money overall. Cities in California (such as Palm Desert, see Chapter 7) and other parts of the country are creating solar power and energy efficiency funding for homeowners, who pay back the money over many years through their property taxes. The U.S. Small Business Administration has a little-publicized 7a loan program to fund energy efficiency projects. The more innovative funding for clean energy and green building that is available, the more rapidly the field will grow and help the economy.

Angel Investors

What exactly is an angel? Angels are relatively wealthy investors looking for opportunities to invest their own money in promising young businesses. To be an angel one must be an accredited investor, a term that is defined in Regulation D of the Securities Act of 1933 and under other applicable securities laws and regulations. Angels have a net worth of $1 million or more, or income of $200,000 per individual for each of the last three years, $300,000 if married. It's the SEC's way of trying to protect those who do not meet these requirements and may not be sophisticated enough in their knowledge of investing to get involved in these transactions.

Angel Investor Case Study
KEIRETSU FORUM

Keiretsu Forum is the world's largest angel investor network, with 17 chapters worldwide, including a chapter in San Francisco for which Colin Wiel is the president. "An angel is an individual who invests in startup companies, like venture capitalists (VCs), but VCs work for a company in the business of investing, while angels invest their own money," says Wiel. Angel investors are very interested in green businesses for investing. "Cleantech is our hottest category," says Wiel, "and it has been growing rapidly in the number of deals we see and those that we find for the last two to three years. This month [February 2009] we have seven cleantech companies that we are screening."

To be considered for investment by the Keiretsu Forum, each company applies through its website, then goes through a two-tier screening process to identify the most promising investment opportunities. Generally the Forum sees 30 to 50 companies apply, and after screening the top five will present at a chapter meeting. "The first stage is a committee review, by groups who specialize in each area, like cleantech or technology companies," says

Resource Guide

To have your proposal considered by the Keiretsu Forum, start the process on its website: k4forum.com. And don't forget to follow Colin Wiel's advice for a successful presentation:

- Cover all of the basic business elements, not just the product.
- Keep the story simple, distilled down to the essence of your business.
- Assemble the best management team possible, and include this in your pitch.

Starting Green

KEIRETSU FORUM, CONTINUED

Wiel. "Two to three people from the appropriate committee review each application, then give them a thumbs up or down to pass to a second stage of screening. At the next stage there are 25 members in a room, and they hear all 10 presentations, then vote on which five will present at the chapter meeting. At the chapter meeting, there are a hundred people in the room, primarily members. Each company makes a 10-minute presentation, followed by a 10-minute Q&A." After the presentations the companies all leave the room, and anyone who is interested in a company forms a team for due diligence.

The end goal of those presenting is to get funding. "Fifty percent of the companies that present at chapter meetings get funded," says Wiel. "It takes about 8 to 10 weeks from the time they do their presentation to the time they get funded." In addition to receiving money, the presenters receive another valuable commodity—insight about how they did. All of the comments the group makes are returned to the companies, anonymously, helping them improve their presentations and their businesses to increase their luck in the future.

Not all angels work together in groups like the Forum; many make investments on their own. Working with a group can change the type of investments made and the size of the investment. "Individual angels more often than not are friends and family," says Wiel. "There is less due diligence, and the dollar amount raised is smaller. Most individuals are investing $50,000 to $100,000." In contrast, the Keiretsu Form typically makes investments of $500,000 to $1.5 million, with investments from angels aggregated. By working in this range of investment, angel groups fill a funding gap left by other options. "In general with

KEIRETSU FORUM, CONTINUED

individuals you can raise up to $500,000, and with a VC you will raise from a couple of million dollars on up. If your needs are in this middle range, it's a very awkward amount of money to raise, and angel groups fill this gap."

Companies in which the angels invest are typically in early stage. They have passed the initial product development stage, or seed stage. "Seed stage is too early for us," says Wiel. "Seed stage companies are still developing their product, and want money for this. Early stage companies already have their product developed, and now want money for growth and marketing. We are generally investing in companies that are already past seed stage."

With the economy suffering in early 2009, many businesses are seeing sources of capital drying up, but many angel investors are still looking for solid investment opportunities in the businesses they review. "We are still actively investing," said Wiel when I spoke with him. "What has changed is that VCs have slowed down dramatically, and startups that might have gone to VCs are now coming to angel groups instead." The valuations of the businesses it is seeing have also changed. "Valuations have come down significantly," says Wiel. "We would see valuations before in the $5 to $7 million range that are now more like $2.5 to $5 million range. In good economic times, companies command higher valuations based on future expectation of outcome. Now, investors are not willing to pay as much."

For those seeking investment, Wiel has a few tips to help their chances for success. "I would say the most important thing is to distill your message to its essence. It's a hard thing to do but important. What is

KEIRETSU FORUM, CONTINUED

the essence of the company? Not everyone knows this. Another important thing is to present the complete story with all of the essential parts. Ten minutes is not a lot of time, but you need to tell the whole story in a short time, touching on all of the major aspects."

The essential components to include in the presentation include:

- Markets, the opportunity
- The product
- Marketing and sales strategy
- Team
- Financials
- Exit strategy
- The deal that you are proposing to investors.

Having a product is important, but it's far from the only thing that investors look at. "One of the most common errors is that the company wants to spend all of their presentation time talking about their product," says Wiel. "They spend seven minutes on the product, and leave out some of the other parts. I would say that the number-one thing that angels care about when making an investment is the team. The strategy

Angels Earn Their Wings

The best angel investors provide more than money. They are not just reviewing you; you are reviewing them to find investors who will bring valuable experience, people you can work with. It doesn't hurt if they have valuable connections in their network that they can plug you into as well. One of the great aspects of angel investors is that they are usually eager to help out, as savvy businesspeople with a great deal to offer.

KEIRETSU FORUM, CONTINUED

will change, and even the product will change oftentimes, but the team will still be there." What are the angels looking for in the management team? Is it all about having a great deal of business experience in the field they are working in? "Experience is not absolutely necessary," says Wiel. "I'm looking for wisdom, credibility, and leadership skills."

Another difference between angels and VCs is their motivation. VCs invest because it is their job—they have a mandate to their investors to maximize returns. Angel investors hope to make money, of course, but it's not all about the money for them. If it was, they could invest in other ways without getting personally involved. They want to feel good about the investments they are making, feel they are helping out. "We want to get involved because we enjoy business, and we want to be proactive and productive," says Weil. "We are very active in helping to support companies, rolling up our sleeves, providing instructions, and maybe serving on the board."

Venture Capital

Venture capitalists are an attractive money source for many entrepreneurs. It is their job to invest millions of dollars in early stage companies. VCs typically invest larger sums than angel investors and are willing to endure higher risk than some investors for the promise of a significant payoff, such as from an innovative clean energy technology. They attract entrepreneurs like moths to the flame.

And venture capitalists are drawn to green businesses. One of the most famous venture firms, Kleiner Perkins in Silicon

Valley, is betting heavily on cleantech, betting that entrepreneurs changing how our energy, our cars, and our fuels are developing some of the biggest opportunities of our time. Their cleantech group includes famed VC John Doerr, who has been involved in the funding of Google and Amazon, and none other than former Vice President and renowned green advocate Al Gore. "Scientific breakthroughs in biology and materials technology mean there's never been a better time to start and grow a great green venture," reads the Kleiner Perkins website. "Greentech could be the largest economic opportunity of the 21st century. It is an unprecedented challenge that demands great innovation, speed and scale."

Hard Times in VC City

As of this writing, the economic crisis has caused some VC funds to have difficulty raising money, putting the crunch on some cleantech companies that need further funding to get far enough along to have products to sell. This could lead to a rough time for VCs and the businesses they invest in.

Many other VCs are also developing green opportunities as well. Andy Funk is the managing director and founding member of Funk Ventures, one of a handful of VCs that focus on socially responsible companies. Funk believes that by investing in these businesses his fund can "give back to people, give back to the environment, and still do well. Everyone can win. This is an industry that can change the world."

While he notes that there is money available for investing, Funk says that much of the capital is targeted for infrastructure development in wind, solar, and geothermal, and not just startup companies. One of his investment targets is smaller projects than most VCs look at, including investments in the $100,000 to a few-million-dollar range that large funds don't invest in.

The money invested by VCs in your business is not free. VCs are in the business of maximizing the return on investments, and they have a reputation for negotiating tough terms. When you are the moth, you might get burned by the flame.

The Inside Story of Raising Money

ADEO RESSI

 It's a common question:"How do I attract investors?" Is there a secret recipe?

As the CEO/founder of TheFunded, Adeo Ressi is helping CEOs and others learn the ins and outs of the funding process with VCs, one of the important components of the investment world. There is some good news and some bad news, according to Ressi. "Cleantech is the second most popular investment category," says Ressi. "Everyone is waiting for your big idea. There is $150 to $300 billion sitting in the hands of investors waiting to be put in the hands of companies that will save us. It is an unparalleled, historic opportunity to get money, go out and change the world. You want investors to come to you. You are the flame and they are the moth." That's the good news. And the bad news? "Raising money is like hazing," says Ressi. But he provides investors with

Resource Guide

As the Founding Member of TheFunded.com, Ressi provides an online forum for entrepreneurs to rank investors, turning the tables a bit on the usual situation. TheFunded is the seventh venture Ressi has started, and provides a valuable inside look into a variety of funding opportunities and insight into the impact of the current economic environment on funding opportunities.

ADEO RESSI, CONTINUED

tips to navigate the process successfully, illuminating how it really works.

One of the first steps in the process Ressi describes is to "demonstrate traction," proving your vision of the company. "The skill of your team is critical to closing a deal, and to realizing your dream." In addition to a team of experts, you will often also have to demonstrate that you have a patent position, you can produce a prototype, and can launch a product.

Also important to funding, as well as the business, is "getting a lot of media." Investors are attracted to businesses that have a high profile. Blogging or publishing are one part of this process.

Next, you need to prepare your presentation materials. Brevity is key.

Tip for Success

Ressi suggests forming a C corp and not an LLC if you plan to seek investment from venture capitalists. The flow-through taxation of LLCs that might be attractive to you will not be attractive to investors like VCs, and will keep them away.

Ressi recommends sticking to no more than 15 slides and keeping the message as simple as possible. "It has to be something people can understand," says Ressi. "They call it an elevator pitch for a reason."

When you are ready, you need to pick your targets. Look for local investors, people in your area. "Get out and socialize with them, going to events," says Ressi. "But don't bother them with your pitch when you talk. It may be hard to resist, but

---

ADEO RESSI, CONTINUED

actually cornering VCs in the elevator with your plan can be annoying to them. A friendly introduction may be good, with follow up." Having someone pin you down at a party with their whole story isn't a big turn-on. "Better than you pitching them when you meet them is getting their friends to pitch your story to investors."

When you do make a connection with an investor and you follow up, you need to make an initial introduction. Then you set up the meetings. "The idea is to maximize face time," says Ressi. "Make sure that you come back again. The purpose of every meeting is to come back to the next one."

At the end of the day, Ressi advises one last thing: Do not compromise your dream. "When it comes to investors and creating your plan, you are the believer, and only you know what to do. Whatever it is, compromise will hurt you."

If you meet with VCs and manage to secure their interest, you may get a term sheet to review providing the terms of the investment they are proposing to make. Ressi has worked with a wide range of CEOs to navigate VC term sheets. They are complex, and you will need a lawyer to fully understand what they are saying.

Tip For Success

"Do you think the first offer is the best offer?" asks Ressi. As is the case with any business proposition, it's best to work from a position of strength. "Negotiate multiple offers," suggests Ressi, to work out the best deal for yourself.

ADEO RESSI, CONTINUED

Working with the right VC firm and under the right terms can provide a useful source of money. Working with the wrong fund or bad terms could be painful. No matter how badly you feel you need the money, be clear about what you're doing when you sign.

CHAPTER

 5

How to Green Your Business Operations and Facilities

In addition to facing all of the same challenges other businesses face like marketing, planning, and raising money, green businesses must also consider an additional factor—reducing the environmental impact of how they do business. There's more to your environmental impact than the product or service you deliver; it includes everything that goes into running your business, all the way from your suppliers to your customers and beyond. It runs through your entire supply chain, including how goods are transported, how customers' orders are stored in warehouses, and how retail outlets sell them. It includes how customers use the product and what happens to the product when they are done with it. This chapter lays out some of the strategies that green businesses of any size can use to green how they do business to become more successful right from the start.

The benefits of greening your business operations are many. By using resources more efficiently and wasting less you can save a great deal of money. The authors of *Green to Gold*, Dan Esty and Andrew Winston, describe the impact of green efforts on the bottom line at some of the largest companies such as 3M, DuPont, and Wal-Mart, which can save billions of dollars by using energy and other resources more efficiently. Small businesses and start-ups may not save billions of dollars, but they can still help their bottom line greatly with eco-friendly practices.

Defining Moment

The practice of looking at the environmental impact of a product from one end of its life to the other, from the raw materials it is made from to its fate when it can no longer be used, is called life cycle assessment. To find out more about life cycle assessment see:

- *Environmental Protection Agency*: epa.gov/nrmrl/lcaccess/
- *Carnegie Mellon Green Design Institute*: eiolca.net/index.html
- *American Center for Life Cycle Assessment*: lcacenter.org/

Another benefit is that greening the work environment can increase employee productivity. Employees in green businesses become excited and more engaged in their work, which helps increase productivity and opens the door to new opportunities. When businesses embrace environmental initiatives, they start to see new directions for the business to grow where once they saw only problems. You can connect with green business partners providing essential goods and services—green phone companies, green banks, green insurance providers, green energy suppliers, and green office supply companies—creating a network of green businesses that help each other.

Startup businesses that are still getting their business together might not have any operations yet that need greening, but you can build green into plans as they go. Big businesses have the advantage of size, but startups have the advantage of flexibility and motivation. Going green in all aspects of your business from the start ensures efficiency savings from day one and a strong green brand that drives rapid growth.

Green Tools for Small Businesses

According to the U.S. Small Business Administration, small firms drive about half of the country's economic output. Small businesses also have a significant environmental impact. If their energy use reflects their contribution to the economy, small businesses are responsible for about 3,500 million metric tons of carbon emissions per year.

Yet small businesses have had little opportunity to take advantage of the latest developments in sustainable business practices in the same way that large companies have. Large companies employ professional sustainability staff and consultants, but small businesses do not have the resources to hire a sustainability consultant nor do they have time to read through all of the greening advice to find which solutions best apply to them.

To solve this pressing problem, Natural Capitalism Solutions, a sustainability consultancy based in Colorado, has partnered with online education firm Cogbooks to develop a web-based tool that delivers the expertise and information normally accessible only from a professional sustainability consultant. Combining

CogBooks' unique personalized learning approach with Natural Capitalism Solutions' world-renowned expertise, this tool gives small businesses access to the specific help and guidance they need to deliver real business improvement.

The tool is aimed at small to medium-sized businesses that want to impact their bottom line by applying sustainable business methods. It would also be invaluable to sustainability consultants looking for supporting tools to help their on-site implementations. The tool is available in modules, each retailing for between $50 to $200 depending on the topic size and number of licenses purchased. For more information, contact Natural Capitalism Solutions at (303) 554-6550, info@natcap solutions.org.

Budgeting Can Help Green Your Startup

As you create a plan for your business, drawing up an operational budget can give you an idea of how much it will take to run your business every month. Your budget is a tool to help you achieve your goals, and if being green is one of the goals of your business, then examining the budget impact of greening your operations right upfront will help you get where you want to go.

A sample business budget in Figure 5.1 illustrates how you can go green without busting your budget. Many people believe that going green will cost a great deal and is not feasible for a small business, but greening your operations can save money in some areas and build productivity in others. The sample budget illustrates the impact of greening a business on its operating budget, showing how much each item may cost before going green and after.

Looking over the expenses in this example, the largest expense is the salaries of employees. This is not unusual for many small businesses, particularly those that are service oriented. Employees

Figure 5.1—**The Impact of Going Green on a Small-Business Operating Budget**

RENT	BEFORE	AFTER
Salaries/wages	$200,000	$220,000
Rent/lease	50,000	52,000
Advertising	30,000	15,000
Promotional supplies	5,000	6,000
Equipment leases	10,000	10,000
Office supplies	2,000	2,400
Travel	30,000	15,000
Meetings, entertainment	6,000	5,000
Company vehicle	9,000	7,000
Waste disposal	2,000	1,000
Offsets		500
Printing	1,000	1,100
Cleaning service	4,000	4,400
Gas and electric	8,000	4,000
Water	1,200	700
Telephone, internet	3,000	3,000
Outreach		5,000
Insurance	5,000	4,500
Repairs/maintenance	4,000	4,000
Taxes and licenses	22,000	22,000
Total	**$392,200**	**$382,600**

are not just an expense however. They are an investment. It may cost more to provide a living wage or health insurance, but the investment can yield great rewards by attracting the best talent, retaining valuable employees, building your brand, and motivating workers. It's good for the employees, good for business, and good for your community.

Your building will probably be another big part of your budget, as it is in this example. A green building might cost slightly more to buy or lease, but since green buildings are much more energy efficient, your gas and electric bill will be lower, producing a net saving. The greener the building is, the more money you will save on energy.

Advertising might be another area where your green business will save money. Green businesses often avoid traditional advertising and instead use low-cost marketing alternatives such as giving out samples, blogging, and social networking to reach their customers (see Chapter 6).

Other items in the operating budget may cost a little more when choosing a greener option. But it's important once again to think of these choices not just as expenses, but as investments. If you invest in greener printed materials, green promotional items, or greener office supplies, these line items in your budget may go up. These items are generally a small percentage of the overall budget though, and as highly visible symbols, they can have a significant positive impact on the image and value of your business.

When you add it all up, while some items in the green budget cost more, the overall budget can be lower by helping your business be less wasteful and more resourceful. And the value of your business goes up if your efforts create a green brand that attracts business. The bottom line is about more than how much you spend—it's about how everything you do builds financial value as well as natural capital and human capital.

Measuring and Auditing Environmental Impacts

When you are running your growing business at full steam, you'll get so caught up in the day-to-day business that you probably won't spend much time measuring your environmental impact, even if you want to. When it comes to talking about how green your business is though, some of your customers are going to look for information to back your green claims up. Any business can say it's green. How do you prove it?

To get a handle on this, many businesses are tracking their environmental impact and doing a green audit to look for areas to improve. Doing a simple audit yourself or with your employees can help get things started. A more sophisticated analysis may require consultants to help out on specific environmental areas (energy, waste reduction, or compliance with laws, for example) or on the overall environmental impact. Even if you are just getting started with your business, taking a look at what is examined during a green audit helps you to know where you are headed.

Getting certified as a green business is an increasingly useful step that helps eliminate confusion felt by consumers and businesses looking for green companies. A growing number of green business certification programs are available. Companies will audit your business from one end to another and provide you with a badge for your website or a certificate for your storefront that tells the world you have met their standards for green. The Green Business Alliance (greenbusiness alliance.com) provides a self-audit form to certify and "Greenify" your business. Additional certification programs can be found at

> ### Resource Guide
> See the EPA *Small Business Source Book on Environmental Auditing*. Published in 2000, it still provides a useful overview of the steps involved in auditing the environmental impact of a small business (epa.gov/sbo/pdfs/audit book_500.pdf).

the Sustainable Business Network of Washington (sbnow.org), which is launching a pilot certification program, and the American Consumer Council (ACC). The Bay Area Green Business Program (greenbiz.ca.gov) provides certification through self-auditing, which is a straightforward process—and inexpensive. Being audited by an independent third party is always a stronger form of certification, however. While the audit and certification often cost a little money, the business it brings in through increased green credibility can make the investment worthwhile.

To know where your business stands today, you can do your own quick audit of your business. The idea is to repeat the process periodically, at least once a year, recording your current perform-ance and tracking improvements in reducing your environmental footprint. The questions may not work in the same way for a gas station, organic produce store, or a dry cleaning service, but in general an audit will walk you through topics such as:

- *Are you in compliance with environmental laws and regulations?* Being in compliance for issues such as handling hazardous chemicals or releasing pollutants is essential before you worry about anything else.
- *Are you using hazardous chemicals, or increasing their use indirectly?* Even if you are in compliance, look for ways to reduce use of hazardous compounds.
- *How are you energy efficient?* The less you spend on energy, the more you can spend on other aspects of your business as it grows.
- *Are you using energy-efficient appliances?* We use tools to get our job done, but are there more efficient alternatives, such as energy-efficient PCs?
- *Is your building energy efficient?* New green buildings are one way to go, but retrofitting old buildings is an even bigger opportunity.

🌿 *Are you producing your own energy?* Can you build solar or wind power into your business plan?

🌿 *What is your carbon footprint?* The carbon dioxide, methane, and other greenhouse gases that we all release are creating climate change. Green businesses need to consider their impact on climate change as an important part of what they do. The biggest sources of greenhouse gases for most businesses will be transportation, and energy use in buildings. Energy efficiency is the most cost-effective way to reduce your carbon footprint, usually. Carbon offsets are used by some businesses to further reduce their carbon footprint.

🌿 *Are you conserving water?* Water is an increasingly valuable resource, and it pays to use water wisely.

🌿 *Are you encouraging ridesharing, carsharing, or telecommuting?* Green transportation does not need to cost more, and can help save money.

🌿 *Are you eliminating unnecessary air travel?* Air travel is expensive and has a large environmental impact. If you do need to travel by air, buying offsets can reduce your climate change impact.

🌿 *Are you using renewable materials?* See if any of the materials you plan to use can be replaced with materials that originate from plants, not fossil fuels. Even better, see if the material can be from plants that are sustainably raised and harvested.

🌿 *How much waste do you produce and where does it go?* Consultants can help with waste reduction and reuse as well.

🌿 *Do you have a recycling program?* Recycling is an easy step, and something people look for.

🌿 *What is the environmental impact of your suppliers?* Your environmental impact does not stop at your door. Businesses are increasingly looking at the impact of what they do throughout their supply chain.

🍂 *Have you looked into green business services such as printing, insurance, and banking?* These partners can help you build your green credibility, and move your business forward with their valuable network of connections.

🍂 *How do you help your employees live better lives?* Green businesses are increasingly expected to help people build healthier lives and more sustainable communities.

Green Your Buildings

The buildings you use in your business will probably be responsible for a large part of your environmental impact because they often waste energy and other resources, and create an unhealthy work environment. Buildings with poor lighting or air quality can be a hidden drag on profits by reducing employee productivity. Employees get sick less often in greener commercial buildings, including fewer respiratory ailments. Because employee salaries are one of the largest expenses for many businesses, increasing productivity in this way can have a large impact on overall business performance.

People often assume that green buildings must be very expensive, but according to the U.S. Green Building Council (USGBC), the initial cost of green buildings is about 0 to 2 percent higher than other buildings, which amounts to little or no cost difference upfront. In addition to being a good investment for the environment, green buildings are also a sound business investment, saving money with reduced energy costs for the life of the building and holding value better for their owner, a factor that is likely to continue or even increase in the future as green buildings become more sought after. Green buildings make a clear and highly visible statement about what your business is all about.

While the definition of green is murky in some areas, the definition of a green building has become much clearer thanks to the success of green building certification standards such as LEED (Leadership in Energy and Environmental Design). LEED was established by the U.S. Green Building Council to represent the top 25 percent of buildings according to points scored in different categories such as siting, energy efficiency, water use, and materials. The more points scored, the higher the LEED rating a building can earn—Silver, Gold, or Platinum. While LEED is the leading rating system in green building certification, there are others such as Energy Star buildings, which are rated according to their energy efficiency.

Some of the features of green buildings that certification standards look for include:

- Better lighting, with more use of natural sunlight
- Energy-efficient lighting—using lighting systems that deliver the most light for the energy they consume and lighting controls to reduce waste
- Better insulation and overall building envelope, saving energy for heating and cooling
- Passive ventilation for cooling and air exchange
- Energy-efficient windows and shading
- Use of building materials that are sustainably produced and do not release hazardous materials into the indoor air environment
- Water conservation fixtures
- Greater comfort due to improved environmental control
- Renewable energy production, such as from solar panels on the rooftop
- Cool roofs, or green roofs, cutting down on air-conditioning needs
- Siting near mass transit
- Accommodations for bike riding
- Space for recycling bins

The USGBC now has a rating system for certification of commercial building performance, LEED for Existing Buildings: Operations and Maintenance. Its features describe not just how the building is designed or built but also how it is used. The overall goal is to improve energy efficiency and reduce waste. Even if you're not trying to be LEED certified and just want to get a feel for what steps you can do yourself, look over this rating system to see what is expected in green buildings (see the U.S. Green Building Council website, usgbc.org).

If you are not seeking a LEED-certified new building and your landlord does not want to spend the money to green your building, don't let this stop you. You can still take many cost-effective steps to reduce energy waste. LEED for Commercial Interiors is designed for this situation, and certified or not, anyone can get started with easy, low-cost steps such as changing the thermostat, weatherstripping, and changing your light bulbs.

Lighting is an important energy expense in most commercial buildings, and inefficient lighting is one of the big opportunities to improve. The ways to improve lighting, making it more efficient and friendlier for employees and consumers include:

1. Use natural lighting to avoid the use of electricity.
2. Use automated lighting controls to reduce waste, turning off lights when they are not needed.
3. Switching to more energy-efficient light sources.

Introducing natural light into a business area with skylights, solartubes, or other means can pay for itself through reduced energy costs; the more that natural lighting can be used, the less electricity is needed. Natural sunlight is also more pleasant than electric light, and studies have found that natural light increases business productivity and can even cause shoppers to spend more. Sensors can be installed that turn off or dim lights when daylight is sufficiently bright, automatically tailoring the light level and electricity use.

Another strategy is to turn the lights off when they are not needed. As obvious as this seems, it does not always happen if people must flip switches. A better choice is making the process automatic by installing timers or occupancy sensors from companies such as Wattstopper or Leviton that automatically turn lights off when nobody is around. Some building codes such as Title 24 in California now require the use of occupancy sensors in new commercial construction or remodeled buildings. While occupancy sensors might not be required for businesses in your region yet, they could be soon, and they can be a good investment even if they are not required, paying for themselves with reduced energy costs.

> ## Go Green, Save Money
>
> Occupancy sensors cost from about $30 to $100 per light switch, and they are easy to install, reducing energy use up to 45 percent (green.ca.gov).

Using more efficient light bulbs and fixtures is the next easy step to save energy and money. You don't have to own a building to invest in new light bulbs. While incandescent light bulbs waste most of their energy as heat, compact fluorescent bulbs use 75 percent less energy. One of the benefits of more efficient lighting is that it generates less waste heat, excess heat that can require more air-conditioner usage. Compact fluorescent light bulbs (CFLs) have come down in price and improved in quality, avoiding the issues that have held many people back from buying them. Although they last 10 times as long, they often pay for themselves in less than a year or two, saving $30 per bulb over their lifetime (energystar.gov). To encourage more efficient lighting, the federal government has passed legislation requiring the phasing out of inefficient incandescent bulbs starting in 2012. Other governments around

Calculating the Impact

For a calculator that will figure out how much you will save by changing your light bulbs, go to energystar.gov. Changing light bulbs is one of the low-hanging fruit in energy efficiency, which is one reason why so many governments are helping drive this change.

the world, including the European Union, Australia, and Brazil, are also taking action to phase out incandescent bulbs in favor of more efficient technologies.

Beyond compact fluorescent bulbs, LEDs (light-emitting diodes) are the next generation in lighting technology. While incandescent bulbs last about 1000 hours, CFCs last about 10,000 hours and some LEDs are thought to last up to 50,000 hours. LEDs have been designed with a unique range of colors, they light up instantly without a warmup period, and they are energy efficient. They also still cost a fair amount for some applications, but their cost is rapidly declining and their output improving. By lasting a very long time as well as saving power, they can avoid the trouble of changing bulbs, particularly in hard-to-reach locations. Wal-Mart is changing the bulbs in their refrigerated cases to LEDs, producing less heat, therefore saving money both on lights and cooling. Exit signs or outdoor signage with energy-efficient LED lighting can even qualify for rebates from your utility.

After lighting, another big energy expense is heating and cooling. According to the Energy Star guide for small businesses, commercial buildings spend about 40 percent of their energy bills on heating, ventilation, and air conditioning. To reduce heating and cooling energy losses look at:

1. Investing in energy-efficient heating and air-conditioning systems
2. Reducing losses in ventilation systems by sealing and balancing ductwork

3. Making sure the building envelope is well-sealed and insulated
4. Reducing heat load by using energy-efficient appliances and lighting in the building
5. Using cool roofing to reflect heat from buildings
6. Using energy-efficient windows and shading

These steps have a wide range of costs and paybacks. When it comes to heating and cooling, the low-hanging fruits include sealing the building envelope, taking care of weatherstripping, sealing cracks, and checking insulation. Insulation is being made from a variety of eco-friendly materials such as blue jeans or recycled paper (made flame retardant) as an alternative to fiberglass, and installing insulation often pays for itself with energy savings in two years or less. Air ducts are often a surprisingly easy and cost-effective fix as well. If the air ducts in a building lose 30 percent of the air going through them, fixing the air ducts can increase the efficiency as much as getting an air conditioner with 30 percent higher efficiency, but at a fraction of the price. Installing fans is another low-cost way to reduce cooling costs.

The more costly steps such as changing your heating or air conditioning with more efficient systems will also pay for themselves in most cases, particularly if other steps such as sealing the building envelope and fixing ductwork are taken care of first. The trend in the past has often been to use equipment larger than was needed. With more efficient ducts and a more

Strategies of Green Leaders

The Rocky Mountain Institute has been a leading proponent of energy efficiency for many years, and its website is a rich resource for information about energy efficiency (rmi.org). Reading through its resources can help you get informed about the opportunities to save money, and decide which energy efficiency measures to take first.

efficient building, a smaller air conditioning unit will be needed, reducing the cost of buying a new one. Whether your systems are new or old, they should also be maintained, cleaned, and filters changed to keep them operating as efficiently as possible.

Adjusting your thermostat, setting it higher in summer and lower in winter by a few degrees, is an easy way to save money and energy. It's hard to please everyone, but changing the thermostat even two to three degrees can save money without producing a big change in the general comfort level. Also, changing your thermostat to a programmable digital version helps to automatically turn off the heat at night or on weekends so you don't have to.

Cool roofing is another energy efficiency move for buildings. In hot climates roofs soak up heat from the summer sun and the heat can penetrate into your building, increasing the money spent on air conditioning. Roofing that reflects heat keeps your roof and your building cooler, so less air conditioning is needed. Cool roofs are required for new or remodeled commercial buildings in California under Title 24 building codes, and other states are moving to adopt cool roof standards as well.

Saving Water

Water is increasingly precious in many parts of the world, and as populations grow and the climate changes, this trend is likely to continue. The UN estimates that by 2030 half of the world's people will live in areas without sufficient water, straining businesses as well as people. Scarce water will mean more expensive water, providing an ever greater incentive for businesses to conserve water.

For offices, the main water use is in the bathroom. Looking for leaks in fixtures is a low-cost way to save a lot of water. A leaky faucet or toilet may not seem like a big deal, but the drip from a leaky faucet can waste thousands of gallons a year. If you have the option, consider installing low-flow toilets or waterless urinals.

Landscaping is another big drain on water. If you are selecting a space for your business or planting landscaping yourself, look for drought-tolerant plants from the Mediterranean, Australia, or South Africa. Change your irrigation schedule, the type of sprinkler heads you use, and the timing for your watering schedule.

If you are planning a business that uses large quantities of water, such as an organic farm, a hotel, beverage production, or paper products, you may need to talk with your local water agency and others to anticipate future decreases in supply and increases in the cost of water. A report "Water Scarcity and Climate Change" issued by CERES and the Pacific Institute (2009) found that water use presents an underappreciated risk for many businesses in fields like these.

Finding ways to innovate in these businesses, getting the job done with less water, could provide a key competitive edge. An investment in water efficiency now will pay off in the years ahead, and the tighter that water supplies get, the more important this advantage will become for your business.

The Long Beach Water Department recommends the following ten steps for businesses to save water (see bewaterwise.com):

1. Make a commitment to water conservation.
2. Appoint a conservation champion.
3. Determine how and where you use water.
4. Learn about conserving water in the business environment.
5. Check your system for leaks.
6. Set a conservation goal.
7. Involve your employees.
8. Install low-flow devices.

9. Be aware of water efficient equipment.
10. Monitor your results.

Spending Less on Energy by Going Solar

Like any business, startups are going to use electricity, and for a green startup what could say green better than solar power? There are not many people who are opposed to producing clean energy from the sun, but many people do believe that solar power is too expensive or not reliable. Luckily, solar is getting cheaper, and in some situations you can get solar power for little or no money down.

Cost has been the main factor holding many businesses back from putting solar panels on their buildings because panels often cost $1,000 apiece, and commercial photovoltaic installations easily cost hundreds of thousands of dollars. Although the upfront cost can keep many from installing solar, many more businesses would sign up for solar power if they can get clean green energy without this initial cost. And this is just what SolarCity is providing with power purchase agreements (PPAs).

Like most solar power providers, SolarCity sells panels and installation services to homes or businesses. This business will receive a big boost from increased government incentives, but SolarCity also offers an alternative. For commercial customers, SolarCity can also maintain ownership of the panels, selling customers the power they produce on a per-kilowatt-hour basis in an arrangement called a power purchase

Market Power

One way for businesses to carve out a market niche is by focusing on projects of different sizes. Sun Edison provides power purchase agreements for commercial sites with larger solar installations, megawatt in size, while SolarCity is working with smaller commercial installations as well as homes, carving out a different niche.

agreement (PPA). In addition to installing the panels, SolarCity monitors and maintains the systems they install to ensure that they keep working. "If the panels don't produce power, we don't get paid," says Lyndon Rive, founder and CEO of SolarCity. "We make our money from a system operating optimally."

With about 40 percent of its business in the commercial side, the target business client is typically in an owner-occupied building. "I personally feel there is a big need for small businesses to go solar," says Rive. "This is a market that is underserved, and they see the value. Often they are family-owned, successful businesses. They own their building, use a lot of power, and are looking for ways to save money."

Power purchase agreements do not require any money upfront and can help businesses save money immediately. "They are small savings," says Rive, "but if they have a choice of clean power versus dirty power, and save money as well, then people will sign up." The locked-in rate can be lower than customers pay their utility today, particularly in many states on the East Coast and California. The utility rates are high and are predicted to continue increasing 6 percent or more per year in the years ahead, while the rate with SolarCity increases only 3.5 or 3.9 percent annually, depending on the region. As time passes and the cost differential increases, the savings grow larger.

SolarCity is doing well helping people and businesses save money. "Businesses look at this, and it might not be a lot of money now, but it's a lot over time," says Rive. In addition to saving money, businesses are also looking at this arrangement as a way to reduce their risk, removing volatility from this component of their future expenses. Removing risk and uncertainty from future energy budgets frees up capital for other uses.

In addition to supplying solar panels, SolarCity performs energy efficiency consulting. Solar power and energy efficiency are natural partners. Weatherstripping, insulation, changing

Starting Green

light bulbs, and fixing air ducts all cost much less than solar panels and can provide a big increase in efficiency with a small investment. Educating consumers with rapid feedback about consumption helps them to change behavior, using power more wisely. "It's amazing what education can do," says Rive. SolarCity expects that this information combined with energy savings tips will help customers save between 5 to 15 percent.

Greener Office Supplies

Millions of people work in offices, either an office at home or in a corporate setting, and the office is where many green efforts start. Wherever your business is, you need pens, binders, shipping materials, desks, chairs, coffee, cups, and other office supplies, so the combined environmental impact of millions of offices adds up quickly. There is more to green office supplies than buying recycled paper, and it's not usually obvious from looking at a pen or chair if it is greener than the alternative. While buying green office supplies may not be your business, it is the business of The Green Office (thegreenoffice.com) and other businesses that identify and sell green office products.

Jesse Gibbs has helped The Green Office move its business forward by helping dispel commonly held misconceptions about green products, such as the idea that green products are always more expensive. Sometimes green products are slightly more expensive, but sometimes green products are far less expensive than the alternative, according to Gibbs. "For instance, a remanufactured toner cartridge is greener than a new one since materials are being reused, and it costs significantly less," says Gibbs. "One hundred percent post-consumer recycled copy paper, another popular green product, will typically cost 10 to 25 percent more than paper with no recycled content."

Another common assumption Gibbs encounters is that green products don't work well. "This is a common misconception," says Gibbs. "Green office products work just as well as their conventional counterparts. The average person would not be able to tell if a given document was printed on 100 percent post-consumer recycled paper using remanufactured toner vs. conventional paper with a new toner cartridge."

Although office products may not seem like a big deal, buying green office products can provide a number of benefits, particularly when viewed as just one part of sustainability efforts. "By choosing greener office products and taking steps to improve practices, businesses and individuals are making an important incremental step towards a more sustainable future," says Gibbs.

As part of the overall sustainability effort, greener office supplies can also help employees. "The benefits of a greener workplace are improved employee morale and health, which can lead to greater worker productivity, higher revenues, and increased operating efficiency. Overall, we feel that creating a greener work environment is an essential investment in the most valuable resource of any business, which is its people."

Printing Green

For all of our technological progress in business in the computer age, we still consume mountains of paper, about 85 million tons of paper each year in the United States conventional paper products can damage the environment through the harvesting of trees and the use of water and bleaching agents to produce paper. To reduce the environmental impact of printing, you can use less paper and print on recycled or FSC-certified paper products from sustainably harvested trees.

> ### Tip for Success
> Using electronic communications can cut down on paper use, especially in areas such as mass marketing. "Electronic communication should be the first means of communication," says Midori Connolly of Pulse Event Staging.

One easy way to use less paper is to print on both sides of pages. Another way to go is to stop printing blank pages, either with a specific software solution or by doing print preview every time you print. Narrowing the margins on your pages also reduces the number of pages printed.

Resource Guide

The City of Portland, Oregon, *Green Office Guide* has a great list of ways for offices to go greener, many focused around using fewer resources and saving money at the same time (resource saver.org/file/toolmanager/ O16F22121.pdf).

Some intrepid office workers are pushing the printing envelope by seeing if they can work without printing anything at all. Having the printer right next to your PC can make printing a little too convenient. If all you have to do is push a button and pick it up from the printer without leaving your chair, it's easy to keep printing papers for a quick read, but moving the printer to another room helps change old printing habits. It's surprising what a difference a few steps can make in your mental balancing of the question whether to print or not. It may be hard at first, but with time you could grow accustomed to life without a printer.

Paper is not the only component of green printing—there is also the ink that goes on it. Toner cartridges have piled up in landfills, but HP now offers a recycling program if you mail back the used cartridges. Staples offers a credit for bringing in old cartridges, and Cartridge Depot and Cartridge World both sell reconditioned toner cartridges for far less money than new ones and provides franchise opportunities for green entrepreneurs.

There are also greener options for print jobs that you send out to printing services. Alfonso Maciel of Green Postcards in San Francisco prints flyers, mailers, brochures, annual reports, letterhead, posters, newsletters, announcements, and business cards. "If it goes on paper we can print it," Maciel says. The cost for greener printing can be somewhat higher, according to Maciel. "We go beyond paper and we have become a union shop, so our costs are higher than most because we pay livable wages, health care, and pension plans." The higher cost can be an investment in your community and business network that pays off in the long run.

Dave Michaels directs sales and marketing for Ecoprint (eco print.com), also a green printing business. The Washington, D.C.–based Ecoprint is a wind-powered business. It is carbon neutral, using recycled and FSC-certified paper and low-impact inks for a wide range of printing services. "Being a green business can win you additional opportunities, earn goodwill, stronger relationships, and increase the perceived value of what you offer," says Michaels. "With the landscape increasingly cluttered with green claims, there is a hunger for authenticity and clarity." Taking solid steps such as working with a green printer helps build a credible green brand.

He finds that the cost of green printing depends on the job, but is generally within 5 to 10 percent of other printers. "We are finding ourselves competitive at run lengths of 5,000 and less. Note that as run lengths increase, the green premium increases due to increased paper consumption." He has found that green businesses must also compete on the quality of their service, not just their environmental performance. "This is a big pitfall of new green companies," says Michaels. They are overly focused on the environment, and not enough on business performance. "Core areas that are important to our clients are quality, turnaround times, and ease of use."

Calculating the Impact

To figure out the ecological impact of your printing, try this calculator at the Environmental Defense Fund (edf.org/paper calculator). It can help you see the impact of the paper you use and make more eco-friendly paper choices.

Recycle, Reduce, Reuse, and Save

The dumpster may not be your favorite place to hang out, but it may be another place to discover opportunity. Whatever is in the dumpster is by definition a waste, and waste is a lost opportunity to save resources and save money. Whatever goes in the dumpster is something you paid for once when you first bought it and then again for the waste disposal company to haul it away. That is a lose-lose proposition.

Recycling more aggressively can cut down the amount of stuff in the dumpster. Recycling bottles with a deposit or redemption value earn revenue, and other parts of your waste stream such as metals, plastics, cardboard, and paper may also be worth money. Consultants from businesses such as Waste Management will go through business waste looking for opportunities to reduce waste and save money.

Terracycle (based in Trenton, New Jersey, on the web at terra cycle.net) has built its whole business around making new things out of garbage, including office products such as pencils made from recycled paper, lunchboxes made from juice pouches, reusable shopping bags made from Target bags, and shower curtains made from Bare Naked granola bags. Started by Tom Szaky in 2002 packaging worm poop fertilizer in old plastic soda bottles, it has since branched out to make a variety of other products from garbage, converting this problem into an opportunity. Its business is a model for taking any waste stream and converting it into new products and opportunities. "There is nothing that cannot be made out of garbage," Szaky says, who forms partnerships with major corporations to take their waste and make a profit from it. "The opportunity to change the biggest companies is massively underserved and in massive demand."

In addition to recycling and reusing materials, you can reduce waste by not using something in the first place. For example, do you need paper towels to dry your hands or can you use hand towels? Instead of paper cups and plastic utensils, try using mugs and regular silverware, and install a dishwasher. The disposable stuff may sound cheaper at first, but the cost of disposable items adds up to hundreds of dollars quickly, even in a small business.

Buying water in disposable plastic bottles is another big econo-no-no these days. An easy alternative is water from new water filtration devices such as the unit offered by AquaPure4Me. These eliminate waste, provide cool, clean water, and allow you to stop spending money on bottled water.

Greening Your Transportation

Transportation contributes greatly to global climate change as well as causing pollution. It also can take a great deal of money for businesses to transport goods and people around the globe. As you start up your business, think of the following strategies to green your transportation and shipping needs:

1. Avoid unnecessary travel by air.
2. Choose rail transport.
3. Use more eco-friendly vehicles with better mileage for ground transport and alternative fuels or electric vehicles.
4. Use car-sharing for business vehicles at home or while on business travel.
5. Consolidate orders and shipping into fewer but larger shipments.
6. Use eco-friendly cab and limo services.
7. For business meetings, conferences, and business travel use environmentally friendly hotels.
8. Reuse boxes and other shipping materials.
9. Source materials locally when possible.
10. Use more webconferencing, teleconferencing, and video-conferencing to replace business travel.

Starting Green

11. Encourage employees to carpool, use mass transit, or bike to work.

12. Encourage telecommuting, where appropriate.

You might not think of your employees' commute as part of the impact of your business on the environment, but encouraging ridesharing, carpooling, and carsharing can help employees and your business. It does not cost a business anything to encourage employees to try ridesharing with businesses such as PickupPal. Based in Canada, PickupPal helps match up those who need rides with others who can give them, including those who want to share a ride to work in the morning. Started in Canada, PickupPal is now also found in a growing list of cities in the United States, Australia, the United Kingdom, and New Zealand.

"In these economic times, providing a carpooling option can boost employee productivity, making it easier and more cost effective to get to work," says Brent Drewry, executive vice president of business development at PickupPal. Joining PickupPal can also help a company achieve sustainability goals that it sets for itself and reports to the world. "We provide web-based reporting, which allows companies to track progress against their sustainability objectives, with metrics such as mileage traveled and carbon avoided through the use of ridesharing." PickupPal will soon also be allowing groups to set up their own Eco Rideshare page and add in social networking links to user profiles.

Resource Guide

Limos and taxis can also be greener when you need them, using the services of businesses such as ECO-LIMO (eco-limo.com), OZOcar (ozocar.com), and Terramoto (terramoto.net). These businesses have the benefit of more efficient vehicles, which lowers their operating costs, and a distinct green brand. Terramoto plants a tree for every trip in one of their fleet of Priuses in San Diego.

Carsharing with businesses such as Zipcar (zipcar.com) helps individuals and businesses avoid the expense of car ownership. Zipcar sells use of its cars on an hourly basis to individuals or businesses who work with them. Cars are reserved online and gas, insurance, and up to 180 miles per day are included in the fee you pay. For business travel, you can get access to cars in cities across the United States, the United Kingdom, and Canada. It's easy to get started, and as an added eco-bonus, many of the cars are fuel efficient.

Shipping is another opportunity to reduce your environmental impact, by reusing shipping supplies, for example. Eco-Box of Texas has built its business around supplying recycled boxes for others to use. Make a space for boxes and packing materials that come with shipments you receive.

Other than biking or walking, the greenest transportation option is staying home, and telecommuting is exactly that. The flexible workplace is the wave of the future. The workplace is less and less about having people who all sit in a room or building together, and more about assembling teams of high-quality people who can do innovative work together no matter where they are. The benefits are not just to the employee—the business can win as well if its employees are happier, avoiding the hassle and cost of commuting.

Try reducing costs and your environmental impact by sourcing materials locally when possible. When the price of oil rose abruptly in the summer of 2008 the cost of shipping rose along with it, making even large companies such as Wal-Mart push for ways to reduce shipping costs. The price of oil will rise again, giving local purchasing a financial edge once again.

Green Meetings and Travel

Your business will probably have more meetings than you realize. There are meetings with partners, dinner with clients, awards

events, promotional events, and even the holiday party. These meetings can be made greener in many ways, saving money, wasting less, and enhancing your image. The Green Meeting Industry Council (GMIC, greenmeetings.info) recommends using compostable or biodegradable materials whenever possible and perhaps even considering nondisposable flatware and dishes.

To green events, you can work with professionals such as Midori Connolly, CEO and founder of Pulse Staging and Events in San Diego, the first sustainable audio-visual staging company in the United States. "There is undoubtedly a business case for greening events," Connolly says. "Normally there are several key points to review when planning a green event. These might include accommodation and venue selection, transportation, food and beverage, office procedures, and communications."

There are many options; the choices made to green an event will depend on the size of business, the type of event, and the resources available. "A small business meeting or event has its own unique considerations," says Connolly. "Generally a budget must be more closely monitored and each dollar maximized."

Calculating the Impact

GMIC has found serving drinks and condiments in bulk reduces waste and saves money. Bulk cream is 62 percent cheaper and bulk sugar 50 percent cheaper than in individual sealed packages, for example.

"Think carefully about the site you choose," says Connolly. Minimizing transportation to and from the meeting helps reduce the environmental impact. "Venues situated at or very near airports are an ideal choice. Most airport hotels are willing to negotiate more on pricing for meetings and events.

When arranging the event, guests will expect organic food, which can be served on a budget. "When choosing menus, work with the caterer to source seasonal, organic ingredients locally," says Connolly. "Rather than individually wrapped meals, use tray-passed or buffet where possible. Finger foods and/or sandwiches eliminate the expense of cutlery altogether."

The impact of meetings can include a great deal of material that is thrown away afterward. Even small actions such as throwing away signs and name badges means throwing away money. "One study showed that collecting name badge holders for reuse at an event of 1,300 attendees can save approximately $975 for the event organizer," Connolly says.

Beyond the event itself, many meetings involve outings, but rides on the local harbor may not fit your budget or a green-themed meeting. "Groups can partake in hiking or walking excursions that are good for their health," says Connolly. "Many city walking tours are available at low cost through the local visitors bureau. Probably the best alternatives for group activities are those that benefit the community where the event is held."

Green travel also means staying at greener hotels. A growing number of hotels are working to help the environment to save money and attract business. When looking for a hotel to hold your meeting or to stay at during business travel, you need to have some criteria to help you make your decision. Kit Cassingham has many years of experience as an environmental consultant to the hotel industry and her database of green hotels around the world, with over 3,800 hotels, is a great place to start your search for a venue.

> ### Tip for Success
>
> "If staying at a hotel, request that your room block not receive the daily newspaper but that a few extra copies be left in lobby areas. The hotel usually charges $1 to $2/day for these papers," says Midori Connolly, Pulse Event Staging.

What should you ask a hotel? Cassingham advises being prepared with questions for the sites you are considering. "They should have a checklist of questions about the green issues that matter to them," says Cassingham. Some of the questions she suggests you put on your list are:

- Do you use only durable serving items: plates, cups/glasses, flatware, and linens?
- Is your food locally sourced and organic?
- Do you compost?
- Do you recycle, and if so, what?
- How much of your electricity is from renewable energy?
- Do you have a sheet and towel reuse program?
- Do you have bulk amenity dispensers (shampoo, soap) in the guestrooms?
- Can attendees opt out of having a newspaper delivered?
- Do you recycle, and if so, are there recycling bins in the guestrooms?
- Do you donate to charity?
- Are your sheets and towels made of cotton or other natural fibers (as opposed to polyester blends)?

> **Resource Guide**
>
> Kit Cassingham founded Sage Blossom Consulting in 1989 to consult with the bed and breakfast industry, and in 2004 she actively merged her environmental conservation and hospitality backgrounds. Her database of green hotels can be found at environmentallyfriendlyhotels.com.

The greenest meeting, and the cheapest meeting, may be the one that doesn't happen at all. Technology for collaboration at a distance has improved greatly, allowing ideas and electronic work to travel around the globe without our bodies doing the same. "The recent leap in quality of videoconferencing lends itself to avoiding the time and waste of travel," says Midori Connolly. "The result is avoiding lost production on travel time; no cost of travel for each attendee. Although there will be energy consumed in running a projector, there is no driving, no flying, no shuttling between airport and destination. If purchasing videoconferencing technology is not financially viable, an affordable alternative is to rent the equipment."

Investing in Human Capital

The most valuable part of a business is not the facilities it owns, its stock, or what it produces, but the people in the company that make it all happen. If you are a firm relying on creative individuals for your success, as most businesses are today, treating people well can attract and retain the best talent. Going green is an effective way to do this, by providing a greater sense of purpose. Engaged employees are not just punching the clock, but care about what they do, are more productive, and stick with your business longer.

There are several things you can do to green the employee part of your business:

- Be flexible about work hours.
- Provide good medical benefits.
- Listen to employees.
- Encourage employees to participate in community events and local charities.
- Offer profit sharing and employee ownership opportunities.
- Encourage physical exercise.
- Provide healthy snack options.
- Be transparent and open in communications within the company.
- Encourage green efforts within your company.
- Avoid too much hierarchy.
- Provide educational support and training.

Christopher John is the managing director of Sedona Green Staffing, in Sedona, Arizona, working with green businesses in

renewable energy and many other sectors. "We are active in the natural resources, nonprofit, government, and business communities," says John. "Sustainability can be a part of virtually every sector."

He has found that green businesses have made progress at introducing work cultures that motivate and engage workers, although producing green products is still no guarantee of cultivating green work practices. "It is about creating an atmosphere where people feel empowered and intrinsically motivated while working in a healthy environment toward exciting goals," says John. "By providing a truly green workplace and management mentality, you are encouraging people to become more aware of themselves and their surroundings. Ultimately, companies across the board are realizing that paying genuine attention to sustainability issues will translate to greater employee recruitment, retention, and productivity."

> **Green Resource**
>
> You can find out more about Dawn Dzurilla and the expertise at Gaia Human Capital Consultants in recruiting for cleantech and renewable energy companies at gaiahumancapital.com.

As a business grows, it often must recruit leaders to executive roles and turn to human capital professionals such as Dawn Dzurilla of Gaia Human Capital Consultants to help put the right leadership teams in place and to develop green benefits and branding. In Dzurilla's experience, green entrepreneurs have some things in common: "They have tremendous vision, think of themselves as leaders, they believe in themselves, they believe in what they are doing and are able to attract those willing to join them on such a quest," she says. Having the right leadership also creates the right culture for success.

There are many ways that a person such as Dzurilla can help companies. "We work with them in many ways, particularly to attract, acquire, and retain their senior leadership and key staff talent," says Dzurilla. It's not only about finding a body, but identifying what they need to do to advance the entire operation."

Those buying green products often expect a lot from green businesses. "At some point many firms want their firm to be recognized for sustainability, for their commitment to the triple bottom line. In certain firms, the culture does not follow where the company is headed," says Dzurilla. "They'll be working on developing some aspect of renewable energy, and meanwhile there are SUVs in the parking lot. You are looking around, and there is no interest in energy efficiency. It gets to be an internal blind spot in their culture."

The impact of your business on people does not end at the front door either. Your business affects the lives of customers, suppliers, and workers throughout the supply chain, hopefully for the better. Considering your business in this broader context helps put things in perspective. What kind of world is your business helping create? Progressive businesses are working with communities around the globe whose lives they touch. Starbucks supports local coffee farmers and invests in their communities, for example. Fair trade is a form of this, helping the farmers by ensuring a fair and steady price for the products, as well as helping Starbucks by ensuring a high-quality coffee supply.

Energy-Efficient and Greener Computing

Computers are everywhere in the workplace today, and they use a surprising amount of energy. A typical desktop PC will use over 100 watts of power, much of which is lost as heat that requires more power to cool the building. There are several ways to use less energy, reduce e-waste, and reduce the carbon footprint of computing without sacrificing the power of computing to move your business forward.

Resource Guide

The Climate Savers Computing Initiative (climate saverscomputing.org) is working to reduce the impact of computers on climate change by making them more efficient. They are targeting a 50 percent reduction in PC power consumption by 2010.

The Climate Savers Computing Initiative is developing computers with smaller power sources that are much more efficient. Using a smaller power source in the design of a PC also results in less heat, allowing the fan inside to be smaller. The Climate Savers Computing website lists the more efficient computer models available, including those from major brands such as HP. According to Bill Weihl, the Green Energy Czar at Google, in the typical PC "half of the PC power is thrown away as heat, before it gets near the CPU." One way to find more efficient PCs is to look for the Energy Star label; Energy Star-rated computers use 15 to 25 percent less energy than other computers. Laptops usually consume less power than desktops.

Weihl says Climate Savers Computing is having an impact. "Climate Savers Computing is going very well. We have over 350 organizations [companies, universities, state governments, and nonprofits] as members, all pledging to buy energy-efficient PCs and servers and to use the built-in power-saving features. And all the major manufacturers now have systems available that meet the Energy Star guidelines and also some that meet the more stringent Climate Savers Computing guidelines—and a road map that continues to increase efficiency each year."

Enano computers are small, lean, and efficient, with the new

Calculate the Impact

To calculate potential power savings from your computers, try the calculator at http://co2freeradicals.org /calculate.html.

models using less power when they are on than standard PCs use on standby mode. Joey Crowell, inside sales representative, says Enano models use 15 watts when idle and 28 watts at full-power use. This compares well with typical PCs that use 40 to 60 watts, even for Energy Star compliant computers. Because Enano computers use less energy, they also produce less heat, saving money for air conditioning. Enano computers are also quite small, saving space, reducing packaging, and reducing the impact of shipping. You can find Enano in the EPEAT database and on its website (enanocomputers.com).

Web servers and the transmission of information around the globe also consume power that is usually from burning fossil fuels, such as most electricity in the world. Information and communication systems are now responsible for 2 percent of global greenhouse gas emissions, according to Enernetics, a Boston-based company working to reduce the impact of computing and the internet on climate change.

Alexander Wissner-Gross is the cofounder and CTO of Enernetics, which has its website at CO2Stats.com. CO2Stats has thousands of websites signed up already, ranging from sites for large corporations such as IBM to medium-sized companies such as Segway to a host of smaller businesses. For small businesses with fewer than 10,000 page views a month, the cost of a plan is less than $5 a month, and even sites with up to a million page views a month only pay a flat fee of $29.95 a month.

The first step CO2Stats takes is to look at where website visitors are located and where the servers for sites are located.

> ### Resource Guide
>
> Another place to find a greener PC is at EPEAT.net, the Green Electronics Council. It evaluates computers from major manufacturers (including Dell, HP, and Lenovo) using environmental criteria, and gives products a ranking of Gold, Silver, and Bronze.

Resource Guide

Green web hosting with a company such as AISO.net or Super Green Hosting makes your website as green as the rest of your business by providing solar-powered, carbon neutral web hosting.

CO2Stats uses this information to check its database of power sources around the world, measuring the climate impact of website visitors. "We identify where the greatest energy efficiency gains can be made," says Wissner-Gross. "There are inefficiencies in both content and distribution. A lot more can be done than might have been appreciated."

Next, CO2Stats works with sites to reduce their energy usage, in part by making sites more efficient. More efficient sites also load more quickly, providing the added benefit of helping retain site visitors longer, which often translates into spending more money. For the emissions that cannot be reduced, CO2Stats purchases green-e–certified renewable energy credits (RECs) such as those from NativeEnergy.

As a benefit of participating, clients are able to post a "Green Certified Site" badge verifying to visitors that they are going carbon neutral with CO2Stats. This badge helps attract and retain business to a site. Wissner-Gross reports, "We've found that when people see the badge, they stay longer."

Green Insurance Providers

In greening your business, you are not alone. There are green businesses you can partner with to provide many of your basic business needs. If you need insurance, why not partner with a green insurance provider? You need a bank, so why not deposit your money with a green bank, helping other green businesses in the process? Partnering with other green businesses can help your brand and provide learning opportunities. It can also provide powerful business connections, helping you plug into the community of green businesses in your local area and in the rest of the world.

Every business has risks and needs insurance, and greener choices for insurance are starting to emerge. Green Business Insurance (GreenBusinessInsurance.com) is an independent insurance agency run by Pat Thompson of Dublin, Ohio, specializing in providing insurance for green businesses. When he looks at the insurance industry, he sees it as one of the industries with the most to lose with climate change and the most to gain by encouraging green alternatives. "We really need to get a handle on this," says Thompson. He believes that green businesses present a lower risk in many ways, and he works with underwriters to translate that lower risk into lower costs by brokering better insurance policies. "The insurance industry has everything to gain by giving businesses and individuals an incentive to reduce carbon emissions and reduce waste," he says. "Positive branding, gaining market share, and reducing the frequency and severity of weather patterns are just a few examples how insurance companies would benefit."

If you green your business, you may be reducing your risks in various ways. Having less organic solvent in your business may reduce your fire risk and reduce the risk of health problems for your workers. And reduced risk could mean spending less on insurance. The insurance business is all about measuring risk and having people pay the insurance company enough to cover their risk. When Thompson walks into green businesses, he has noticed they tend to be well-run, run by people who are thinking ahead. "I think green businesses are inherently better managers of risk compared to standard businesses and

> ### Tip for Success
>
> One benefit of policies with Travelers is that in the event of a loss, its policies provide for replacement with green materials.

deserve lower rates," says Thompson. "I can usually negotiate lower rates for the green policyholder."

In addition to working with green business owners, Thompson also works with nongreen businesses to encourage them to convert, lowering risk to provide a win/win for all involved. Although the insurance industry tends to be conservative, the business benefits of going green will encourage more insurance agents to join him.

Going Green and Clean with Green Cleaning

The indoor environment can include chemicals we are not aware of and may not want in our air, both from the materials in the building and from the chemicals used in cleaning. The chemicals in common cleaning products can be a harsh, nasty mix and may be related to health issues for those who use them. The cost of these products includes not just the product itself but also indirect costs due to cleaning-related health issues, environmental costs, and costs for water treatment systems.

Tip for Success

If your business is in a LEED-certified building, you need to use certified cleaning products to maintain your building's LEED status. Green Seal products are certified as containing safe ingredients (greenseal.org).

If you hire a service to do your cleaning, consider a green cleaning service such as Ecoclean Services in San Diego. Owner Carrie Cortazzo provides services that are not harmful to the environment in buildings or the broader world. In the bigger perspective, the benefits of green cleaning include "longer healthier lives, reversing the effects of global warming, and last but not least helping keep our water waste streams cleaner for less money to be spent to get it clean to reuse," Cortazzo says. "Eco-friendly products are not harmful to pets or human health while conventional cleaners do cause problems over time to our skin and lungs." The cost of a green cleaning service is about the same as for conventional cleaning, Cortazzo reports. "For professional cleaning service the cost for conventional runs approximately $30 per hour in San Diego, and eco-friendly cleaning ranges from $32 to $40 per hour depending on the company you choose."

Building a Carbon Neutral Brand with Carbon Offsets

Reducing your environmental impact is the place to start for any business, including the many low-cost suggestions described in this book. Try as you might though, you will probably not completely eliminate your environmental impact. You can change your light bulbs to energy-efficient compact fluorescent bulbs, but they still use electricity, some of which probably comes from burning fossil fuels.

Some businesses are not content to just do better when it comes to helping the environment. They want to be the greenest possible shade they can achieve, and this entails becoming carbon neutral, taking their net emissions of greenhouse gases all the way to zero.

Because most of us cannot completely stop using energy from fossil fuels, another way to go carbon neutral is to pay others to remove greenhouse gases from the atmosphere using carbon offsets. Carbon offsets are an indirect way for a business to reduce its greenhouse gas emissions, paying someone else to reduce theirs. If I need to fly on an airplane from Los Angeles to Boston, and the trip cannot be avoided, I can still avoid contributing to climate change by working with a company that pays a farmer to collect the manure from his pigs and ferment it into methane that is captured. (If you did not pay him to do this and the

More Options

In addition to buying offsets, another option for getting to carbon-neutral is buying Renewable Energy Credits (RECs) from NativeEnergy or others. RECs pay for the additional cost of some renewable energy projects, helping make new projects possible.

manure produced methane on its own that escaped into the atmosphere, the methane contributes to climate change.)

The Carbonfund (carbonfund.org) has a program specifically for small businesses to offset their emissions. Through its Carbonfree Partner program, businesses fill out a worksheet and purchase offsets to zero out any greenhouse gas emissions they are responsible for. For businesses with less than 20 employees, they can purchase CO_2 credits for about $10 for each ton of carbon dioxide avoided. This means a business with 5 people, which will produce about 35 tons of carbon dioxide a year, can offset all of their emissions for $350 a year, a relatively small expenditure.

Terrapass is another business selling offsets for businesses. It supports the green efforts of clients in other ways as well. It has a portfolio of offset projects that are domestic, voluntary, and verified by third parties. The offset projects include wind power, farm power (methane capture from dairy farms), and landfill methane capture. These are all projects that are happening today and provide cost-effective reductions in greenhouse gas emissions. Mira Karp, the manager of sales and business development at Terrapass, says that it encourages energy efficiency as well, providing clients with products and information to cut back on greenhouse gas emissions. "It's definitely something we talk about with all of our clients," she says. "We have seen that Terrapass customers are people who are purchasing offsets as part of a more comprehensive environmental strategy, which includes conservation and energy efficiency."

A variety of small businesses buy offsets from Terrapass, calculating first the amount needed using its online calculator. "People break down their emissions by category, so they can see where their footprint is, and where they can do better," says Karp. Terrapass offsets at present are $13.12 per metric ton of CO_2. One of the upsides of working with Terrapass is that you can display a Terrapass Carbon Balanced Business badge on your website to let business partners and customers know that you have taken this important step.

Buying offsets does cost a little, but provides real value for a business. According to Karp, the benefits are many, depending on the company and what they are trying to achieve. "The owner may feel like it's the right thing to do. It helps with marketing; customers want to patronize a company that takes green issues seriously. Some green businesses see regulation coming and are getting ahead of the game."

Resource Guide

Offsets can be a little confusing for many the first time around. See more about how Terrapass offsets work and their benefits to businesses at its website (terrapass.com).

6

Green Marketing and Communications

So you've got your green biz dream, you've got your product or service ready to go, and you're ready for the customers to come running. But they don't. You feel like you're on one side of a plate glass window waving and shouting at the people rushing past on the sidewalk outside, but nobody is turning to look. How are you going to get their attention and convince them to do business with you? You can have the greenest, most exciting, and innovative product around—and you probably do—but if people don't know about it or don't understand what you're saying, they're not going to buy it. It's time to talk marketing, to start thinking strategically about how to get the word out and bring in business.

It's easy to become so excited about your product that you lose sight of the importance of marketing. After all, if your product saves the planet, why wouldn't everyone automatically pick up on it?

We've all heard people say "These things will sell themselves." Having a great product is important. One of the benefits of green products is that they often earn a loyal and vocal base of customers who help sell them, almost as if the product really was selling itself. But usually there is a lot more to it than that. Usually there is a passionate, creative, and committed entrepreneur in the middle of the crowd of customers telling his story and getting others to listen.

To tell your product's story, you need to know the story well and be good at telling it to anyone willing to listen. Who is the product for? What do customers like to eat, how much money do they make, and what kind of pajamas do they wear? Where are they, and how can you reach them? What do they dream about, and what do they hate? Having a clear idea of your target market helps you to find the best way to reach it.

One issue holding your product back may be that customers have just not heard of it. It's as if you were speaking the wrong language. Another issue is that they might have heard of it, but they are not sold on it. They don't understand why they should spend their money on it. It's not the right thing for them. What are the benefits of your product, and how are you talking about them? Are you giving people what *they* want, or what *you* want them to want? What is your brand?

Surveys routinely find that a vast majority of Americans say they are concerned about the environment and will spend money according to environmental values. For example, an early 2009 survey commissioned by Green Seal and EnviroMedia Social Marketing found that an astounding 82 percent of Americans said they were buying green, even in the worst economy in decades. What else can you get 82 percent of Americans to agree on? Presidential elections these days are won by a few percentage points and called a landslide.

The funny thing is that these numbers just don't jibe with how people actually spend their money. In most product categories green is still a niche: Less than 1 percent of our energy is solar, and 3 to 4 percent of our food is organic. If you drive down the road today, you don't see 82 percent of Americans driving eco-friendly cars or 82 percent of homes having solar panels. What's going on here?

It seems that people respond one way in surveys, based on how they would like to act; they often spend their money another way. Somebody is not telling the whole story. It's easy to say you care about the environment in a phone survey—who doesn't? But spending your money is another thing entirely. And that is where the green rubber hits the road.

One explanation might be simply a matter of convenience. "Green products are rarely on the shelves where consumers shop," says Josh Dorfman, author of *The Lazy Environmentalist* (Stewart, Tabori & Chang, 2007) and CEO of Vivavi. "People do not want to go out of their way or be hassled just to do the right thing for the planet. It's up to green businesses to make it as easy and convenient as possible for consumers to shop their stated green values."

So beware of survey results that are incredibly optimistic and tell you exactly what you want to hear. Basing your marketing plan on results like these may not turn out the way you hope.

The Green Market

What is the green market? There have been a variety of answers. People generally look for a simple answer—seeking the X in "X million consumers buy green products." The more people look into it, the more complex the answer seems to get. Green people are not all the same, and people who buy green products are not necessarily even all that green themselves. They have a multitude of motivations and lifestyles. People buying organic food are not necessarily the same as those investing in energy efficiency improvements in their homes. Going green is not an all-or-nothing response. Some people buy green for emotional reasons, some for their health, some because they're worried about the future for their kids, and some to save money.

I do believe that there is a core group of committed green consumers, the true green believers. They believe in going green as a deep article of faith, and they believe it is the answer to much of what they think is wrong in the world. They bought solar panels years ago, without worrying too much about the cost. If someone explains why a product is good for the planet and for those who live on it, these people will listen and often buy it, even if the product is more expensive. The problem for entrepreneurs is that this group is relatively small, a few percent of Americans. Granted, this is still millions of people, and plenty of successful businesses have been built selling to this group. But it is a niche, and far from the whole story.

One commonly discussed green consumer group is LOHAS, an acronym for people with Lifestyles Of Health And Sustainability. In 2006, the Worldwatch Institute reported that the LOHAS market in the United States spent $300 billion and included 30 percent of U.S. consumers. Others put the amount spent at closer to $200 billion. LOHAS are a broad group buying a great variety of products and services—organic food, yoga, alternative medicine, hybrid cars, eco-travel, green building, solar panels, green clothing, and the list goes on. Some have described companies selling to this group by how they do business—in an ethical and eco-friendly manner—rather than by what they sell.

I Googled "LOHAS" while writing this book and found over 2.8 million hits, a healthy number. The LOHAS idea has been around a while now, but groups tied to LOHAS, such as the LOHAS Channel, *LOHAS Journal,* the LOHAS Consumer Report Series, the LOHAS Forum and Business Conference, and of course, LOHAS.com, seem alive and well. Some green marketers say LOHAS is an outdated concept, but perhaps these are people moving on to market the latest concept.

The Greenest Americans

In the afterward of *Strategies for the Green Economy* by Joel Makower and Cara Pike a variety of market segments is described based on The Ecological Roadmap, a study by Earthjustice. Using over 900 questions, 1,900 people were interviewed and a variety of values were tracked and analyzed. Three groups in their analysis were seen as the most promising green market segments: the Greenest Americans, The Postmodern Idealists, and the Compassionate Caretakers.

The Greenest Americans, 9 percent of people interviewed, rank the environment highest on their list of values. "This group of largely older, highly educated, white Americans represents the best market for the best green products," writes Pike. "When trying to reach the Greenest Americans,

Market Power

It's common to assume that demographics predict how people are thinking and how they will spend, but this is not always true. In *The Gort Cloud* (Chelsea Green Publishing, 2009), Richard Seereini says that green is not a demographic, to be described by age groups, income levels, or ethnicity, but a psychographic, defined by attitudes and values.

keep in mind that they do their homework and research their green choices. They are four times more skeptical of advertising than the average American and care little about brands. As a result, they are unlikely to take marketing claims at face value." The study found that this group makes environmental factors an important part of purchasing decisions, and many have the money to buy the products.

Postmodern Idealists are another important green group described by Pike. They are young people with high incomes and strong environmental values. They are strong individualists, believe in diversity, and consider labor practices an important part of going green. They are also drawn to technology-oriented products such as solar gadgets. It is not a large group. It totals just 3 percent of Americans, but the many students and young people in the group may provide a continued opportunity in the future as their earning power grows.

Compassionate Caretakers are one of Pike's larger market groups, and include about 25 percent of all Americans. A majority of Compassionate Caretakers are women, and they are very socially engaged in their communities. They don't think of themselves as environmentalists, placing kids and families higher on their list of priorities. They are busy and will buy green if it fits into their life and works. "If you can catch their attention, green messages tied to children, family, and health will resonate with Compassionate Caretakers," writes Pike.

Going Mainstream: The Un-LOHAS

There are a small percentage of Americans who will buy green even it is more expensive, perhaps 5 percent. These are the true believers, the Greenest Americans. But that leaves another 95 percent of people who generally won't. Opportunity Green 2008 at UCLA, the panelists including Josh Dorfman (author of *The Lazy*

Environmentalist) and Zem Joaquin (founder of EcoFabulous), all agreed that price is still the key factor for most consumers, and if the price of buying green is higher, 95 percent of people won't buy it (the number here is not exact). For green to truly go mainstream, it must get over this obstacle.

For green products to break out of their niche and go mainstream, they have to be great products with a combination of features, design, and price that draws consumers in. "The key is to rid yourself of any notion that you will have success simply because your product or service is green," says Dorfman. "Create and deliver products and services that are exceptional in addition to being green and you'll stand a good chance of reaching a broad base of consumers."

Can education change this observation? Sometimes, but the customer has to be hooked first before a little further information can reel them in. "It's much easier to educate a consumer about environmental values when the consumer loves your product or service," says Dorfman. "People are very open to discussing the benefits of sustainably harvested or reclaimed wood when purchasing our furniture when they have already fallen in love with the design of the piece. If they haven't fallen in love with the design, they're generally not interested in being educated as to its environmental benefits. The simplest way to succeed is to not ask the consumer to change but rather to deliver green products and services that surpass a consumer's expectations."

Advertising and Public Relations

Advertising and public relations are two strategies for entrepreneurs to get their story told to a much broader audience than they can probably achieve on their own. Working with a public relations firm requires an investment, as does buying ads, but the investment could pay off significantly. A little bit of PR can go a

long way to get you noticed more rapidly in the media than would otherwise be possible. And media exposure provides credibility, validation by a third party that you are the real deal.

As a partner in Signature Green Public Relations and Marketing (signaturegreen.net), David Mleczko has a great deal of experience in helping green businesses find the most effective strategy to advance their business. "It's a tough call knowing whether to move forward with an increased marketing investment for your growing business," says Mleczko. "Any marketing investment is going to compete with precious resources needed for other vital operational challenges."

The key to working out the best strategy can be seeing what works, and to do this you need a way to measure success. "What's your return on marketing dollars spent? This is where many business owners get stuck," says Mleczko. "Public relations results are tough to measure and quantify. Some measure the success of public relations by comparing it to the cost of advertising while others look at the reach and frequency of advertising compared to media coverage based on circulation or viewership."

The benefits of public relations can extend beyond increased sales at the moment, increasing the profile of your business far down the road. "With an effective PR campaign you should see a bump in inbound calls, more traffic on your website, and rosier sales reports from your retailers as stories hit the papers and airwaves," says Mleczko. "But the value goes far beyond the stories printed and aired. A good PR firm, with the right messaging and positioning, will help build your brand with consumers for the long haul."

"It's really important for small businesses to build rapport with local media outlets and expand from there," says Dorfman, author of *The Lazy Environmentalist*. "A good local story can do wonders for a business. I started Vivavi in Washington, D.C. Within a month of our launch *The Washington Post* covered our

TOP TEN GREEN PR TIPS

The top ten factors that David Mleczko of Signature Green Public Relations and Marketing suggests you look for in a public relations firm before you start doing business with it are:

1. Hire a firm that will take the time to really understand your business and target audiences for growth.

2. Find a firm with experience in growing smaller businesses. You are not Fortune 500 (yet). Will it keep in touch and strategize with you along the way as your business and opportunities evolve? Ask for references on this question specifically.

3. Is it strategic? A shotgun approach of blasting news releases out to the media may not work as well as a laser-like strategy to reach customers and retail partners.

4. Contacts are important, but look out if a firm promises you coverage, or drops fancy celebrity names. Who you know is worthless without a newsworthy story to tell.

5. Look for a "clip" book with examples of its success for other clients. Check out a client's online press room.

6. See how well it understands environmental issues and can articulate them. Check out its client list for any "bad guys."

7. Talk about branding, asking how the firm sees positioning your unique product and "green" value in your competitive space to gauge its creativity and strategic brainpower.

8. Look at the size of the firm, to make sure that you and your business don't get lost in the shuffle.

TOP TEN GREEN PR TIPS, CONTINUED

9. Look for a point person with whom you will be dealing. Ask who will manage your account and how long he/she has been with the firm and in the PR business.

10. Find out the term of an agreement. For how long will you be locked in, and how do you get out if the results don't pan out?

---

retail website. Granted, *The Washington Post* is a very large home-town paper, but we were able to get incredible marketing mileage out of that article. Bottom line is that good press boosts a company's credibility, and every small business needs to establish credibility as fast as possible."

Create a Website

Just about any business today has a website. It's so easy and inexpensive to put a website together that there's no reason not to, no matter how small you are. A large percentage of people today search for just about everything on the web first, often through Google or Yahoo. The Yellow Pages are getting to be old news, I'm afraid. Some small businesspeople are intimidated by the idea of setting up a website, but it's not as daunting as they think. To have a simple professionally crafted website put together can cost a few thousand dollars, and there are green web design firms that specialize in dealing with green businesses and understand their needs and markets. In addition to supplying green web hosting, for example, Greenest Host also features Greenest Design, with CEO Mike Corrales (full disclosure—

this is the business that designed the Starting Up Green website for me).

If that sounds like a lot of money still, then you can do it yourself. Domain registrar Network Solutions provides not only domain registration but also hosting and website building tools for you to do it on your own. Even if you have very little money and few computer skills, you can figure out how to use the tools they provide for web design. I'm no computer whiz myself, but I put together the site for 75GreenBusinesses .com using their tools. (It's nothing fancy I know, but it seems to get the job done.) You can use one of their preconfigured layouts as a template to get started and drop building blocks into place. Supplying content is more of an issue than the design.

> **Tip for Success**
>
> The web has been around for a while now, so the selection of choice domain names is getting a little picked over. Strings of a few words can still work though.

One of the keys to getting your site together is picking a domain name. It needs to be clearly connected to your business. If your business is called EcoBlabbers and your domain for its website is HighEnergySpeakfest.com, then the connection between the two is too obscure, hurting your ability to draw traffic. If you sell green tennis rackets, don't call your website BallGreens.com—see if GreenTennisRackets.com is available first. Having a good domain name can even be a part of choosing your business name.

Once you have a website, you need to promote it. Google provides some handy tools like Google AdWords that allow you to selectively place small ads on relevant sites, targeting certain keywords. You can start running ads for little money, paying per click. Simple in principle, volumes have been written about strategies to promote your website through tools like AdWords.

Blogging for Dollars

A blog is like a journal kept on the web, with frequent entries. For your business blog, you could write about what you're having for breakfast, but unless your business is breakfast food it might be better to write about the news, opinions, and events related to your business, things your customers would want to know. Part of the goal is for people to get to know you better and relate to you by bringing them into your thought process. For the blog to be worth your while and attract people to it, you need to have something to say of general interest and you need to say it reasonably often, adding to the blog at least once a week. People will be most interested and follow your blog if you talk about things that are on their mind.

More Options

Check out my own blogs at 75greenbusinesses .com/blog and on Fast Company where I'm an "expert blogger" on green business.

When you have a blog, people who like it will set up a feed through an RSS (really simple syndication). Feeds provide them with updates every time you post something to your blog. If people start to follow your blog, that draws traffic back to your site and increases awareness of you and your products.

Blogging was a new phenomenon a few years ago, but now it's almost a given that your business will have a blog. It takes a little time to put together a post, but blogging is free. "Such methods are not merely important; they're essential," says Josh Dorfman. "In today's marketplace, you're operating at an extreme disadvantage if you're not taking advantage of free tools to build a relationship with your customer. This applies to all businesses, not just green businesses."

In addition to writing for your own blog, you can also work to get attention on other people's blogs. Getting others to talk about you on their blogs can provide validation of your business. The information about you on the web is not just you talking about yourself, but others saying good things as well. Some of the most popular green sites are read by hundreds of thousands of people or more.

Influential and highly read green blogs to target include:

- 🍃 Treehugger
- 🍃 Inhabitat
- 🍃 Ecopreneurist
- 🍃 Trendwatching
- 🍃 WorldChanging
- 🍃 EcoGeek
- 🍃 Jetson Green
- 🍃 The Lazy Environmentalist

There are also green news sites, such as:

- 🍃 GreenBiz.com
- 🍃 Sustainable Industries
- 🍃 Renewable Energy World

Frankly there are a ton of blog sites, and the number is growing all the time. The sites to target depend on your business. If you are developing a green gadget, the wind-powered blender, try Eco-Geek. For hot green style and designs, try Ecofabulous. For your cleantech business, you need to get your story in Renewable Energy World. In general, of course, the more blogs you get on, the merrier.

But you don't have to stick to sites that are labeled green. There is a big mainstream world out there beyond the green one. The really big jackpot is to get into mainstream media. If you've got a good story and you can make it relevant to benefits beyond the environment, such as saving money, living well, and taking care of our kids, then go for the nongreen mainstream bloggers.

The Gort Cloud

Richard Seireeni's recent book *The Gort Cloud: The Invisible Force Powering Today's Most Visible Green Brands* put a name to something that I was starting to sense but had not yet put my finger on. In it, Seireeni describes how green entrepreneurs are connected to a variety of groups that share common interests and interact closely with each other. This network of interacting groups and people is "The Gort Cloud." He tells the story of several entrepreneurs that have successfully tapped into this network to spread their message, reaching a much broader group than would otherwise be possible. The Gort Cloud can also help connect entrepreneurs to those with valuable skills and services that can help advance your business.

If the right people like what you have to offer and talk about your work with others, the message can spread rapidly. Whether they were consciously aware of it or not, many green leaders such as Jeffrey Hollender of Seventh Generation or Tom Szaky of Terracycle who are adept at communicating have used their connections in this cloud of interactions to communicate a brand without spending a great deal.

Making Connections

The various groups that connect with each other to make the Gort Cloud include:

- Government (EPA, FDA, Department of Energy, state governments)
- Nonprofits (Sierra Club, NRDC, Union for Concerned Scientists)
- Businesses
- Schools
- Blogs
- Customers

This does not mean the connections happen on their own. Some entrepreneurs have innate skill at talking to others in this way and creating a compelling story that others want to hear. Others might need to strategize a bit. Try to avoid appearing overly contrived because being authentic is a big plus in many green eyes and ears.

One way or another, you need to make a connection using whatever resources you've got. Join groups, blog, meet people for coffee, call the local paper, have your friends tell their friends, do something crazy that catches everyone's attention. Do whatever it takes to be known. This is all part of reaching out into the cloud.

In *The Gort Cloud,* Seireeni tells the story of Dr. Bronner's Soap. Over many years Dr. Bronner's has built a solid and growing reputation around the quality of its organic soap. Given samples, people come back for more and stick with it, paying 30 percent more for the product compared to some of its competitors. Dr. Bronner's spends little on advertising because of the success of its other promotional work—its ad budget for 2008 was $12,000.

Social Networking Media

After blogging came social networking, where online communities of people who share something in common can interact electronically. The common interests can vary dramatically, and can include green topics. Social networking can be a very easy way to make new connections, to stay in touch, and to rediscover old connections. Old friends I haven't talked to for 20 years found me on the internet this way, and I've made great new business connections as well. Social networking is not something I have grown up with like some younger folks, but slowly I have found it can be useful.

One caution—some of these social networking sites such as Facebook can also become huge time sinks, and given the nature of the beast, sometimes it's hard to tell what's a sink or not. Some discipline might be in order to use the tool productively and not twitter your life away.

LinkedIn

LinkedIn is a business-oriented social networking site. It was originally little more than your CV posted online, but it has grown

and added new functionalities. One practical aspect of LinkedIn is that it helps you stay in touch with people in a mobile workforce as they move from job to job. Previously, if people left their business, their old e-mail would go dead and so would their phone number, and that could be the end of your connection to them. With LinkedIn, your contacts can update their e-mail and other information to keep their network intact and stay in touch even as they move around. As a business-oriented social networking system, LinkedIn tends to be more about the work you are doing and not so much your personal life. You won't find pictures of crazy college parties in LinkedIn. You will find people you have worked with previously but lost touch with, and they will find you.

LinkedIn groups can be a useful way to connect with people interested in environmental business. For example, the GreenBiz group in LinkedIn now has over 10,000 members, sharing discussions, jobs, and news.

Facebook

Facebook started on college campuses, out of the founders' dorm room, and it still has a portion of its system devoted to the antics of college kids. I wasn't sure about getting into Facebook, but my attitude has changed somewhat. It's still a different crowd than LinkedIn and a lot more informal, but it also has a useful side for businesses.

One big attraction of Facebook is that it's free, one reason it has a bajillion members. People mix business and personal connections and links. The sense of closeness with a big group can be attractive, but can also be deceiving. Another reason people like Facebook is because it makes them feel closer to those who share pictures, messages, and other tidbits about their personal lives. I advise a little caution before you let your hair down too far. If you are using Facebook for business, be careful about what you say and post. Assume that the world inside Facebook is a public one.

Twitter

Twitter is suddenly a huge phenomenon, exploding out of nowhere it seemed. It's a combination of social networking and instant messaging to groups. Each entry, called a "tweet," is limited to 140 characters, about one sentence. Such short messages are a natural progression and an inevitable one for the age of the Blackberry, iPhone, and instant messaging. We communicate in shorter and shorter bursts, and we want more and more frequent information.

There are many who swear by Twitter for small frequent updates on what their friends and acquaintances are up to or for business info, like Stocktwits. To tell you the truth, I'm still figuring Twitter out. There's not much you can say of consequence or with much insight in so few characters, other than providing a link to a blog or a news story. It's like a media aggregator, with every person creating her or his own mini news channel. I'm afraid it's a little noisy in there, with all of the tweeting and retweeting, and it can be hard sorting through it all. There are many green businesspeople in Twitter though including me and many of the people I talk about in this book.

> ### Ghost Twittering
>
> I recently read that some celebrities hire people to enter tweets for them. Maybe green celebs will want some green ghost tweeting work to be done as well.

Green Meetings

Another valuable way to connect with potential customers, partners, and media is at conferences, meetings of local groups, and networking events. No matter how electronic things get, there is

something in us that still feels the need to see someone in person before we do business. Maybe it's just human nature to want to shake hands and look people in the eye before we do business together.

There are a growing number of green business conferences. One way to attend is to just register at the meeting and walk around talking to people. Another is to buy a booth, and if you have a lot to say and the right connections, you might just get in as a speaker.

Resource Guide

The USGBC holds one of the largest green building events, the Greenbuild conference, which grew to 28,000 attendees in 2008. As recently as 2002 the meeting only had 4,189 people registered, which shows the explosive growth of the green building field in recent years.

Green America (formerly called Coop America) sponsors multiple green business gatherings called Green Festivals at different times of year in different cities. Green businesses can apply to join Green America's Green Business Network for a small screening fee ($95 in early 2009) and membership dues, which provides a free listing in its National Green Pages, the opportunity to exhibit at Green Festivals, networking opportunities, and other benefits.

I can't list all of the green business meetings out there, but there are a few that deserve special mention. I've greatly enjoyed West Coast Green, a green building conference and much more, that covers a broad range of topics related to the growth of sustainable businesses. Its amazing lineup of speakers in recent years has included Al Gore, Van Jones, Ed Begley, Hunter Lovins, Sarah Susanka, Eric Corey Freed, David Suzuki, and a host of other shining green luminaries and helped energize attendees to get out and make a difference.

Opportunity Green, founded by Mike Flynn and Karen Solomon, has been held at UCLA in November in recent years.

It also talks broadly about the growth of sustainable business-es. Innovators like Tom Szaky (founder of Terracycle), Graham Hill (founder of Treehugger.com), Zem Joaquin (founder of Ecofabulous), Josh Dorfman (author of *The Lazy Environmentalist* and CEO of Vivavi), Chip Ridgeway (VP of Environmental Programs at Patagonia), and many others have offered valu-able insights about the dos and don'ts of growing a sustainable venture.

More informal networking oppor-tunities are also being organized by Green Drinks (greendrinks.org). Green Drinks groups now meet once a month in hundreds of cities around the world, talking about environmen-tal topics or whatever else comes to mind and sharing a drink together, getting to know each other, and swap-ping business cards. Sometimes a speaker will be featured. Because a great deal of business is still local, meetings like these are a good opportunity to see what new and interesting businesses are in your area, and perhaps connect with some customers as well.

> ### Resource Guide
>
> EcoTuesday, founded by Oren Jaffe and Nikki Pava, organizes green networking events in a growing number of cities, for example, San Francisco, Los Angeles, and Washington, DC. Groups meet every fourth Tuesday.

The Eco Investment Club (ecoinvestmentclub.com) has members around the world bringing together investors and entrepreneurs interested in fostering green businesses as both great investments and the right thing to do. Yeves Perez is the CEO of EINI, the parent company of the Eco Investment Club, and drives its mission forward with meetings and programs that bring together key people in emerging cleantech hubs like San Diego. One of the innovative programs Perez has created is his ClimateChangers designation, being used to recognize people like Bob Noble, CEO of Envision Solar, "businesspeople who

have demonstrated an eagerness to reduce carbon emissions in their industry of practice, and the knowledge and creativity to achieve that goal."

One of the requirements for being a ClimateChanger is meeting an educational component. It's necessary to take valuable courses like "Climate Change and Business—The ROI for Going Green," a two-day course offered by Scripps Institution of Oceanography and the Rady School of Management at UC San Diego. Another offering is the "Eco Investors Bootcamp" in San Diego, which includes classes and tours of green businesses to get people up to speed on the state of the green business community.

Building a Green Brand

Advertising is all about creating a brand, right? But what is a brand? It's an intangible, without physical form, but it often has more value than all of the buildings, machines, offices, and other tangible assets a company owns.

A brand is closely related to the motivation people have to buy something. It often relates to a feeling they have about a product, a feeling derived from the brand. The brand includes the logo, images, songs, trademarks, and experiences that customers associate with a product or service. The point of branding is to make customers associate your product (or service) with something they want to have, something they see enough value in to purchase. Good branding drives sales. It keeps your product from being a commodity, interchangeable with every other product in your category, and not valued highly.

What about building a green brand? Sustainability is an essential part of the brand, of course, but images of butterflies and dandelions might not be enough. As green consumers get more sophisticated, the message needs to get more sophisticated.

It's not enough to just say something is green—why is it green and how green is it?

Labels and certifications are part of green brands, creating shortcuts to understanding the environmental benefits and avoiding jargon. But with the proliferation of labels, there is a big risk of losing sight of the overall story. The field is crying out for some simplification.

For the broader market, the mainstreaming of green, the green message may only be brought on at the end. How does it benefit customers and how is this communicated? The strategy for this market might be to not worry about creating a green brand, but just concentrate on creating a great brand. A great brand has all of the virtues—the right price, function, features, style, and environmental benefits as well. People driving the Prius aren't all out to save the planet. None of them are opposed to it, but they also like the fact that the mileage saves them money, that the car is surprisingly roomy inside, that it has four doors, you can carry stuff, and the car is reliable.

Joel Makower explains in *Strategies for the Green Economy* (McGraw-Hill, 2008) that consumers for the most part still want the same things as always: "They want what everyone in developed economies want: comfort, security, reliability, aesthetics, affordability, status, and pleasure." Most consumers are not captivated solely by the environmental benefits. "They want to know: *What's in it for me, today?*" So, images of butterflies and dandelions might have their place in ads, but they won't work for everyone by a long shot.

Avoiding Greenwashing

Green marketing has changed. As more businesses have tried to position themselves as green, there has been some backlash from skeptics. Of late there has been a great deal of talk of

greenwashing, with skeptics accusing firms of making misleading or exaggerated claims about the environmental benefits of their products. This does not mean that green businesses should give up, but they do need to be careful in the message that they use to reach consumers.

EnviroMedia has a listing of greenwashing examples in its Greenwashing Index (greenwashingindex.com). People get to vote and comment on the examples of ads they feel are the most disingenuous, as well as the ads they find the most authentic. Ads from oil companies, coal, and some power generators tend to get tarred and feathered on the site as the "worst offenders."

One target of greenwashing accusations, for example, has been producers of bottled water who reduce the amount of plastic in each bottle by 30 percent. Most consumers aren't really

GREEN LIST

According to Terrachoice Environmental Marketing (sinsof greenwashing.org), greenwashing can be broken down into seven categories, "The Seven Sins of Greenwashing." They are:

1. Sin of the Hidden Trade-Off

2. Sin of No Proof

3. Sin of Vagueness

4. Sin of Worshipping False Labels

5. Sin of Irrelevance

6. Sin of Fibbing

7. Sin of the Lesser of Two Evils

buying this one as being very green, with bottled water being inherently not very sustainable compared to filtered water.

To make statements about the environmental benefits of products, the claims should be measurable, clear, verified by a third party, and relevant. For example, if you make a statement about your window cleaner being free of chlorofluorocarbons, this is true but irrelevant because window cleaners never contain CFCs. Its like saying a soda is health food because it's fat free, even though it's loaded in high-fructose corn syrup, and never had fat in the first place.

Your ads and other marketing might still focus on brief memorable messages and images, but having more in-depth information about environmental impact available on your website can at least allow those who are interested to verify for themselves what you are up to.

The concern about greenwashing is great enough that some businesses have shied away from talking about their environmental efforts. When Ray Anderson was first developing his plan to transform Interface into a sustainable floor covering company, he forbid his team from talking about the changes until the work was well underway (See *Mid-Course Correction*). This is one of the keys that others have discovered to avoid greenwashing as well: "Do first, talk later."

Because no business is perfectly sustainable today, talking about your environmental benefits can inevitably reveal not just the progress made but also the distance still left to go, leading some of the more vociferous critics to point their green accusing finger at you. If companies must be perfect to speak of their progress, the bar is getting set

Resource Guide

The U.S. Federal Trade Commission has even gotten into the act, reviewing the rules for ads regarding environmental marketing claims. You can read the rules at: ftc.gov/bcp/grn rule/guides980427.htm.

too high, I'm afraid. There needs to be a reasonable balance between making real progress and claiming more than you should.

Sustainability Reporting

In addition to reporting their financials, a growing number of businesses are creating an annual report summarizing their environmental efforts. There is no regulatory requirement in the United States for companies to report this information, but many companies have decided to do so to inform shareholders, for public relations purposes, to attract investors, and to track their progress toward environmental goals. Some of the largest businesses now put out a sustainability report annually. In the absence of mandatory requirements, the content varies widely. You can easily find examples on the internet. Some are very detailed in their measurement and reporting. Others have minimal data and maximal photos of green-looking things.

Personally, I like to see a transparent and substantial sustainability report, one that provides useful numerical data about environmental performance rather than a public relations-oriented effort. ShoreBank Pacific provides a good example with their own Sustainability Report for 2007–2008 posted on their website (eco-bank.com/SBPNews/sustainableReport.php).

The Global Reporting Initiative (GRI) provides a framework for standardized sustainability reporting (globalreporting.org/Home). Having a standardized format adds value, just as it does with financial reports, allowing the progress of businesses to be tracked and compared. The more sustainability reports are standardized in how they provide this data, the more useful the data will be to shareholders and the business itself as a guide for further environmental progress.

Green Promotional Gear

Promotional items like pens, mugs, and shirts can be a good way to increase your business profile, but for green businesses promotional gear poses a dilemma. Like everybody, green businesses need to promote themselves, but promotional gear that is bad for the environment or wasteful may hurt your image rather than help. Businesses like Proforma Simonetta Freelance or EcoImprints provide promotional items that are greener than the usual promotional items: shirts from organic cotton, soy candles, and pens made of recycled material.

How do eco-friendly promotional materials benefit a business? "We sell promotional items and apparel," says John Simonetta, owner of Proforma Simonetta Freelance. "These items really have to do with branding. If you are a green company, your uniforms should be green, your promo items and giveaways should be green, your annual report, brochure, business cards should be green. Say a company spends $250,000 on updating its energy usage at its plant. How many clients actually see the plant? In addition to doing the hard work of greening its infrastructure, a company also needs to green its outward-facing components, and that is often print, promotional, and apparel."

One common assumption about green promotional items is that they are more expensive, but this is not necessarily the case. "Pricing is compatible if you are comparing two like goods, for example, a pima cotton polo shirt and a soy flax shirt are similar in quality and price," says Simonetta. "However as most eco-clothing (recycled poly, soy flax, carbon fiber bamboo, organic cotton) is currently better quality then most cheap cotton shirts, the cheapest shirt is normally standard cotton. Same for totes, printing, and promo items. A corn plastic coffee mug is cheaper than a petroleum plastic mug of the same weight; however, the cheapest mug will normally be a cheap, petroleum plastic mugs. If you are comparing quality, pricing is really on par, and this is not something that was true even 18 to 22 months ago."

Giving Back Can Help Your Business

A key message of the environmental movement is that we're all in this together, living together in the same communities and sharing the same planet. It's an easy message to relate to, and one of the reasons many people are involved and committed to greening their business. By reaching out and giving something back to the world, your business can deepen its connections in the local community and the broader world, and reaffirm its mission. It also lets people know that you are putting your money where your mouth is.

Many green businesses donate time, goods, or money to causes they believe in, and support nonprofits that are aligned with the business they are in. For example, if you are an organic food company, you might give back to organizations that support organic farming and farmers. The group 1% For the Planet is an alliance of over 1,000 businesses that give 1 percent of their sales to environmental causes. These businesses benefit from knowing that they are helping to make a difference, and they benefit from being green leaders. They can display the 1% For the Planet logo on their website, letting others know of their commitment.

You can also give back in other ways. You can give your time to local groups and activities, or to schools, encouraging kids to seek a brighter future by learning and working with green businesses. You can encourage your employees to give, allowing them time to get involved in these activities, even during work hours. However you do it, you might find that whatever you give is returned manyfold.

Getting Creative—Green Guerrilla Marketing

In the absence of a great deal of money to spend on marketing, small businesses need to get creative to reach their market. Here are some marketing ideas based on what others have done.

One common marketing technique is giving out samples. Go out to markets, fairs, and anywhere that people who might be interested in your product gather and give out a sample, along with information about where it can be purchased. Giving out coupons is another hook, especially when partnered with the sample. If your product is as good as you think it is, having it in their hands or in their mouths (where appropriate) should go a long way toward convincing customers to get on board.

In his book *Stirring It Up* (Hyperion, 2008), Gary Hirshberg recounts several adventures in green guerrilla marketing, starting with handing out Stonyfield samples at the local grocery store. "We had no cash or credit and only two yogurt demonstrators, Samuel and me," writes Hirshberg. "Our entire sales kit consisted of the table, a homemade sign, the yogurt, the maple syrup, and one apron." At one point a Boston radio DJ commented that he would rather eat camel manure than their yogurt, in response to which Hirshberg secured camel manure and drove from New Hampshire to Boston to provide the DJ with the choice. The yogurt won, as did Stonyfield when it got tons of air play. In Chicago they handed out yogurt cups and coupons to train commuters. In Houston they inflated car tires and

> ### Tip for Success
>
> "Find ways to piggyback with other companies that have larger marketing budgets," suggests Josh Dorfman. "We furnished a model unit inside the Riverhouse luxury green condo building in New York City, which enabled us to leverage the Riverhouse's marketing dollars and mailing list to reach our target market."

gave out more yogurt. Over and over, the key for Stonyfield was having a great product and connecting with customers directly.

In *The Gort Cloud,* Seireeni relates the story of Spencer Brown, the founder of Earth Friendly Moving, which produces moving boxes from recycled plastics, reducing the amount of cardboard sent to landfills. "The best way to reach green consumers is viral marketing," Brown says in the book. "The green community talks. They love to share and expose their new finds." They set up displays in yoga studios, spoke in classrooms on Earth Day, and some of their contacts started talking about them on Treehugger and MySpace, spreading the word. He tells the story of Earth Friendly Moving everywhere he goes.

Green Leader Insight

JOEL MAKOWER, EDITOR OF GREENBIZ AND AUTHOR OF *STRATEGIES FOR THE GREEN ECONOMY*

While the green business world is loaded with opportunity, realizing that opportunity can still be a challenge. As one of the best known green business experts, Joel Makower has been helping businesses large and small navigate their way in the growing green world for more than 20 years. In addition to acting as the executive editor of GreenBiz.com and directing events produced by Greener World Media, which he co-founded, he is the author of the recently published book *Strategies for the Green Economy*.

Makower sees two kinds of opportunities for entrepreneurs to join the green business world. "You can create the green version of an existing business model or you can invent something new—a new product,

---

JOEL MAKOWER, CONTINUED

technology, or service," says Makower. "Almost every business has some kind of green counterpart these days." Still, it's not just about being green, according to Makower: "I don't know if most people want to start a green business, but if they want to start a business, creating a green version may be a part of the value proposition."

When it comes to connecting with customers, he sees saving money as one of the key business drivers, noting that few will make purchases based purely on the environmental benefits of products. "Green tends to be a tie-breaker, or a bonus of some sort," says Makower. "Anything you can do to help people save money and reduce costs will do well. For consumers at least, saving energy is the easiest way to also save cash."

In addition to saving energy, reducing other types of waste can also provide an important opportunity. "For the large companies, businesses like Waste Management help customers manage their materials more efficiently, a new business model for them that is very different from their traditional model of being a waste hauler. They found that there were upstream opportunities that help their customers cut costs and improve efficiencies. It's possible that you can create those kinds of opportunities for smaller businesses, focusing on one niche, on one type of business. Businesses have started out doing this for hospitals, for example, consolidating their purchasing for bed sheets, cotton swabs and other material, keeping things in stock, and handling waste. From there, they work to reduce waste."

As the green economy grows, so have the opportunities, and Makower notes that products like energy-efficient lightbulbs and green cleaning products like Green Works from Clorox are moving out of a green niche

JOEL MAKOWER, CONTINUED

into the mainstream. But beyond this Makower finds other seldom appreciated opportunities out of the limelight. "The real opportunities are not in what consumers buy," says Makower, "but in less obvious things behind the scenes. There's a company here in Oakland that created a 100 percent recycled paper alternative to the clothes hanger, and is marketing it to clothing manufacturers like Nike and Gap, selling millions of them. It's the niche opportunities like this that are largely untapped."

Talking with customers about your product can be tricky still, balancing the need to provide clear information about environmental performance without driving customers away with too much information. "The overall rule is to be specific, but not so geeky that people don't get it," says Makower. "You need to allow people who want this information to get it—online is the easiest way, 'to find out more click here.'" The wording of claims needs to be crafted to deal with the increasingly sophisticated consumers by providing access to clear verifiable information. "It's important to avoid general claims like 'eco-friendly, or 'Made with mother nature in mind,'" says Makower. "You need to be specific about the attributes. Relatively few people ask a lot of questions or really look for detailed information, but they tend to be vocal if they find you being disingenuous, so it's best to address them."

Most consumers are looking for honesty and transparency to help judge your performance on eco-issues. "There are three key questions that I ask: "What do you know, what are you doing, and what are you saying?" says Makower, "First, consumers want to know that you understand your environmental impacts. Most companies do not know

JOEL MAKOWER, CONTINUED

them, or they know just the part contained within their walls. Sometimes the activities that take place within your walls are a small part of the story. For traditional blue jeans, for example, the biggest life-cycle impacts come from growing cotton and washing jeans at home—two things that jeans manufacturers don't control."

The next step is to look at what you are doing about it once you know where you stand. "Do you have a plan? Does it have tangible goals and timetables?" asks Makower. "Even if it's years in the making, what are you doing?" And then, to look carefully at how you discuss green steps forward. "Are you talking about these things openly and honestly, not just claiming 'Hey, we're green,' but saying 'Here's what we are doing, what we're committed to, and where we are in the journey.'" I think a customer wants to know that you understand their problems, have a plan in place to do something about it, and are talking honestly about it."

In the end Makower has found that in his experience the decisions about buying green products are about much more than the environment. "The real question is 'How does green equal better?' That is, how does making the green choice become a no-brainer, because it's just clearly the better choice? That's where we need to get, that you choose green dry cleaning because it cleans better, not just because it's green. You buy the green car because it's more fun to drive or a better deal. Until it's about that, it's going to be a niche audience."

"That's the bottom line," Makower summarizes. "The question should be 'How can you make green a no-brainer?'"

CHAPTER

7

The Role of Government:

Carrots and Sticks

Green businesses are not growing in a vacuum, and actions by government are a key influence, shaping and encouraging their growth through a combination of regulation, legislation, and financial incentives. Government creates the rules that shape the business landscape, tilting markets one way or another. The influence of government in our economy and our lives is pervasive, in our food (regulation by the FDA, USDA, and the Organic Food Act), air and water (EPA, Clean Air Act, and Clean Water Act), energy (DOE), and buildings (local and state building codes). The goals of governments, ideally, include stimulating long-term economic growth, protecting resources for the future, and providing for the health and welfare of people. All of these goals are aligned with the growth of green businesses.

The government mandates and incentives supporting green business development include:

- Bans and fees imposed on disposable plastic shopping bags
- Requirements for biofuel production
- Mandates and incentives for the development of renewable energy
- Gas taxes
- Climate change legislation and international agreements
- Restrictions on the use or release of toxic chemicals
- Species and habitat protection
- Funding for green job training
- Preferential bidding for green businesses by government procurers
- Inclusion of environmental protection in international trade agreements
- Funding for research in areas like high-performance batteries
- Labeling requirements for organics (Federal National Organic Program)

Resource Guide

Compliance with environmental regulations is a business necessity, and there are a wide range of regulatory requirements for various industries. See the Business.gov website for a summary of compliance issues, particularly for small businesses (business.gov /business-law/environ mental-regulations /general-info.html).

- Tax incentives for clean and green energy measures such as residential energy efficiency
- Energy efficiency incentives for homes
- More stringent building codes
- Fuel efficiency standards for cars
- Take-back programs for electronics to reduce hazardous electronic waste
- Waste reduction, reducing the amount of construction waste allowed in landfills, for example
- Pollution prevention through the Clean Air Act, the Clean Water Act, and other legislation
- Water conservation through rebates for water conservation fixtures, incentives to change your landscape, and even fees and fines for large water usage as water supplies shrink

This list is only a sample, and it is growing all the time. While most industries work strenuously to avoid increased regulation, green businesses have at times taken the unusual step of lobbying for more regulation of their industry. The organic food industry lobbied for increased regulation, for example, working to make sure that the word "organic" was protected by a clearly defined legal meaning, avoiding some of the confusion that had previously developed around the use of the word, potentially hindering development of the market for organic food.

Green businesses and nonprofits continue lobbying for laws and regulations to support environmental progress. Groups like the Natural Resources Defense Council (NRDC) often spearhead the effort to influence government, pushing for action on important issues

More Options

The Environmental Defense Fund and the Union of Concerned Scientists are advancing environmental issues that stimulate the growth of green businesses, including action on climate change.

like climate change. The NRDC has lobbied and produced reports analyzing a broad range of environmental issues, including protection of the oceans, curbing water pollution, supporting renewable energy, protecting wetlands, regulating toxic chemicals, limiting oil drilling, and supporting energy efficiency. The potential for action on climate change has forces on all sides moving to advance their positions, sensing that crucial decisions will soon be made.

Resource Guide

The diverse members of the USCAP have published a variety of materials about the solutions they advocate for climate change at its website: us-cap.org. Seeing the recommendations of this influential group may provide insight into the kind of climate change legislation we are likely to see.

In an important shift, an increasing number of businesses now see that government action on climate change is not only inevitable, but desirable. They have started working together to encourage progress for both economic and environmental protection. The U.S. Climate Action Partnership (USCAP) of which the NRDC and The Nature Conservancy are a part also includes major corporations like Ford Motor Company, Xerox, DuPont, Johnson & Johnson, and Duke Energy as members, with all of the diverse partners collaborating to find productive solutions that will work for everyone.

The tools at the government's disposal are essentially a variety of sticks and carrots. The sticks are regulations, mandates, and laws that require adherence to environmental guidelines, with penalties imposed in the event of failure to do so. The carrots are incentives, in the form of grants, tax credits, loan guarantees, loan programs, and rebates.

The most likely approach to climate change now appears to be a cap and trade–based system. In cap and trade, those emitting carbon dioxide have a limit imposed, a cap, on how much greenhouse gases they can release. If they exceed their cap, they must buy carbon credits on the market (a carbon market) from others who were more successful in cutting their own emissions. That is where the trade part comes in. The price of carbon on the market responds to supply and demand. Over time, the cap will be reduced enough to stabilize the amount of CO_2 in the atmosphere and slow the rate of climate change. The scientific consensus appears to be that we need to reduce carbon emissions by 80 percent or more by the year 2050 to avoid more severe climate change, and this figure often appears in various government efforts.

> **More Options**
>
> A variation on cap and trade being suggested by some politicians is called cap and dividend, in which the money for carbon emissions is returned to Americans, offsetting any increases in energy costs. See capanddividend.org.

The impact of a cap and trade system is to put a price on producing and releasing carbon dioxide or other greenhouse gases into the atmosphere and contributing to climate change. The higher the price is for emitting carbon dioxide, the more of an economic incentive there is to emit less. There is a broad consensus among many groups like the USCAP that cap and trade allows for the open market to innovate and find the lowest cost methods to maintain economic productivity, while reducing greenhouse gas emissions. In such a way cap and trade harnesses the power of the market to speed the transition to a low-carbon economy.

Europe has had a cap and trade system, the European Union Emissions Trading Scheme, which is designed to reduce EU emissions in conjunction with EU participation in the Kyoto Protocol. Some say that the EU trading scheme has not had a significant impact on greenhouse gas emissions, although the market is still young and valuable lessons were learned from early experiences of having the price of carbon fall after handing out too many credits.

While many different parties are advocating for a U.S. cap and trade system, and a cap and trade system seems like the most likely form of broad U.S. action on climate change, there are still some key details to be worked out. One detail is how the carbon credits will be distributed: will they be auctioned off by the government to anyone who needs them or will they be handed out to businesses and utilities? Those who are invested in carbon-intensive industries (coal, coal-fired power plants, steel, cement, aluminum) are pushing for credits to be handed out rather than sold, which they say would impose an unfair burden. A compromise on this point seems likely. The system could start with some credits handed out but would be phased out over time. Then businesses and utilities would have to start buying them, creating more pressure to release less carbon.

Market Power

Scientists and nonprofits like the Environmental Defense Fund are exploring how market-based approaches can be applied to other environmental problems such as rain forest protection and fisheries protection to stimulate the search for entrepreneurial solutions.

Action on climate change, renewable energy, and energy efficiency are the focus on some of the largest government impacts on green businesses. California passed AB 32, the California Global Warming Solutions Act of 2006, which requires that the state reduce greenhouse gas emissions to 1990 levels by 2020. Because greenhouse gas emissions are steadily growing, this goal requires at least a 25 percent reduction from current levels. From there, the greenhouse gas emissions are required to fall still further, down to 80 percent below 1990 levels by 2050. The California Air Resources Board (CARB) is still working out the plan for implementation of AB 32, with preparations moving forward to begin implementing caps on the largest sources of greenhouse gas emissions by 2012, setting up a cap and trade system that creates economic incentives to provide cost-effective ways to reduce carbon emissions and then looks to innovative entrepreneurs to help produce solutions that meet this market need.

California has also been a leader in the adoption of renewable energy, providing generous support for solar in the so-called Million Solar Roofs Initiative passed in 2006, with $2.9 billion in funding for the development of 3,000 megawatts of solar photovoltaic systems at homes and businesses. Such government support is one reason why the number of solar installations in California doubled in 2008 over the year before, driving the growth of jobs and businesses in the solar industry. Another key initiative California has pushed for is the right to regulate carbon dioxide emissions from vehicles as a pollutant, a move the EPA blocked for the last several years, but which is now being reexamined and which may be supplanted by more aggressive action at the federal level.

Strategies of Green Leaders

"Some have challenged whether AB 32 is good for businesses," said California governor Arnold Schwarzenegger at the signing of AB 32. "I say unquestionably it is good for businesses. Not only large, well-established businesses, but small businesses that will harness their entrepreneurial spirit to help us achieve our climate goals." The website for CARB (arb.ca.gov/cc/cc.htm) has more information on the current status of AB 32 implementation.

In the Northeast, the Regional Greenhouse Gas Initiative (RGGI) has already set up a cap and trade system to reduce emissions from the largest emitters in several states in the region. Periodic auctions of carbon credits are now underway and are starting to put a price on emitting carbon in this region.

Climate Change Regulation by EPA

The EPA is currently taking a variety of steps to get more involved in the fight against climate change. The Supreme Court has ruled that the EPA can regulate greenhouse gas emissions under the Clean Air Act, and the EPA has now ruled that greenhouse gas emissions are pollutants that endanger public health and well-being. Having the EPA in the game increases the pressure on Congress to advance legislation on climate change.

One of the impacts of a cap and trade system is the opportunity it creates for businesses that develop innovative low-carbon solutions. For example, if you have a cement plant and the cost of operating is increased because you must now buy carbon credits to allow for your emissions, you have a financial incentive to invest in lower carbon technologies.

A broadly implemented cap and trade system may provide incentives for not just the most carbon-intensive industries but also a broader swath of businesses that emit carbon directly or indirectly, which includes just about everybody. Businesses in energy efficiency, green building, fuel efficient vehicle production, and renewable energy production would benefit from increased adoption across the United States.

The October 2008 "Bailout" Bill

Remember when a billion dollars sounded like a lot of money? The Emergency Economic Stabilization Act of 2008 (the bailout bill) provided $700 billion in funding for relief of the troubled financial system and also included a number of provisions related to renewable energy and other green business initiatives:

> 🍃 *Production tax credit for renewable energy.* Extends the production tax credit, providing up to 1.5 cents for each kilowatt hour of electricity produced and sold from wind, solar,

and other forms of renewable energy, including wave and tide energy.

🌿 *Extension of solar investment tax credit for eight years.* Provides a 30 percent investment tax credit for solar energy and fuel cells, and a 10 percent investment tax credit for microturbines for the next eight years. Small wind is added, and the $2,000 cap on the residential credit is removed, allowing for the full 30 percent tax credit on these systems.

🌿 *Carbon sequestration from coal.* Adds $1.5 billion in new tax credits for coal projects to demonstrate carbon capture to fight climate change.

🌿 *Credits for carbon dioxide capture.* Provides $10 per ton for carbon dioxide that is captured and used in oil recovery and $20 per ton for CO_2 permanently stored.

🌿 *Biodiesel tax credits.* Extends a $1 per gallon production tax credit for biodiesel and the 10-cents-per-gallon credit for small biodiesel producers through 2009.

🌿 *Energy-efficient buildings tax deduction.* Extends for five years tax deductions for energy efficiency upgrades in commercial buildings, up to $1.80 deduction per square foot with certain efficiency targets being met.

🌿 *Smart grid.* Accelerates depreciation rules for smart meters and smart grid equipment.

🌿 *Recycling.* Allows accelerated depreciation for recycling equipment.

🌿 *Qualified energy conservation bonds.* Allows for a new type of bond to be created, to finance climate change initiatives.

Resource Guide

A useful site for news and information about government action on renewable energy and the opportunities this creates for green businesses is Renewable Energy World (renewable energyworld.com).

The Federal Stimulus Package and Beyond

When the economy took a nosedive at the end of 2008, many wondered if governments might back away from commitments to renewable energy and action on climate change. Instead, the federal government is providing greater support than ever for businesses in clean energy, energy efficiency, and other green businesses.

The stimulus package passed into law in February 2009 (officially called the American Recovery and Reinvestment Act of 2009), provides about $80 billion altogether for renewable energy, energy efficiency, mass transit, updating the electrical grid, and research. "Targeting the recovery with green businesses is the most practical way to get the economy going," says Byron Kennard, executive director of the Washington, DC–based Center for Small Business and the Environment (aboutcsbe.org). Small businesses are always engines of economic growth in hard times, and green businesses in renewable energy and energy efficiency provide economic activity now and a lasting economic benefit in the future. Solar, wind, geothermal, biofuels, and energy efficiency could create millions of jobs in the years ahead.

"In this recession, small businesses are likely to lead the nation's recovery again by creating green jobs and clean energy innovations. In fact, a green entrepreneurial boom is in the offing," says Kennard, because of opportunity to make money, because of the necessity of addressing climate change, and because of the commitment so many people have to helping the environment. "For many, protecting the environment is a cause that arouses passion, and passion is a key element in business success," Kennard goes on to say.

Speaking at an online town hall meeting on March 26, 2009, President Obama discussed his commitment to green businesses to help solve America's economic crisis. "Our success will also require freeing ourselves from the dangerous dependence on foreign oil by building a clean-energy economy, because we know that with this will not only come greater security and a safer environment, but new high-paying jobs of the future to replace those that we've lost," he said. "That's why it's so important to train our folks more effectively and that's why it's so important for us to find new industries—building solar panels or wind turbines or the new biofuel—that involve these higher-value, higher-skill, higher-paying jobs."

Some of the green measures in the February 2009 stimulus package include:

- *Grants instead of tax credits.* These grants allow developers of renewable energy projects to apply for a grant to receive money within 60 days of starting to produce power, rather than waiting for a tax credit. Some investors who cannot use tax credits at the moment will have more incentive to fund projects with a grant like this.

- *Larger credit for alternative fuel pumps.* For 2009–2010, increases tax credit for alternative fuel pumps in gas stations from 30 percent to 50 percent.

- *Manufacturing credit.* Energy-related manufacturing receives $2 billion in credits, at 30 percent of the cost of the project. This money is designed to target factories retooling to make parts for renewable energy hardware, electric grid, or new energy-efficient cars.

- *Plug-in vehicle credit.* Higher credit for plug-in hybrid cars, starting at $2,500 per car, and increasing as the size of the battery in the car increases.

- *Extension of the production tax credit.* Electricity from renewable sources of all types is now eligible for a 30 percent production tax credit through 2012 for wind and through 2013 for several other forms of renewable energy (methane from landfills, wind and wave energy, biomass, waste to energy).

In addition to tax cuts and credits, there is also a variety of direct spending on green projects in the bill:

- Weatherizing homes—$5 billion
- Federal building efficiency—$4.5 billion
- Electrical grid—$4.5 billion for development and upgrade of the electrical grid, to start to create the "smart grid"
- Research funding—$2.5 billion for energy efficiency and renewable energy research
- Mass transit—$8.4 billion
- High speed rail—$8 billion
- State energy grants—$6.3 billion

The act also includes renewable energy loan guarantees—$6 billion in loan guarantees for renewable energy projects—and clean energy renewable bonds. It creates $1.6 billion worth of bonds that finance renewable energy projects, targeting utilities, Indian tribes, state and local governments, and cooperatives that produce electricity.

One of the important components of the bill for solar entrepreneurs in the current credit crisis is the ability to apply for a cash grant instead of a tax credit, thus attracting more investors to support the development of solar power projects. "Instead of a 30 percent tax credit you can get a 30 percent grant," explains Lyndon Rive, CEO of SolarCity in Foster City, California. "For every $10 you spend buying a system, you get $3 one way or another, getting a check back from a cash grant instead of a tax credit if you want" (Entrepreneur.com, March 9, 2009).

Solar energy is a low-risk investment, about as safe as they come, but the $6 billion in loan guarantees in the stimulus package is another key aspect of keeping renewable energy growing. At a time when investors are holding on tightly to their money, having the government back up loans for renewable energy will get lenders back in the game, leading to more solar power systems and other forms of renewable energy being installed.

A wide range of businesses benefit from such measures. "You will see tremendous growth and hiring in green collar jobs," says SolarCity's Lyndon Rive. "In most states the businesses that will benefit are all renewable businesses in wind, solar, and geothermal, including manufacturers, distributors, installers, and the entire value chain." The bill also provides $500 million in funding for so-called green collar jobs, such as the many people who will be involved in energy efficiency retrofits and installation of solar power projects.

All of these measures will help green businesses large and small. As important as the efforts to support green businesses in the stimulus package are, they are only the first step. A national renewable energy portfolio standard, requiring that utilities nationwide supply at least a minimum portion of their power supply from renewable energy like wind and solar, is also supported by the Obama administration. National action on climate change is still to be agreed on although a solution appears more likely than ever and may happen sooner rather than later (see the interview with Hunter Lovins starting on page 192).

The situation is changing rapidly, but even if an agreement on climate change is reached and federal legislation passed (or should I say *when* it is reached), the work will not be over for government or for business. As with AB 32 in California, passing the measure is only the first step. As great as this challenge will be, implementing action in the United States on climate change is an even greater challenge—and a great opportunity. And we will all be eager to see what happens in the next round of negotiations toward an international climate agreement, slated to arrive at its conclusion in Copenhagen in December 2009. A successful agreement needs to include the United States, China, and other major emitters of greenhouse gases if it is to succeed, and a great

deal is riding on the outcome of these talks, for businesses and people around the globe.

Case Study
PALM DESERT, AN OASIS OF GREEN ENERGY

While national and global action on climate change progresses, cities and states have gotten into action, including relatively small cities like Palm Desert in Southern California. Palm Desert, just east of Palm Springs, has a population of about 50,000. Although it is not a big city, it has taken on a big challenge. Palm Desert's director of energy management, Pat Conlon, has taken on the goal of reducing the city's power use 30 percent in just five years. The steps that Conlon and Palm Desert are taking illustrate the important role of government at all levels to create incentives and strategies to grow green businesses by helping everyone use energy more wisely.

"We started January 1, 2007, and we are on track to reach our goal by December 31, 2011," says Conlon. It all started with California's negative experience with deregulation of the electricity market, which led to brownouts and soaring power prices. "Back when we had the utility crisis with deregulation, Governor Davis sent out a request to cities to save 15 percent of their energy on city buildings." Having achieved this goal easily, the city decided to go after a stretch goal, reducing power use citywide by 30 percent. "We are slowly but surely making our way toward the goal," says Conlon. "The goal is to save 215 million kilowatt hours, citywide, on everything, not just government buildings. We are including houses, churches, schools, stores—everything."

Conlon has found that two messages work together to drive uptake of energy efficiency: first, that people can save money by joining the

PALM DESERT, CONTINUED

effort, and second, that they can help the environment as well. With both messages together the town has found its programs have more of an impact on a broad audience, while consumers have been less receptive to a message about climate change alone.

"In Palm Desert we use a lot of energy, primarily for air conditioning," says Conlon. "We use 150 percent more power than comparable homes or businesses elsewhere in Southern California because of our climate zone." In the summer, homes can spend $600 to $1,000 a month on their electricity bill, so people are highly motivated to save energy.

In general, the two keys to encouraging energy efficiency are information and money. "For our energy programs, we have a menu of options," says Conlon. "We entice people to invest in energy efficiency with rebates and incentives. We have been offering free in-home and in-business energy surveys, or audits." In the energy survey, its contractors go through a home and change light bulbs, change shower heads, weatherstrip doors, tune up the air conditioner, and educate the property owner. "We can drill down precisely to where energy goes, and find the cost-effective measures the homeowner or business owner can do to save energy." See settosave.com for the energy efficiency surveys that Palm Desert is performing.

With 4,200 surveys under their belt, Conlon noticed a trend. When they did a follow-up call to ask homeowners how they liked the survey, homeowners would almost always respond positively. But when homeowners were asked if they followed up with any further energy efficiency improvements that were suggested, few had actually done so.

PALM DESERT, CONTINUED

People give a variety of reasons why they had not invested further in energy efficiency, but they all lead back to money. If finance is the main block to progress, Palm Desert needed a loan program that would get around this, and it found a solution in Berkeley.

"The City of Berkeley had a neat idea, doing a solar program by lending money to homeowners and putting the loan payments on their property taxes," says Conlon. Helping to write AB 811, Palm Desert started their energy loan program called the Energy Independence Program in September 2008. The town got rolling so quickly with the program that it has been hard to keep up with demand for loans to pay for performance air conditioners, energy -fficient windows, insulation, general energy efficiency work, and solar power systems.

The process of applying for the loan is designed to be as simple and straightforward as possible. "The loan is between the homeowner and City of Palm Desert, and you apply online," says Conlon. "The interest rate is 7 percent, carried for up to 20 years, with payment of the loan on their property taxes." There is no credit score involved, and as an assessment on the land, it doesn't care about loan to value ratios as would be the case for a home equity. If the owner wants to sell his house, a buyer can assume the assessment, unlike a home equity line that must be paid off. The interest on the loan is even tax deductible. The only catch is that to qualify, the loan must be an energy efficiency upgrade, it must be for an existing building, and the property must be free of any liens.

So far the funds for the program have come from a fund for energy efficiency paid into by investor-owned utilities in California such as SDGE

PALM DESERT, CONTINUED

and PG&E. These funds already exist, so the program does not involve a rate payer increase.

Homeowners are not the only ones who win with the program. It is also creating opportunities for the businesses taking care of the solar power installation and energy efficiency upgrades. "Contractors are dancing in the street, and they are the ones who are the most anxious to take advantage of the loan program," says Conlon. "When we started we had two local solar contractors in town, and today we have over 26." The new contractors include people who were already electrical contractors, often working in new construction. As construction has slowed and the program in Palm Desert emerged, they moved over to solar. Air-conditioning contractors also love the program, of course—the city has not had to do any work at all to promote the program because contractors like these are doing the job for them. "It could not have come at a better time for these guys," says Conlon.

All in all, the program has been a big success. It's going so well, in fact, that other cities in California, like Solana Beach and San Diego, are following its example, and Palm Desert is putting together a road map to show others how to do it. "The law is in place allowing all cities and counties to do the loan program, and the mechanics of the program are straightforward," says Conlon.

These programs are making great progress, but they are only part of the story. Palm Desert is putting together a sustainability plan, with the energy program just one component of its overall sustainability goal. "We have water conservation, natural gas fleet vehicles for public transit, and we have a very successful recycling program, with over

PALM DESERT, CONTINUED

65 percent of solid waste recycled, and climbing to over 70 percent," says Conlon. The more cities that pursue programs like these, the more that government, businesses, and consumers can work together to create opportunities and help the environment for the greater good of all.

The Green Legal View
Aleka Eisentraut and Richard Lyons of
Wendel, Rosen, Black & Dean

Founded in 1909, the law firm Wendel, Rosen, Black & Dean of Oakland, California, is celebrating 100 years as a law firm in 2009, but it is not resting on its laurels. In 2003 Wendel Rosen became the first law firm in the country to be certified as a green business through third-party verification, taking numerous steps to reduce its environmental impact. It is printing less, using 100 percent postconsumer recycled paper, and using energy-efficient appliances. While Wendel Rosen practices law in many areas, its green business practice has become very influential in the green building community as well as the natural food and sustainable agriculture sectors. Aleka Eisentraut and Richard Lyons are members of Wendel Rosen's green business practice, interacting closely with green entrepreneurs to help them deal effectively with challenges and avoid common problems.

"This focus on sustainability contributes to our success because we have shared values with our clients as people who have been operating in a green sustainable manner for many years, before it was a marketing thing to do," says Eisentraut. "We care about the same things they do. It also helps us save money, helps with recruiting, and keeps people interested in staying."

Working with a green law firm like Wendel can make a real difference for businesses in many fields. "One thing that helps businesses is to have a law firm with customers who have gone through the same issues and knows how they are resolved," says Lyons. "The businesses that come to us get the benefit of hundreds of thousands of dollars spent by other people dealing with similar issues. If it's renewable energy, knowing about tax credits is important. If their business is in food, we have knowledge about the laws around labeling and pure food issues." Working with green businesses throughout their community, they have also found that they can help their clients by making valuable introductions, connecting them with others through their network in the San Francisco Bay Area or the East Coast.

Businesses in the natural food industry have many practical legal considerations Wendel helps them deal with, for example. "Many food producers use co-packing arrangements where product is produced by someone else, but sold under their own brand," says Lyons. Working through the contracts behind these arrangements, they understand the concerns involved. "If you're making a generic cracker, you might not care where the wheat comes from. If it's natural, you may care a lot."

Whatever the industry, businesses all face common concerns when starting up, such as choosing a name for their business. Even a seemingly simple decision like this can benefit from having a lawyer involved. "Finding the name for their business is one of the first things people do, and even then it's helpful to consult about this kind of important decision," says Lyons. "We advise people if the name they want is common while another one is distinctive, they will be better able to protect it under a trademark." A unique consideration for many green businesses is how they can build their values into the business by creating a B corp,

or beneficial corporation, with bylaws stating explicitly that minimizing adverse effects on the environment is as important for the business as increasing profitability. "Having this written into the bylaws helps protect management and directors from liability and sets expectations for investors about what their business is all about," says Lyons.

Another key business ingredient is money, and raising money involves legal papers with important implications for the future of a business. "The terms of investment are always very complicated," says Lyons. "We are in a position to say that a term sheet is reasonably balanced, that in one case the terms are very favorable to your company, or we might find that they are very investor-oriented. We can alert a client that if they sign a term sheet, they could lose their company."

Despite the importance of these papers, a lawyer is not always involved until it's too late. "People don't understand everything that is going on there. They know about running their business, but they don't have experience with a five-page term sheet," says Lyons. "Sometimes people avoid lawyers because they think they will save money that way, and then they get themselves in trouble." While a high level of trust is a wonderful thing many green businesses share, leaving these factors to trust alone is not a great idea. "The relationships are often better than in other areas of business, but still you need to write down clearly what you intend, and do this with a lawyer."

In the green building field, green leases are an emerging field that Wendel is helping to advance, creating leases that encourage both landlords and tenants to optimize the resource efficiency of buildings. Again, consulting with a lawyer can often pay for itself. "We often have clients come to us with an executed letter of intent for leased space, but the letter excludes important areas and we have to renegotiate during the lease negotiation phase, which ends up putting the tenant at a disadvantage and makes the lease negotiation process more lengthy and, therefore, more expensive," says Eisentraut. "It's always best to advise with a lawyer before signing a letter of intent. Green leases are pretty specialized."

There are a few ways for tenants to create a more sustainable space for their business, notes Eisentraut. "One is to negotiate directly with their landlord or property manager to get them to green their building. If they band together with other tenants, they can negotiate together or they can have their space certified as LEED for Commercial Interiors." LEED for Commercial Interiors is designed for businesses that are not located in green buildings and requires little from a landlord. Another option is to get certified as a green business, being audited for measures such as efficient energy and water use. "Getting certified sends a message that you are operating your business in a sustainable manner," says Eisentraut.

Municipal ordinances in places like San Francisco are requiring increased adoption of green building methods, increasing the need for green leases for businesses, such as with the LEED for Existing Buildings Operation and Maintenance (LEED-EBOM) certification that focuses on operating buildings and on maintenance. "Just because the building is green does not mean that it will be operated in a green manner; the landlord will have to make sure tenants are using all of the systems in the way they are supposed to be used," says Eisentraut.

For tenants to change how they operate their business there needs to be a strong connection between how they use power and how they pay for it. "A lot of times several tenants share one power meter, so you can't tell how much power each individual business is using, and if a business saves energy, they don't reap a lot of the reward," says Eisentraut. In general, the party spending the money to upgrade a building or premises in order to make it more sustainable should see the benefits.

Beyond buildings, the actions being taken by governments at all levels to address climate change are altering the legal and business landscape. The state of California has led many efforts in the United States to take on climate change, including the influential bill known as AB 32, the California Global Warming Solutions Act of 2006. "We have followed AB 32, including all of the sub-hearings, for the commercial real estate industry, to advise them on what the commercial real estate landscape will look like, how it will be affected," says Eisentraut. "People are looking forward to a national cap and trade system, which seems likely. A couple of firm clients have joined the California Climate Registry, a program for early adopters, to position themselves to benefit from government action on climate change. If there is regulation on climate change and there is a cap on greenhouse gas emissions, if you are small and green you may be poised to benefit from being an early actor."

Interview with Green Leader Hunter Lovins

While there are a lot of new faces these days in the green business world, Hunter Lovins is no newcomer to the scene. She has been leading the way for years, taking a stand and speaking out about the business case for sustainability. As one of the co-authors of the 1999 green business classic *Natural Capitalism* (Back Bay Books, 2008), Lovins bucked the dogma widely held in business circles that helping the environment and building strong businesses don't mix. The book has served as a visionary guide for many green entrepreneurs, inspiring the green business revolution that is now unfolding. She has also co-founded the influential Rocky Mountain Institute, leaders in the effort to develop a more efficient and greener economy, and is currently one of the founding professors at the Presidio School of Management program offering an MBA in sustainable business management.

As the president and founder of Natural Capitalism Solutions, Lovins is continuing her work, advising businesses and governments on solutions that build strong economies, profitable businesses, and a healthy environment for future generations. With example after example, she shows not only that it could work, but that it is already working, with businesses saving billions of dollars by becoming more efficient with resources.

GLENN CROSTON: *Where does government action on climate change stand today?*

HUNTER LOVINS: Prior to the election, states and cities were taking a leadership role. Over 900 mayors have pledged to have their cities meet the Kyoto goals. Boulder, Colorado, put in place a small carbon tax, with the money to be spent to cut carbon emissions. San Francisco has a small carbon tax on business as well. Various other cities are looking at doing the same, creating revenue programs to pay for cutting carbon emissions. Programs like these provide incentives for businesses to use energy more wisely.

There are also regional initiatives like the RGGI [Regional Greenhouse Gas Initiative] with 10 Northeast states participating. RGGI imposed a cap and trade regime covering the largest emitters of greenhouse gases in these states, with regular auctions of carbon allowances underway that have already raised millions of dollars for climate protection and renewable energy.

AB 32 in California is putting in place a cap on greenhouse gas emissions. CARB [California Air Resources Board] is about to release regulations to implement AB 32, which will likely include some form of auction and trading regime like RGGI. Meanwhile CARB has been issuing clean air standards aimed at carbon and other pollutants.

Since the 2008 presidential election, the EPA has gotten in the act and started issuing regulations, as well. It's not clear yet

whether the regulation of carbon as a whole will be under the EPA, which a lot of businesses believe would be a bad idea, or if Congress will establish a national climate regime. Republicans want a carbon tax, increasing the price, while more progressive people prefer a market-based approach. As we speak, the Waxman Markey American Clean Energy and Security Bill is about to be voted on in Congress. I think it's likely that some market-based system will be implemented. It might not succeed this year, though it it would sure be nice for the United States to go to the climate talks in December 2009 in Copenhagen with a climate protection regime in place.

If the United States does not act, cities and states are likely to act more aggressively. Most of the Western states have said that they will join in with whatever California comes up with, probably resembling RGGI. Midwestern states have also said that they will implement their own initiative to reduce greenhouse gas emissions. Pretty quickly anybody who does business in more than one state will face some form of carbon regulation.

What will a U.S. cap and trade system look like? My guess is that it will be a bit of both giving away carbon allowances and auctioning them off, at least to start. Some accommodation will be made for carbon-intensive industries in the Ohio valley. Best case, the regime will set a low cap first that would decline over time.

Internationally, Britain and the EU have a regime. Initially, the European system gave out too many allowances, but that market is now back on track. Now even China and India are setting up exchanges to trade emissions. As the science news gets ever scarier in terms of how bad the climate crisis is, there will be increasing pressure for the U.S. Congress to put in place real climate protection as well.

CROSTIN: *How can climate change regulation put a price on carbon without slowing the economy?*

LOVINS: It depends on how things are done. California targeted the "significant" sources. Based on prior drafts of the bill and the California Climate Action Plan, the five industry sectors of oil and gas extraction, oil and gas refining, landfills, power generation, and cement production are likely to face mandatory reporting and reduction requirements. Any company that uses large chunks of coal-based electricity or carbon-based fuel is in the gun sights. The interesting question is whether it will be an upstream cap, targeting the 200 to 500 biggest emitters, or a midstream cap that caps all businesses, or a downstream cap that catches all users. Most regimes are upstream or midstream, but if the science continues to look as grim as it does, we should target everyone, whether you drive a gas-guzzling car or run a welding shop that uses natural gas.

Economists argue that if you go upstream, increasing the price of carbon fuels, it will trickle throughout the economy, but price does not determine everything about action. In the Pacific Northwest, when the WPPS (Washington Public Power System, an effort to build nuclear plants) failed, the price of electricity doubled. Several utilities put in place programs to provide information, training, and access to help customers implement energy efficiency, and achieved a huge uptake of energy savings even though prices only went from 1 to 2 cents per kilowatt hour. In Chicago at the same time, electricity was 17 cents per kilowatt hour, but there was essentially no uptake in efficiency because the information and assistance programs were lacking. Like the proverbial frog that sits in slowly boiling water and never jumps out, customers facing slowly rising energy prices tend not to change.

Starting Green

Without the right incentives, higher prices hurt the economy before they change behavior. Those who say fighting climate change will wreck the economy reach that opinion by looking at historic increases in price, at the elasticity of the power market, and how little behavior was changed by price alone without the incentives and opportunity that could have changed behavior dramatically at far lower prices.

Well-structured incentives can save a lot of energy. Southern California Edison found that it is much more effective to give out compact fluorescent light bulbs than to build a new power plant. In Oregon, studies found that per megawatt saved in a community, you will generate $2 million in increased economic activity and create over half a million dollars in increased business income.

Conversely, our failure to implement energy savings is hurting the economy. Today Americans are borrowing $2 billion a day to pay for imported oil. This is surely one cause of the economic crisis. If we invest in weatherizing homes, putting solar in neighborhoods, and building wind farms that are cheaper than new coal fired power plants we can rebuild the economy *and* slow climate change.

The Center for American Progress recently released a "Green Recovery" paper laying out a lot of these numbers, showing how cutting energy use will help the economy. There are studies now for 20 different states showing that climate protection will grow the economy and create jobs. A study in California found that fully implementing AB 32 would add $78 billion to the state economy and create 400,000 new jobs.

There are opportunities for small businesses, too, to take advantage of these trends. I teach at Presidio School of Management. The clean-tech businesses my students are getting started are having no problem raising money from VCs, and from the more traditional financing from friends and family.

CROSTIN: *What is the business impact of reducing greenhouse gas emissions?*

LOVINS: The early adopters who got in and cut greenhouse gas emissions have profited from it. Cutting emissions cuts wastes, which cuts costs and improves operations. From 2000 to 2005 DuPont, which committed to cut emissions 65 percent below its 1990 levels, saved $3 billion by cutting emissions by 80 percent. In 2007 DuPont was saving $2.7 billion a year, which was equal to its profit; it is profitable because of its carbon emissions savings. ST Microelectronics declared that by 2010 it would be carbon neutral with a 40-fold increase in production. Although not initially sure how to do this, figuring it out increased corporate innovation, taking ST from the No. 12 chipmaker in the world to the No. 6. The company gained market share.

A recent AT Kearny study showing that sustainable businesses are up despite the downturn reinforced earlier studies by Goldman Sachs finding that leaders in corporate sustainability have 25 percent higher stock value than competitors. *The Economist* Intelligence Unit found that the worst performing companies in the economy were most likely to have nobody leading sustainability in the company.

Small businesses can do the same. Our web-based learning tool, "Solutions at the Speed of Business," is available from nat capsolutions.org. It shows business owners how to cut their emissions profitably as they strengthen their business and protect themselves from whatever regulatory regime emerges over the next few years.

CHAPTER

 8

Starting a Green Franchise

Millions of people dream of starting their own business, but as attractive as setting your own hours and calling your own shots can be, not everybody does. What's holding people back?

One stumbling block is that people are not sure what type of business they want to start. They know they want to run a business of their own, but don't have a clear vision of what the business would be. Another difficulty is putting all the pieces in place to get started. Then if you do get a business off the ground, another challenge is creating a recognizable brand that people relate to and that attracts their business.

One way to start your own business is to develop an innovative new product or service, which often requires considerable time and money. You can develop a business that is the green version of an existing business, but with your own unique twist on it, your own brand. Developing a brand is like developing a new product in some ways, and can still take time and money. A third option is to jump-start your business by building a business around an existing product and brand—by buying a franchise.

A franchise is a business in which you buy the right to sell the products or services of an established business using their marketing, trademarks, and techniques. According to *Franchises and Business Opportunities* by Andrew Caffey, a "franchise is a long-term business relationship in which the purchaser (the 'franchisee') is granted the right to operate a business under the trademark of an established business owner (the 'franchisor') and use its business techniques."

Resource Guide

There are various legal definitions of the franchise concept. For more details on franchising, there are a wealth of resources available, such as *Franchises and Business Opportunities* (Andrew Caffey, Entrepreneur Press, 2002) and the *Franchise Bible* (Erwin Keup, Entrepreneur Press, 2004).

What this means in practical terms is that a franchise is an opportunity to establish a partnership between you (the person who wants to start a business) and someone with an established business. Because this is a legal relationship, both parties have duties and obligations. As the franchisee, you will generally be required to operate according to the specific standards of the business you buy into, including the products, the appearance of retail outlets, pricing, trademarks, and how you operate. You will not have total freedom to do as you want. For example, if you are buying a fast food franchise, you will most likely have to use the franchise menu as well as its logo, its designs, its color schemes, and so on. But that's why you buy the franchise after all, isn't it?

There are many benefits to buying a franchise compared to starting a business from scratch. The first is that you don't have to start from scratch. You buy a franchise because it is already a proven concept. Starting a business from scratch means you have to plot every step on your own, not knowing how it will turn out. Buying a franchise does not guarantee success, but most franchises have a support structure and the experience of others to draw upon, perfecting the recipe for making that particular business stick. Statistics have shown that all of this makes the failure rate for franchise businesses much lower than for businesses started from scratch.

Defining Moment

In addition to franchises, there are also "business opportunities," which are a very broad concept. A business opportunity could be buying vending machines that allow you to begin a business. There is no trademark involved (you can put your own business name on your vending machines if you want), unlike a franchise, and there are no restrictions on how you run your vending machine business.

That said, a franchise will probably still take a lot of work to make it profitable. Ask yourself two questions before you start are:

1. *How much do you know about the line of business?* If you are buying a restaurant franchise, you might want to learn more or even work in restaurant if you haven't already.

2. *Have you done your own research into the market in your area?*

Tip for Success

When it comes to raising money to start your franchise, different franchise operations have different expectations and strategies. Some will expect you to provide the startup money yourself, out of your own savings and assets. Others will help arrange third-party financing.

Money-wise, when buying a franchise, the franchisee generally pays an initial franchise fee and an ongoing royalty payment. The initial franchise fee will often be in the range of tens of thousands of dollars, and the royalty payment is an ongoing percentage of sales, a single-digit percentage generally. In some cases, you might be required to buy product from the parent organization. This is a point to investigate, to make sure that the pricing is not so high that it would prevent you from making a profit. If the franchise is for organic fast food burritos, and you find that the franchise agreement requires you to buy burritos for $6 each but you can only sell them for $8, you may have trouble making money.

In return for your fees and payments, you get:

- The ability to use trademarks associated with the franchise brand
- Established products and services, saving you the trouble of product development
- The benefits of selling an established brand so you can hit the ground running
- Ongoing promotional efforts and materials the parent organization may provide
- Business leads forwarded for your area
- Training and expert help

When you contact an organization about franchise opportunities, you will have to fill out some forms, and then it will look you over to see if you are a good fit. One thing it looks at is your background and financial status. Because you are going to represent its business, it wants to get to know you a bit, trying to see if you will fit in with the organization and will succeed with your business.

There will be phone interviews and probably in-person interviews. This is not just for franchise's benefit—this is your chance to ask questions as well. The franchise relationship is a two-way street, and you have a lot on the line, more really than the franchise owners. At the end of the day it will be your time, your money, and your business.

Uniform Franchise Offering Circular (UFOC)

As the process progresses and you get ready to purchase a franchise, there will be franchise documents for you to review. Franchisors are required by the Federal Trade Commission to present franchisees with documents that disclose the full nature of how franchising works with their organization. These documents are the Uniform Franchise Offering Circular (UFOC) and have the following sections:

- 🍃 *The cover page*, with the name of the business and the cost of the initial franchise fee.
- 🍃 *Information about the franchisor.* It's a good idea to read this carefully, but don't restrict your investigation of the franchisor to the UFOC—look for other clues on the internet or by talking to existing franchise owners.
- 🍃 *Business experience of the franchisors, including officers and executives of the company.* Bankruptcies in the last ten years by the franchisor also must be disclosed.
- 🍃 *Pending litigation must be disclosed.* If there is a lawsuit, be wary. This could impact your business if the lawsuit goes the wrong way.
- 🍃 *The initial franchise fee and other fees.* The organization can charge fees for a variety of components of the relationship,

such as an annual renewal fee, an advertising fee, or a training fee.

🍃 *Expected overall business operating costs.* The fees you pay are not your only expenses. In addition to these, you will have to pay for the space you lease, employees, and materials. Buying a franchise and paying the expected fees does not include the cost of these items.

🍃 *Specifications about where and from whom you can buy materials.* Again, look out for hidden costs.

🍃 *Your obligations as the franchisee.* Are these manageable? This is where existing franchise owners can help you understand the particular system.

🍃 *The franchisor's legal obligations.* Will it provide you with materials, training, or other support?

🍃 *Territory.* Franchises often come with a specific territory. You don't want to buy a franchise and have someone else buy and set up the same franchise right across the street.

🍃 *Intellectual property rights.* You will have the right to use trademarks and other things that contribute to the brand of the franchise.

🍃 *How long the contract lasts, and how problems get resolved.*

One of the warning signs of danger when considering a franchise is the hard sell. Is the franchise representative saying there is a one-time only offer, if you act immediately? A legitimate organization should have no reason to be in a big hurry to get you to sign and hand over the money. Signing the UFOC is a major commitment—consider having a lawyer knowledgeable about franchises read over the document before you sign. Whatever franchise you are thinking of, take your time to look into it, doing your research before you sign anything or hand over any money.

In some cases you can negotiate portions of the UFOC before you sign. You only get one chance, and it does not hurt to ask if you are uncomfortable with portions of the agreement. Some portions, like use of trademark, will not be negotiable, but other aspects, like fees and territories, might be.

Franchising Your Own Business to Grow

If you have developed a business that is successful, one way to expand it is to start selling franchises. You can grow without a large amount of your own capital, because the franchisees invest their money to start a location, and without the necessity of managing each location directly. There are legal hurdles to overcome to be able to sell franchises, and financial and personal considerations, but for many entrepreneurs who have started successful businesses, it is the best path to rapid growth.

Green Franchise Opportunities

An increasing variety of green franchise options is available, with something in just about every field. I describe a few here, but this sampling is by no means comprehensive. More green franchises are showing up all the time. These examples are just to give you a feel for the types of green franchises that are available, how they work, and what they have to offer.

The Cleaning Authority—Green Cleaning Service Franchise

The Cleaning Authority was founded in 1977 and provides cleaning services for homes across the country. It started selling franchises in 1996, and today there are over 180 around the country. Recently the Cleaning Authority started switching its services to provide green cleaning, using Green Seal-certified cleaning products that have been designed and tested to avoid the use of potentially toxic ingredients. It also uses vacuums with HEPA filters to avoid putting dust and particulates into the air, another

common problem with indoor air quality. Although the company did not start out providing green cleaning services, all new franchises are following this model and older franchises are being converted as well. The initial franchise fee is $30,000 to $55,000 (Cleaning Authority website), and the total investment to start the franchise business is estimated at $83,000 to $142,000, including costs such as a computer, leasing office space, washer and dryer, travel for training, working capital, and a mailer fee.

Cartridge Depot—Recycled Toner Cartridge Franchise

Ink and toner cartridges for printers can waste resources and the millions of cartridges that end up in landfills every year create an environmental problem. Given their expense, they can also be a drain on the finances of a business. Cartridge Depot has built its business around providing refilled and reconditioned cartridges that are much cheaper than new ones, less than 50 percent of the cost in most cases. With the technology Cartridge Depot provides, cartridge quality, one of the concerns in the ink and toner cartridges business, is ensured.

The initial franchise fee is $29,000, and the total initial investment a franchisee should expect to make is about $85,000 to $106,000. The royalty fee is a flat $600 per month, rather than the more common percentage of gross sales. Cartridge Depot provides training at its main facility, working one on one with new franchisees, and supplies ongoing technical support. It also provides help with bookkeeping, marketing, and finding business leads.

Pizza Fusion—Eco-Friendly Pizza Restaurant Franchise

Along with the greening of other industries, the food service industry now has greener options as well. Pizza restaurants are one of the most popular categories for U.S. restaurants, and Pizza Fusion with its green pizza franchising opportunity is rapidly expanding. Founded by Michael Gordon and Vaughn Lazar in Ft. Lauderdale, Florida, Pizza Fusion uses organic ingredients, its delivery vehicles are fuel efficient hybrid cars, and the restaurant locations are certified LEED green buildings, designed to be energy efficient and built with recycled eco-friendly materials. It also uses green cleaning methods in its locations, uses recycled paper products, and gets involved through events in its communities to encourage the spread of greener living and eating habits. Its pizza just happens to be mighty tasty as well as eco-friendly.

The initial investment fee with Pizza Fusion is $30,000, and the total amount of money you should expect to invest to get a restaurant franchise going is about $305,000 to $465,000. The royalty fee is 5 percent of gross sales and advertising fees are 2 percent of gross sales (Pizza Fusion website). Those interested in a franchise should have $100,000 in liquid assets (not borrowed money) and $300,000 in net worth. Pizza Fusion does not provide financing, but it can help connect you with third-party financing such as SBA loans for building and equipment.

In the initial review process, you fill out an application and then visit the corporate offices so all parties get to know each other. After a background check, you'll find out if your application is approved. If it is, you move on to sign the franchise agreement and pay the initial franchise fee. You proceed for training, and start getting a site ready to join the rapidly growing ranks of Pizza Fusion locations.

Green Key Real Estate
GREEN REAL ESTATE FRANCHISE

Founded in 2005 in San Francisco by Chris Bartle, Green Key Real Estate is helping buyers and sellers of green homes by specializing in green real estate, but its work extends farther. Green Key is also using education and action to make homes greener. As the CEO and president of Green Key Real Estate, Bartle is now bringing this opportunity to other entrepreneurs through franchising.

For Bartle, Green Key's mission is clear—"To green every home that we sell." To help make this happen, Green Key commits 10 percent of its commissions from every sale to greening the home that is involved. Bartle wants the world to know that if you work with Green Key your house will be greener. "We find that sellers like our work and take advantage of this upfront. They put our green efforts upfront as a marketing tool for sellers. They say, 'Mr. Buyer, it will be this much greener, at no cost to you.' This gives our brokers a competitive advantage."

The money it puts into greening homes may not cover all of the work that is needed in each home, but it can have a big impact on getting things started. "We start with a home performance audit, and for small homes 10 percent of the commission will be just that. For larger homes, we do testing and some of the retrofit work, getting the ball rolling by putting our money where our mouth is." The greening of a home does not stop with the work that Green Key does. "The process also includes money that our clients put in, based on the education we provide about green homes and energy efficiency," says Bartle. "As a company we have a well-established network of architects, designers, and service provides to help people green their homes."

GREEN REAL ESTATE FRANCHISE, CONTINUED

One of the most common features people are looking for in green homes today is energy efficiency. "The second consideration is indoor air quality, with people who want healthy air for their kids, or for elderly folks," says Bartle. "Some people have specific chemical sensitivities, and can't have formaldehyde or mold." Buyers also look for water conservation features like low-flow fixtures, water-saving irrigation systems, and landscaping with plants that require minimal watering.

LEED certified homes are still uncommon, but other green home rating systems are available, such as Green Point-rated homes certified by Build It Green. "Even home builders are adopting it," says Bartle. "All of our agents are eco-brokers, and certified as green building professionals by Build It Green," a California-based green building certification group. "They are well versed in all thing green, and go through additional training we help provide."

Green homes are increasingly viewed as the future of the market, and not just in San Francisco. While some green entrepreneurs feel that they must stay small and local to stay true to their cause, Bartle felt that creating franchises provided an impact far beyond his original green real estate brokerage. Expanding its reach beyond to its original office in San Francisco, Green Key now has three franchises in the San Francisco area. "We're also making traction with folks in other places around the country, in 32 states," says Bartle. "There is no other national franchise in green real estate that we know of. Green building is catching on everywhere, even in the reddest of states. It's not a political thing and not a hippie treehugger thing. It spans the spectrum of beliefs. Once you learn about indoor air quality, nobody wants to live in a toxic home."

GREEN REAL ESTATE FRANCHISE, CONTINUED

Bartle has found that the target market for franchises includes two groups. "The smaller portion is brokers and agents that are currently identified as green. They've been the green agent in their company for years, running a boutique. We're saying to them, 'We are aligned—let's join forces and work together.' The larger segment is everybody else." The broader group of agents and brokers are now seeing green as an important differentiation, as the future of their business. For this group, screening is important. "We screen them with a questionnaire, and we get to know them. When we are building a brand, we can't have people who are just talking the talk and not really believing in what we are doing."

Buying a Green Key franchise at present costs $9,800, as an introductory offer. "This will probably go up," says Bartle. "In this economy though we don't want the fee to be a deterrent. There is also a 4 percent of revenue royalty fee, and no annual renewal fee. It's a very affordable franchise package, compared to others. If they already have an existing entity, they may already have some of their expenses like insurance taken care of."

"After screening, we have a couple of visits, often at their site, and then at our site," says Bartle. "They meet other people, and we get them up and running with our library and marketing, If we are going into a new geography, we integrate the MLS, and the whole startup process is 30 days."

Green Key also provides training about green building, through programs put together by others. "The NAR (National Association of Realtors) has a new training program for realtors in green building that

GREEN REAL ESTATE FRANCHISE, CONTINUED

is very accessible," says Bartle. To help franchisees learn more about Green Key, Green Key provides internal franchisee training about how to be a part of Green Key, covering its operations and how it supports franchises.

Green Key is not just selling green, but working green in its office, ensuring that in its interactions with clients and the business community its green brand is thoroughly credible. "We also use carbon offsetting with a company called 3Degrees, based in San Francisco," says Bartle. "As new agents come on, we do an audit of energy use, and add that in, and corporate pays that. All of our agents are carbon neutral, and all offices are certified green businesses, if there is a program in their area. They could also use the San Francisco Green Business Program checklist to certify their program. We look at cleaning, energy use, water, and everything else to be as green an operation as possible."

Like many green businesses, Green Key has found that education is an important part of what it does. By educating brokers and homeowners, its franchises are helping spread the word about green building throughout their communities.

Green Landscape Maintenance—Franchise Opportunity with Clean Air Lawn Care
Interview with Gerry Keane, President

Our lawns and landscaping are not a passive part of the environment. Maintaining landscaping can have a surprisingly large impact on the environment. According to the EPA, using a gas-powered mower for an hour emits the same amount of hydrocarbons

(precursors to ground-level ozone) as a SUV driven 23,600 miles. And it's not just the mowers—leaf blowers, fertilizers, and weed control can all take their toll.

Gerry Keane and his associates started Clean Air Lawn Care in 2006 to offer a more environmentally friendly landscape maintenance service. Simple steps like cutting grass taller helps soil to retain water and makes it harder for weeds to grow, reducing the need for other means of weed control. Using solar power electric mowers and organic lawn treatments, the business has rapidly grown into a national presence in landscape maintenance and a solid franchise opportunity for green entrepreneurs eager to make a difference.

Keane and Kelly Giard (CEO) got their start thinking that there must be a way to create a more environmentally friendly lawn care business. "We had friends with a daughter in the environmental field looking for something to do," says Keane. "So we got some electric gardening equipment and a truck, and it took off."

They quickly rolled out the business to 10 locations around the country in communities like Seattle, Denver, Austin (Texas), and Portland (Oregon). "Those 10 locations took off with minimal dollars for marketing and advertising, just getting known through things like Treehugger and Green Drinks events," says Keane. "The PR engine is kicking in with appearances popping up on *Fine Living*, HGTV, and the Franchise 500, which has been great."

The focus of business has been residential, with an increasing percentage of commercial work, schools, and government. "It's a premium service because of what we are offering, but the cost is competitive compared to normal lawn care service," says Keane. "Most people we are targeting are green minded and are more comfortable doing things the right way rather than hearing a big lawn mower. We're only going after 1 percent of the market really, but still that's a big market and a big opportunity to change things."

Their business is also helped by regulations and incentives an increasing number of cities are putting in place to encourage people to switch from polluting gas mowers. "We support swap-out programs, where people can change old polluting equipment for newer cleaner machines," says Keane. "We also do educational programs about why electric equipment is better. Our goal is to not just build our business, but to help create change."

The equipment they use has been a key part of greening their franchises. "We use all electric equipment instead of gas-powered appliances, including mowers, trimmers, and blowers, and we have solar panels on our trucks that power the equipment," says Keane. "We can operate the whole day with the equipment we have in the truck. Some people at first said it couldn't be done, but the machines are durable, getting daily use for commercial businesses, up to an acre with the electric mower." Even the trucks used are small and fuel efficient, and the business offsets gas usage as part of being carbon neutral.

Keane, Giard, and the rest of their team are still adopting new measures to expand their business and reduce their environmental impact. "We added granular organic treatments for lawns to our mix of services in 2008, becoming the single source people need for their landscaping," says Keane. "Adding treatments to the services doubles the business model right off the bat. We are working with other green businesses, helping them reduce their carbon footprint by working with us."

In addition to changing how their service is delivered, they have created a business where people love to work. A visit to the headquarters for Patagonia, a green leader in outdoor clothing, inspired many of their recent efforts. "It is amazing," says Keane. "No offices, everyone in the same space working together, on-site day care, and people working just because they love being there."

After their visit to Patagonia, Clean Air Lawn Care created a new corporate location of their own, purchasing a Victorian

home next to a river along a park. "We wanted to create a work environment where work doesn't feel like work, where people just don't want to leave," says Keane. "It was a monumental move for us, but it has really paid off. As we green our business with things like the new building, we are seeing increased productivity, and retention is a nonissue, because people want to be here. They don't want to leave. We have a kitchen, with a little greenery, and people come in early to eat here rather than having breakfast at home."

This culture has proven to be a big selling point with people seeking franchise opportunities. "When you're recruiting, awarding franchises to people, and attracting new partners, how you present your organization is everything," says Keane. "We don't just want someone to write a check and buy something to be a part of the business. We want this infectious sense of 'Wow.'"

One factor to consider when looking into buying a franchise is location. "A franchise needs at least 32 weeks of mowing per year," says Keane. The strength of the green market also varies from region to region. "We are seeing increased business coming from areas that you would expect, like California, Texas, Florida, Oregon, Washington, and the Northeast, areas that have a lot of interest in green business, the change agents. As the green wave spreads, we'll see more interest in other areas, too. We've mapped out 500 franchises as our goal. If we meet that mark, we've had a big impact on greening the U.S. lawn care business."

For those who are interested in buying a franchise, the process starts with a qualification process to see if people fit the culture, know how to run a business, and have the financial status to start a successful franchise. "We require people coming in to have $50,000 cash available and $100,000 gross. We want to avoid getting people starting a business who have made a mistake," says Keane. "Then people get invited to Discovery Day in Fort Collins where they spend time with Kel, have dinner, talk, and interview people. They also get to go out in the field, to see what that is like." If people are awarded a territory then they sign and move forward with a seven-day training course, putting together a marketing plan, and learning how to use the bill payment system.

Clean Air Lawn Care provides a few options for the fees associated with buying a franchise. "People can start with a $15,000 initial fee and 9.5 percent royalty, $25,000 initial fee with 8.5 percent royalty, or $35,000 initial fee and 7.5 percent royalty," says Keane. "Some people have more money available and want to pay more upfront, while others have less cash on hand, so now we can work with all of these people." In addition to the franchise fee, people need money to get started with the truck, solar panels, marketing, and ads, which all adds up to another $15,000 or so of other startup costs.

The relationship continues once a franchise business is started. "We help franchises in many ways, including taking care of billing, marketing, and advertising," says Keane. "We get discounts on products, such as a deal we worked with Patagonia, and importantly, we help them understand how to get started, removing the fear about how to get the business rolling. We help with PR, and we have a database of leads we've formed over time. We work with our marketing goddess on a plan for each franchise, looking at what we have tried in that region to see what did not work and what did work. Our support team is always there, talking to franchises about how we can help. Their success is our success."

Beyond the financial issues and business experience that franchisees need to have, they all have their own unique life stories. "Some people call them the '29 forever group,' people who think they are young even as they get older, who are outdoorsy, athletic, and don't want to get old," says Keane. "We have stories on our website about the motivations the franchise owners

have. One was traveling 150,000 miles a year and wanted to make his own hours and spend more time with his kids. Quality of life is an important part of the demographic, but they are definitely green-minded folks who want to run their own business while doing something for the world." This is something they share with green businesses everywhere.

CHAPTER

 9

Starting an Energy Efficiency Business

We live, work, play, and shop in buildings, spending most of our lives in them. In addition to having a big impact on our lives, buildings also have a big impact on the environment. They are responsible for almost half of our greenhouse gas emissions (Architecture 2030), much of this the result of wasted energy that requires more coal and natural gas to be burned than would otherwise be necessary.

Constructing more energy-efficient buildings and retrofitting older buildings could be the cheapest, most cost-effective way to reduce greenhouse gas emissions (Commission for Environmental Cooperation).

Chapter 5 highlights some of the strategies to improve buildings. This chapter discusses some of the ways you can help reduce this waste—and build a business. With billions of dollars spent each year on wasted energy and with increased government incentives to improve efficiency, making buildings more energy efficient is a massive business opportunity and one that is getting more attention from all quarters.

The wave of shining new LEED-certified buildings growing across the country and around the world is one way that greener buildings are contributing to the economy and the environment. The ultimate in green buildings is a carbon neutral, or "net zero" building using energy efficiency and renewable energy to reduce the building's carbon footprint to zero. As important as these examples are, however, new buildings are only a small part of the problem compared to the millions of existing buildings that leak energy. These older buildings provide an even bigger opportunity for increased energy efficiency.

Government Support

The state of California has emphasized energy efficiency since the 1970s, with the California Public Utility Commission providing incentives for utilities to encourage efficiency. Through a variety of creative energy-efficiency programs in the ensuing years, and with increased efficiency emphasized in Title 24 building codes, California power consumption has stayed flat while power use in the rest of the country steadily increased. Today, power use in California is twice as efficient as the national average. The California experience can be replicated nationwide with the right incentives, and there are increasing signs that this is in the works.

One sign of the importance of energy efficiency is the support the federal government has committed to provide for energy efficiency efforts. The 2009 stimulus package has provided $5 billion for weatherization of low-income homes, $4.5 billion in funding for energy efficiency retrofits in federal buildings, and tax credits for a wide range of energy efficiency upgrades in homes.

Energy Efficiency Opportunities

The growing interest in energy efficiency will help businesses such as energy efficiency auditors and contractors. Energy efficiency auditors inspect homes and other buildings and suggest ways that they could be made more efficient; contractors go ahead and make these changes happen. In the November 10, 2008, *U.S. News and World Report,* energy efficiency auditor was listed as one of the best small businesses to start, with a low entry barrier, and only $10,000 needed to get started.

As the founder and CEO of Sustainable Spaces in San Francisco, Matt Golden has grown his business making homes more energy efficient, healthy, and comfortable for the people that live there. Golden describes the emphasis on energy efficiency retrofits in the 2009 stimulus package: "Low-hanging fruit programs such as low-income weatherization are an admirable way to start—they create jobs and help people lower energy bills, and can help our nation achieve a lofty goal of retrofitting 2.5 million homes in the next few years, hitting an annual run rate of 10 million homes improved by 2020."

The number of jobs and businesses created by energy efficiency work could be significant, providing one of the key arguments for investing in energy efficiency as a nation. "As the housing market struggles and hard times hit the construction industry,

many workers have lost their jobs," says Golden. "But there is hope in green collar jobs. With some retraining, these millions of talented workers can sharpen their trades and learn new skills to help us build this new industry. It could also create 1.25 million sustainable jobs, and as many as 8 million total jobs if manufacturing and other supporting industries are included."

The Green Collar Economy

Green collar jobs are the 21st century equivalent of blue collar manufacturing jobs in the 20th century, providing good wages and stable work for millions of people who will be installing solar panels, weatherizing buildings, and building wind farms.

And the jobs are created efficiently, with a large number of high-quality jobs created for the amount of money invested. "A number of studies show that every $1 million invested in retrofits creates approximately 12 direct jobs," says Golden. "By this estimate, investing on the order of $10 billion a year in retrofits, as proposed here, can be expected to directly create close to 120,000 direct jobs a year and 600,000 over five years, with a large share of these jobs in relatively high-paying occupations" (*The Direct Impact of Home Building and Remodeling on the U.S. Economy*, National Association of Home Builders).

The work to encourage energy efficiency is continuing, with additional legislative efforts being pushed forward, Golden describes: "For middle class homeowners, Congressman Peter Welch (Vermont) recently announced a national energy efficiency program—The Retrofit for Energy and Environmental Performance (REEP) initative, which could provide homeowners and businesses with access to direct cash incentives, interest rate subsidies, and credit support based on the percentage increase in energy efficiency they achieve. This program is included in the House Energy and Commerce Committee's upcoming bill, the American Clean Energy and Security Act of 2009."

The money spent on energy efficiency could have a sizable payback for all of us, driving the growth of businesses in the field and providing a big step forward in the fight against climate change. "If the U.S. is able to retrofit 128 million homes, as the DOE would like to do at the pace of 10 million a year, it would have measurable impact," says Golden. Such an investment could create a 25 percent reduction in the carbon emissions of U.S. homes at an average cost of $5,000 to 6,000 per home. Overall, this would produce a 5 percent reduction in the U.S. carbon footprint, according to Golden, the equivalent of taking 50 percent of our cars off the roads or everyone switching to hybrid vehicles.

As businesses involved in energy efficiency grow, they will stimulate other related businesses as well. "The first wave is the people doing the hands-on work in the field with green-collar jobs in renewable energy or green building," says Eric Corey Freed, author of *Green Building and Remodeling for Dummies* and Principal of the Organic Architect design firm he founded in 1997 (organic architect.com). "The second is the people doing the marketing, websites, accounting, hiring, and whatever else businesses need behind the scenes." And the waves don't stop there. Like many green entrepreneurs, Freed believes that education is needed to drive the continued growth of green businesses, creating the opportunity for those that can provide this important resource. "The third wave is teaching, at all levels," says Freed. "We need people that take all of this information and make it available in an easy way for all sorts of green building topics, and other sustainable business areas" (Entrepreneur.com, March 9, 2009).

Starting an Energy Efficiency Auditing Business

One type of energy efficiency related business is auditing, inspecting homes and buildings for energy efficiency and identifying

opportunities for improvement. To start an energy efficiency auditing business, you'll need training, some instrumentation (depending on the kind of audit you do), transportation, and clients. If you already work in the building industry or in one of the trades such as working as an HVAC contractor or electrician, you already have a big head start.

If you don't have a background in energy efficiency and want to be an auditor, then it's time to take a class or a workshop and read up on the topic in some good books. If you are an auditor, you probably won't be implementing all of the work that you describe during your inspection, but having a solid practical under-standing of the many factors involved will help your business. Classes and workshops on energy efficiency are sprouting up every-where, including on the internet and at community colleges, non-profits, and special courses. Any program, course, or conference about green building will also contain a strong emphasis on ener-gy efficiency. Some places to look for training in your region are:

- 🍃 The Housing and Urban Development website (hud.gov/offices/cpd/affordablehousing/training/web/energy /help/courses.cfm)
- 🍃 UC Davis Energy Efficiency Center website (eec1.ucdavis .edu/education/)
- 🍃 The Department of Energy list of weatherization training centers across the country (apps1.eere.energy.gov/weather ization/training_centers.cfm)
- 🍃 The Department of Energy list of adult education and training in energy programs (eere.energy.gov/education /adult_education.html)
- 🍃 The California Center for Sustainable Energy for informa-tion and regular free workshops in San Diego related to renewable energy and energy efficiency

For proof of your energy efficiency skills, you can get certifi-cation from the Residential Energy Services Network (RESNET), becoming a certified RESNET building rater (sometimes called a HERS rater, for Home Energy Rating System). Getting certified provides credibility. To be certified, you need training from a RESNET accreditied training center, which covers a long list of practical topics:

- building issues (insulation, windows, ducts, thermostats)
- how to do a home inspection
- financial issues related to energy efficiency work
- calculating volumes and areas of spaces
- how to analyze and report home performance

The RESNET website (resnet.us) has all of the information you need to get started, including information about training, classes, and testing. After taking a course, you will need to take the RESNET National Rater Test, which includes multiple choice and true and false questions. The test takes two hours and costs $50. A passing score is 80 percent, and candidates are informed right away if they have passed. The Study Guide for the test is available free online, and while it's just an outline, it provides a quick overview of the kind of information you would be expected to understand.

Resources and Strategies for Auditing

An auditor can either do a technical audit or a less technical audit. Some strategies integrate the auditing service with other services, such as having the same business do auditing and contracting work.

A nontechnical audit starts with a simple visual inspection of a building, using a checklist and interviewing the homeowner. The auditor in this case would do a walk-through, checking the types of lighting that is used, looking for cracks and sound weathersealing, looking at the insulation in the attic, and looking at utility bills, for example. For the nontechnical audit, you need little more than a car, an office with a computer, a good eye,

training, a checklist to work off of, a report template, and knowledge of what to look for.

If you have a business in which you are already traveling to people's homes for other purposes, adding a less technical audit may not require any additional resources really, except a bit of your time. One opportunity that has been explored by Geopraxis is to build an energy efficiency audit called the EnergyCheckup into home inspections for real estate transactions. Because home inspectors already go to homes as part of real estate transactions, they are familiar with building systems and can add this as part of the service they provide. Green Irene Ecoconsultants include energy efficiency as one factor in their Green Home Makeovers and Green Office Makeovers, doing a non-technical audit and providing helpful suggestions.

If you are already knowledgeable about building systems, and have a service to offer (like duct repair, or installing insulation), you might offer a free audit to get started with customers. To be credible though, the audit should not just be a sales pitch; it should provide an unbiased appraisal of what each home needs.

A technical audit gathers more data about a home using instruments like an infrared camera and the blower door test. An infrared camera is a specialized camera that can see where heat is escaping from a home, which is a useful tool for the auditor and can help to drive home the efficiency message to potential homeowner customers by allowing them to see the problems on

Tips for Success

Among the benefits of working in the energy efficiency auditing field (as described by Pro Energy Consultants' website):

- A high hourly rate paid for home audits
- Low overhead expenses if you run your business from your home
- Pay for performance, so you don't have to worry about managing accounts receivable

the camera. The blower door (see the section on Pro Energy Consultants) is a large fan mounted in a doorway to test the integrity of the building envelope by measuring the resistance to blowing air through the door. By feeding this data into a software system you can predict the steps needed to increase home efficiency, balancing cost and savings that can be achieved.

A business performing a technical audit provides a more detailed report to homeowners, with a thorough analysis of a home's performance, but such a business also require more resources to get started, approximately $10,000 to $30,000 for the initial investment, and additional resources for your:

- Office (for a home office, minimal expense)
- Employees (if you have someone answer the phones, for example)
- Vehicle
- Marketing

Your Product

For auditing, you will generally provide information communicated directly with homeowners and verbally by a written report. The more quickly the report is delivered the more effective it will be. If you can actually walk with the homeowners and point out the problems to them, following up immediately with a professional-looking written report, it will have more of an impact than a report delivered weeks later (or not at all). The written report also helps to justify the expense to the homeowner.

The Price Is Right

The pricing of reports from efficiency audits would depend on the amount and quality of data provided. For a non-technical audit of a home based on visual inspection, the cost may be about $100 or even less. For a technical report, including analysis with infrared camera and blower door, the audit will probably cost a few hundred dollars, depending perhaps on the size of the building being inspected.

The report from an energy audit should include an action plan, and may suggest specific contractors to carry out the work. If you do form partnerships with contractors, it could help bring in business, but be careful about whom you recommend and how you recommend them. It's best to form relationships with people you really know and are confident will do great work.

For marketing, there are a few strategies to connect with homeowners without spending a great deal. Advertising yourself on Craigslist is easy enough. If you have an existing business in HVAC or a related field, contact clients with a mailer to inform them of your new service and how it can save them money. Go to local home improvement events for homeowners and to green fairs. Give talks at the local schools; the kids will talk to their parents about your business. With all the interest in energy efficiency these days, see if the local newspaper or TV station is interested in talking to you and running a story, which lets even more people know how you can help them. Doing an audit for a well-known figure in town can help make the story appealing. Know any celebs in need of weatherstripping or insulation?

Case Study
PRO ENERGY CONSULTANTS FRANCHISE

Some energy efficiency auditors work locally one building at a time or with crews in one city. Pro Energy Consultants has bigger dreams, selling franchises across the United States so entrepreneurs can build their own energy efficiency businesses. The company was created by partners Mark Canella, Kris Simonich, and Derek Sola. Canella had run his energy auditing business in Cleveland for 13 years and is an expert in his field. Pro Energy Consultants began rolling out

PRO ENERGY FRANCHISE, CONTINUED

the franchise business in the fall of 2008, and it now has ten franchisees signed up across the United States, with more signing up all the time.

When a Pro Energy Consultant is working with a client, he or she goes to the client's home and conducts an energy audit. "The visit includes consulting, listening and talking with the homeowner, and the technical component, the audit," says Simonich. "When people call for an audit, they are motivated by various factors that the consultant needs to understand. "We put on our consultant's hat and listen," says Simonich. "We need to talk about 'Why are we here?' Clients are motivated by the energy cost pain, spending more on energy than they want, or the comfort pain, that rooms are too hot or too cold." The third factor motivating clients is their green conscience. When consultants sit down with clients, they analyze utility bills and talk about problem points, allowing clients to provide information that often leads to the best solutions.

After talking, consultants undertake the actual technical audit featuring the blower door and the infrared camera. The blower door is a large fan that is sealed in a door frame and blows air out, measuring how hard the fan has to blow. The easier it is to blow air out, the leakier the house must be. As the fan blows air out, air gets back into the house through other routes, exaggerating the air exchange and highlighting problem areas that can be identified with the infrared camera.

The infrared camera visualizes areas where unusual heat differences occur, the focus of many problems in homes. "The camera is the piece everyone gets excited about," says Simonich. With the camera in hand, the consultant explains simple principles with the homeowner looking over his shoulder, helping the client make sense of puzzling energy costs or

PRO ENERGY FRANCHISE, CONTINUED

discomfort. "We walk around with the homeowner, educating them," says Simonich. "At the end we will have to explain our findings, reading from the blower door and the camera, boiling it down to very simple principles."

After the audit, the consultant creates a plan for the homeowner. "We can tell them what to do and how much it would cost," says Simonich. "The reality is that it's not the big expense of the repairs that makes a big difference. People already know if they need windows. It's the small repairs that give them the biggest return on investment, those little $1 to $2,000 repairs they would never know about and never fix without the audit." Consultants can help to coordinate these smaller repairs with contractors in their network.

With the economy taking a dive, the interest in saving money has never been greater. "In Cleveland, for example, our record months were September, October, and November of last year, 2008," says Simonich. "The more that people realize they are staying in their house, the more cost conscious they become. With the economy down, the business is consumer driven; people are clamoring for it."

To get started, those interested in buying a franchise need to go through a four-to-six-week qualification process to get to know the founders and start what will be a long-term partnership. Once franchisees complete the process and are awarded the territory, they sign the agreement and pay the initial investment of $29,900, which includes payment for the infrared camera and blower door.

The next step is completing two training courses, one on the internet and one with a printed manual. Although some interested in a franchise might worry that it requires an extensive technical background, Pro

PRO ENERGY FRANCHISE, CONTINUED

Energy Consultants provides franchisees with whatever information is needed. "We like people to be on board for about a month before bringing them out for training." Next, franchisees travel to Cleveland for three days of practical hands-on training, including everything from mock audits to practice dealing with homeowners.

With the training under their belts, consultants are ready to start their business, including an eight-week mentoring program with scheduled conference calls with trainers. The mentoring program helps reinforce training and get things off to a smooth start.

Franchisees continue receiving support for their business. There are:

- An 800 number they can advertise, routing customers back to their business

- A company web page that allows customers to input their zip codes and directs them back to their local business

- Participation in vendor purchasing programs, providing a better deal than they could receive on their own

- Protected territory and ongoing support

- Research and development as the business grows, introducing new revenue streams and strategic partnerships

There are still new avenues to explore, with energy auditing as the springboard to additional business opportunities. "Going forward, the audit is just an entrée into other things," says Simonich.

The opportunity to fix our homes and make them more efficient is a huge one, and there's plenty of room to grow across the country.

Starting Green

Energy Efficiency Contractors

Once an auditor examines a home and provides a list of actions to be taken, somebody has to go ahead and do the work, creating opportunities for home efficiency contractors, the people who do the retrofit work in homes to make them more efficient. Contractors doing energy efficiency work will need all the tools of the home trade, a contractor's license, a truck to get around, and an office. They will also need a way of attracting business (more on this later).

For contractors, the product they sell is the work done on the home. This work could be viewed as a checklist based on the information the auditor provides, but you add more value by viewing the work as part of an integrated system, including the home and the homeowner. Discuss the list with the homeowner, identifying items the homeowner considers the highest priority, that fit in her or his budget, and that provide the most energy efficiency bang for the buck. Verifying energy savings adds value, providing some before-and-after readings of home performance and estimating the money savings that can be expected. In some cases you might also form partnerships with others to distribute or sell their energy efficiency products. There are a variety of novel insulation products available, for example, as well as lighting solutions, lighting controls, and other efficiency products.

The type of work energy efficiency contractors do includes:

- Installing insulation
- Changing lighting
- Installing lighting controls
- Changing thermostats
- Installing a whole house fan or attic fan
- Repairing air ducts
- Insulating pipes and ducts

- 🍃 Weatherstripping
- 🍃 Installing daylighting
- 🍃 Installing energy efficiency appliances
- 🍃 Installing energy-efficient heating and cooling systems

If your current business is in heating and cooling systems or in the building industry, moving into energy efficiency contracting, or emphasizing efficiency in your existing business, could be a smooth transition. Being up to date on energy-efficient heating systems, ventilation, air conditioning, and heat pumps is important. Air ducts are an important part of energy efficiency, and knowing the correct ways to appraise the problems and fix them is another opportunity. After this, energy efficiency in the building envelope is important as is reducing wasted electricity. Some businesses that are already working with HVAC systems will probably build on what they already have and rebrand themselves as a "Green HVAC" business, focusing on energy-efficient HVAC equipment and developing a partnership or expertise in fixing air ducts or insulating buildings. It's helpful, however, to avoid being too narrow in your focus, to have a view of whole-house performance to integrate all of the possible routes to efficiency.

The Market

Homeowners who seek out energy efficiency auditing and contracting are motivated by saving money, as well as making their home more comfortable and helping the environment. Most people are interested first in saving money, health and comfort, with the environmental benefit as the green icing on the cake. Including the message about saving money will be a key part of the marketing for your energy efficiency business.

Who is the market? Saving money is always a popular topic, even with people who are not very concerned about the

environment. The interest today in saving money is greater than ever for a broad cross section of society. Saving money is in. Very in, and I have a feeling it will be this way for some time to come. Having impressive statistics, graphics, and testimonials about the money people save on their energy bills will help to get customers to sign up.

If you are already a contractor, your past customers might provide a list of potential leads. How many people you have worked with installed new heaters or air conditioners? A heater will be relatively expensive compared to the value from insulation and fixing air ducts, so if they bought a heater they might be willing to invest a little more to get much greater value out of their previous investment. How many people put off buying a new air conditioner because it was too expensive? They might be willing to invest in lower cost energy efficiency improvements, which will often provide a more rapid return on their investment.

If you don't have a list of contacts ready to go, you can partner with another business that does and that is constantly in the business of driving out to people's homes, such as a heating and cooling contractor. They get the call for a heater repair, and you provide another option that can be packaged along with the repair or replacement of the heater. Including energy efficiency steps at the same time may allow for a smaller heater to be used, reducing the cost, and saving money for the homeowner. Electricians, plumbers, roofers, and others could also provide potential partners.

Market Power

One of the key selling points for energy efficiency contracting should be the many ways of lowering the cost of doing efficiency improvements in homes and businesses. Don't forget to talk with customers about tax credits, rebates, and other incentives for energy efficiency work.

Financing Efficiency

In the long run the money spent on energy efficiency in homes and businesses saves money by helping people waste less, but this still requires an upfront investment that can hold people back. Removing this initial finance barrier is often the key to unlocking the greater potential for energy efficiency. Creative financing is being explored in many ways to overcome this barrier and further the growth of the energy efficiency industry.

On-bill financing being piloted in places like San Diego, California, allows business customers to finance certain energy efficiency improvements. With on-bill financing of energy efficiency projects, utilities help businesses fund improvements that are paid back through their utility bill, helping them save money overall. Another unique way to finance energy efficiency is being developed by cities in California and other parts of country through special financing districts. The city creates a pool of money which homeowners can apply for to pay for energy efficiency in their homes. The money is paid back over many years through their property taxes. The U.S. Small Business Administration has a little-publicized 7a loan program to fund energy efficiency projects.

> ### Resource Guide
>
> A variety of government grant and loan programs for energy efficiency are summarized at: business.gov /expand/green-business /grants-and-loans/.

GREEN SKIES ENERGY EFFICIENCY CONTRACTING BUSINESS PLAN*

Vision
Within the next five years grow Green Skies to be the leading energy efficiency contractor in Phoenix with $4 million in annual sales, helping homeowners and businesses to save money and fight climate change.

Mission
Providing greener buildings for comfort, savings, and a greener world.

Objectives

- Grow sales to $4 million by Year 5, then 25% a year.

- Break-even in Year 1, achieve Year 2 net profits of $75,000.

- Price projects to achieve minimum gross profit of 15%.

- Get 5 mentions in print, radio, and TV, and 20 mentions on internet in Year 1.

- Achieve average gas and electricity savings of 30% for homeowners.

- In Year 5, identify 22,000 leads and 5,500 customers.

- Avoid 350,000 tons of client CO_2 emissions in Year 5.

Strategies

- Build reputation by greening operations and delivering on promises.

GREEN SKIES BUSINESS PLAN, CONTINUED

- Increase market awareness through relationships with realtors and energy audit firms.

- Ensure high quality work using energy audits, follow-up, and certified workers.

- Ensure profitability by choosing the right customers, buying smart, and pricing profitably.

- Use technology for marketing, client education, and to design work for the greatest savings.

- Target older neighborhoods with higher incomes to increase sales.

Plans

- Design a service package and pricing by September Year 1.

- Launch website by December 15 in Year 1.

- Start web marketing in February Year 2 and complete in July Year 2.

- Develop co-marketing plan with an energy auditing firm by March Year 2.

- Attend Earth Day with booth in April Year 2.

- Attend regional building conference in May Year 2.

*Modeled after *The One Page Business Plan* by Jim Horan.

Interview with a Green Building Leader:
Eric Corey Freed

Eric Corey Freed is an architect, author, and educator leading efforts to green our buildings and our economy. As principal and founder of organicARCHITECT, a design firm in San Francisco, he is a well-known and highly regarded green architect. Through frequent speaking engagements, design work, consulting, and educational work he has reached out to the growing green building community and helped it to grow. He is the author of *Green Building and Remodeling for Dummies*, and has two more books— *Sustainable Schools*, and *Green Home Green Pockets*—coming out at the end of 2009. I spoke with him about the opportunities in green building and the rest of the green economy.

While the down economy has hit the building industry hard, Freed has found that the green building market is doing relatively well, particularly in specific areas. "For example, building owners looking to stand out in the market are turning to greening buildings," says Freed. "There's also a pickup in the business for large commercial projects, where green building is a good differentiator to stand out in a tough market."

Another motivation for green building is to save money. "We estimate that on average that it costs about $4 per square foot to get LEED certified," says Freed, "but it pays for itself at a rate of $67 per square foot including energy, according to the USGBC." The emphasis on saving money is particularly strong in the down economy. "The downturn forces people to rethink priorities," says Freed. "I've seen a definite transition from green finishes, which might be seen as a luxury, to saving energy and saving water." While the down economy is rough for many businesses, it creates an important opportunity for businesses that deliver energy efficiency. "We'll see a boom in companies like Sustainable Spaces that address energy efficiency in buildings," says Freed. "We'll see businesses like this around the country."

Saving energy is not just a fad though. A long-term trend that will keep the green building movement growing will be the rising price of electricity in the years ahead. "When gas was $4 a gallon, businesses had to change, and people were choosing smaller cars and smarter driving habits. The same goes for electricity," says Freed. "When we have a carbon tax, when the cost of electricity goes up from 12 cents to 24 cents a kilowatt hour, everyone will have to address energy efficiency. Not from an abstract carbon footprint perspective, but from a tangible impact on bottom line."

Government action is also playing an important role in stimulating long-term growth of the green building industry, Freed has found. "We can't solve climate change, spread green building nationwide, or provide clean energy without government help from solar rebates to changing laws for soapy grey water. All of these things have to be addressed. I've started compiling a list of building codes that need to be changed, and I'm working with San Francisco in changing them, working one-on-one to remove the blockades and barriers. I'm working locally, but ideally we can do this at the state and national level."

Building codes may not always receive a great deal of media, but they have a major impact on green building, sometimes helping it and sometimes holding it back. "Here in California we have Title 24 building codes requiring improved energy efficiency," says Freed. "Why can't Title 24 be enforced nationally?" Even in a place like San Francisco that is very commited to green building, there is still work to be done though to improve codes and how they are enforced. "The Mayor of San Francisco is very committed to green building and had a press conference where he said we have a new law that you can't use grey water (soapy water) in your backyard," says Freed. The city building inspectors, however, didn't have the authority to implement this. "Figuring out these things here in San Francisco, we can transfer them to state and national level," says Freed.

The continued growth of the green building industry will create opportunities for a broad range of workers and businesses. "I would say that there are opportunities for any trade that is loosely connected to energy or utilities including water or sewer, whether manual, blue collar work, companies that are leasing solar equipment, or Joe the plumber," says Freed.

Along with the need for businesses that improve energy efficiency, there is also a need for ways to measure the impact of these improvements. "This is a subset of the back-end functions businesses need," says Freed. "Like the work of Agilewaves [the energy information company], providing feedback information and education about green performance can help change behavior for energy use or consumer spending."

The many workers and businesses moving into the green economy will also increase the opportunities for related businesses. "Contractors, electricians, plumbers, or other existing members of the service industry making the transition to the green collar economy also need to be thinking about marketing, billing, websites, and other supporting activities," says Freed. "Along with the surge in companies that are part of the green economy, there will be an equal surge in companies like these that are fluent in the language of sustainability, such as marketing companies that know how to speak to consumers about these things."

All of these workers making the move toward sustainability create challenges and opportunities in education and training as well. "Every building project has trained professional inspectors," says Freed. "What if we trained them to inspect other building techniques, such as green building methods? We'd suddenly get the entire building industry trained in two years." And the training is not just needed in the building industry, but in every industry. "We need good teachers. We need everything from basic eco-literacy in elementary schools to green MBAs. We have a few schools like the Presidio [School of Management] offering a green

MBA, and Harvard and others schools are toying with it. But every MBA program will offer a green option, and this will become the norm, not just for the elite but for everyone."

The change to a green economy sometimes requires a change in thinking. While some believe that the green economy is for environmentalists, Freed believes that the opportunities are for everyone. "I've been in this for nearly 20 years, and the true environmentalists are really dedicated to the idea that we want everybody to get involved," says Freed. "The idea that we're some elite country club couldn't be further from the truth. We need to make every building a green building and make every business a green business. We need to get everyone involved."

For all of those considering a green business, Freed offers a few tips. "First, and this is very important, be humble," says Freed. "There is nothing wrong with saying 'We know we're not perfect.' You can say, 'These are the things we're doing, and here's what we want to do that we haven't figured out yet,' but not make broad claims about being green. Look at the most admired companies working on sustainability, like Interface. [Founder] Ray Anderson will be the first to tell you all the things he's doing wrong, and things he is still figuring out. Be humble and honest."

Consumers expect honesty, and transparency. "When somebody comes out and says 'We're a green company' and it's one green product, then they really can get in trouble with consumers," says Freed. "They would be better to lay it out, to be honest and open, and say, 'Well, we've only got one green shoe today, but here is where the problems are. We'll keep working on it.' Businesses don't like it, but there's nothing wrong with saying 'We don't know how to do that yet.'"

Wrapping up our interview, Freed reflected on the years invested by the many businesses and activists in the green community to get to this point, and the many years ahead still.

"These things take time," says Freed. "It doesn't happen overnight, but plant these seeds now and it will happen. The more seeds you plant, the better, as long as they are the right seeds to help create the change."

CHAPTER

 10

Starting a Green
Retail Business

Most of the objects in our daily lives come from retail businesses: furniture, food, books, or clothing. A third of the new businesses started each year are retail businesses, according to the *Retail Store Startup Guide* (Entrepreneur Press). Many entrepreneurs share the dream of setting up their own little shop. Get a space, buy some stuff, put it on the shelves, and the customers come rolling in, right?

Unfortunately it's not always quite that simple. There are some key questions you need to think about before you start ringing up the sales. Will you be starting a new business from scratch, or buying a retail franchise or a business opportunity? What type of products will you focus on? Green clothing? If so, for what market and what type of clothing? Outdoor? Upscale eco-chic? Recycled clothing for resale? Or maybe home products? Will you have a brick-and-mortar location, a physical storefront, or will you have an internet store only, as many businesses do today?

While some issues are common to all retail businesses, others are unique to green retail. Presumably your green store will sell green things. But how are they green? There are a variety of ways to be green and different shades, with different levels of messages about the health and environmental impact of goods. You need a clear vision of your business, and that means sorting through the many possibilities to have a specific concept.

Business Basics

If you are selling retail, you will need a seller's permit. The details will vary in different areas, but you've got to have one.

Another key question is about your market. A clear vision of your customers helps you decide the right goods to put on your shelves. Who are you selling to and what are they looking for? Is it the core green group that values the environment above all else? Or is it the larger number of people who value the environment but look at the price of goods as the major factor in their buying decisions?

The other big question about your store is the store itself. With the green label can come high expectations; many customers will expect everything about your store to be green, from one end of the building to the other. Some may be keen to look for nongreen aspects to raise the rallying cry of "greenwashing!"

Ultimately the same rules that apply to any retail business will apply to your green store. There's just the addition of the green issues. If being green is part of your concept, it will be integrated into your products, your location, your marketing, your employee policies, your store, and your suppliers. One thing being green does not do is to release you from working to make sales and earn a profit.

The main costs of starting a small retail business are:

- Store space, either leased or purchased ($1,000 to $10,000 a month)
- Store interior ($10,000 to $100,000 upfront to get started)
- Inventory (variable, depending on what you are selling. This is a big wild card.)
- Salaries, payroll taxes, and other employee expenses (for a few employees, $1,000s to $10,000s per month)
- Other operating expenses (insurance, utilities, $1,000s per month)

Your specific costs will depend on these variables. There are startup cost calculators available on the internet or in business planning software kits. As you work through your business plan, you should have a pretty good idea what your store will look like and what it will cost you to get started.

Green Products

The products that you sell define what your store is all about; they need to be carefully thought through as part of your strategy. What is unique about your store's offerings that will bring customers to you and not your competitors? What simple central concept holds all of the products together and draws in traffic?

One strategy for a green store is to build a unique green counterpart of an existing retail business. In some cases being green might be enough to create a whole new concept. If you are

building the first green pet store in your town, providing eco-friendly dog food and treats, this niche may be distinct enough to attract traffic from pet-loving environmentalists who have not found these products elsewhere. An organic bakery, organic café, or organic butcher shop might provide a similar opportunity to carve out a retail niche by moving to the green side of existing businesses.

Here are some ideas for green stores to think about. The list is potentially endless, but you can write me if your store is not on the list:

- Green building supplies
- Salvaged and eco-friendly building supplies
- Eco-friendly pet store
- Herbal remedy store
- Second-hand clothing franchise
- Solar gadget store (sort of the green Brookstone)
- All bulk food store, to reduce packaging
- Organic meat butcher shop
- Office supplies
- Energy efficiency device store (combined with service offering in energy auditing)
- Electric scooter store

One of the concerns about selecting green products for your store is the confusion in identifying what makes some products greener than others. Certification schemes have been created for many types of products to make selection of green products easier for businesses and for consumers. Having a label that says "Certified Green" in a credible way is much easier than having to screen each product one at a time to see where it came from, how it is made, and where it will ultimately go, determining for yourself its environmental impact. Many certification schemes are used primarily for one type of product, like paper or cleaning products. Third-party certification helps to ensure that every-thing is on the up and up, although the proliferation of certifica-tion standards at present can create confusion as well.

Some certification standards are:

- *FSC.* Forest Stewardship Council certified wood and wood products (fscus.org)
- *LEED.* Leadership in Energy and Environmental Design, developed by the U.S. Green Building Council (usgbc.org)
- *MSC.* Marine Stewardship Council, for the certification of sustainably harvested fish (msc.org)
- *Green Seal.* Certification of a variety of products that avoid the use of hazardous chemicals, particularly household cleaning products (greenseal.org)
- *Green-e.* Provides certification of offsets and renewable energy credits (green-e.org)
- *Energy Star.* Energy-efficient certification for appliances, with the EPA (energystar.gov)
- *Organic.* From plants and animals raised without synthetic pesticides, hormones, antibiotics, fertilizers, or other syn-thetic chemicals (ccof.org)
- *Fair Trade.* Providing reasonable payment for goods, best known for coffee, but also used for handicrafts, choco-late, tea, and several other foods (transfairusa.org)
- *Cradle to Cradle.* By MBDC, for eco-friendly products of reusable materials (c2ccertified.com)
- *SMART certification.* For building products, textiles, clothes, and flooring (sustainableproducts .com/mts/smartstandards.html)

New certification schemes are appearing all the time it seems. Cradle

> ### Getting Certified
>
> A database of green labels and certifications from around the world can be found at globaleco labelling.net.

to cradle certification is well known but has not been broadly adopted. It is derived from the McDonough and Braungart book of the same name. The idea of cradle to cradle is that nothing goes to waste, that all of the products we use can be reused with downcycling, that is, losing quality with each round of use until they can no longer be used. SMART certification by MTS is an up-and-coming certification method that also examines product life cycles, but some believe it is more accessible and may prove more broadly applicable.

Just because something is not yet certified does not mean it is not green, particularly products from smaller vendors. Getting certified can in some cases cost a product developer a fair amount of money, at least for a small business. In the absence of a certification for the products you want to sell, deciding if a product is green or not will be a judgment call. One help is to look for specific claims and wording, things that can be measured and verified. For example, it is better if a product says "made from organic cotton" rather than a broad statement about being "eco-friendly" or "all natural." As nice as these terms sound, they lack substance and specific legal meaning, and may sometimes be deceiving.

If you are to talk about products' environmental impact as well as their other features, you need to be educated about these products. People are sure to ask, and it will help in some cases to seal the deal. Talk to your suppliers about where things are made, how they are made, what they are made of, and what will happen to the product when people are done with it. There are not a lot of perfect options, but some are clearly better than others. Recycled materials are better than virgin materials. Goods made from petroleum products seldom win many green points. Goods with a long lifespan, durable products, are green because they avoid using resources for replacement. Products that can be recycled and reused at the end of their first life to have a second or third life are very green. Used goods are almost always eco-friendly, because they require virtually no new resources. Although they have generally been considered not too sexy, used goods have surged in popularity in the current economic environment.

The trick is getting the right combination of price, product quality, and environmental quality that works for your customers. Organic products that are good for the environment but don't work well are not big sellers. Green products that are priced competitively, work well, and are good for the environment will prove big winners.

The Green Store Itself

Along with the goods you sell, the environmental impact of your store will help build credibility and attract customers. Many of the routes to green operations discussed in Chapter 5 will apply to your store, including energy efficiency, water conservation, and leasing a green building, if possible. Also, you might use green display materials such as those that ECOR is developing (ecorglobal.com). These materials are made from recycled materials such as paper, cardboard, agricultural fibers, and "Bovine Processed Fiber." Paint the store with low VOC paint, use recycled building materials where possible, use energy-efficient lighting, and have window shades to cut down on heat from windows.

In thinking about how you position your store to find your niche, you are going to look at your location and your region and the competition you will face. You might think that your competition is other green retail outlets in the same category, but this might not always be the case. If you are thinking of a green grocery store, for example, you may envision Whole Foods as your competitor. But is there a Whole Foods nearby, or are you really competing with the regular grocery store right across the street,

the farmers' market, or the CSA that brings fruit and vegetables right to the door?

Who your market is will say a lot about where you locate your store. Are you providing a product that commands a premium price? Perhaps it is innovative and not available elsewhere? Are you relying on its environmental benefits as the main selling point? You should probably locate in a more upscale type of neighborhood. Going for the cheapest lease may put you in the wrong neighborhood for your market.

Internet or Brick and Mortar?

Internet selling has grown enormously in recent years. The costs for getting an internet store started are lower, because it avoids the need for a large inventory, store lease, and other expenses that come with a storefront, and building a store on the internet can move forward with lightning speed compared to setting up an old-fashioned storefront. Building a brand on the internet can take advantage of the vocal green bloggers, spreading links to your webstore like confetti.

And yet there are still old-fashioned stores out there, with buildings, and shelving, and a cash register—the works. It's not as if brick and mortar has gone the way of the dinosaur. One reason is that people still like to feel, touch, and smell some products before they buy. In psychological tests, people will pay more for objects that they have touched, and select them preferentially over those that they just read about on the computer screen.

Having It Both Ways

Some entrepreneurs have both online and storefront locations. Livingreen has stores providing green home products in Los Angeles and Santa Barbara, California, as well as an internet store where you can buy many of their products.

Case Study
STARTING A TURNKEY ONLINE ECO-STORE WITH ONLYGREEN4ME™

One option for a ready-to-go online store is provided by OnlyGreen4Me,™ giving entrepreneurs the means to get their own Eco-Store up and running quickly.

Although straightforward in principle, starting your own retail outlet is not trivial. It takes time and energy to sort through the great variety of green products available, identify those you want to sell, and work with each supplier to get started. Working directly with each supplier, you need to negotiate pricing, as well as managing payments, shipping, inventory, and software for transactions. The more vendors you work with, the more time it will take to get started, and time is money. If you have a brick-and-mortar operation, you will also need to acquire and outfit space, take care of hiring, and other complications.

OnlyGreen4Me is making it easier for eco-entrepreneurs to create their own online Eco-Stores. "OnlyGreen4Me delivers a fully functional, e-commerce Eco-Store with over 7,000 third-party certified eco-products from nationally recognized companies," says Pete Green, founder of OnlyGreen4Me. It makes setting up a store easy by eliminating inventory, shipping and handling, billing, and collection. With such a broad range of green products, for both the home and office and with the software for an online store ready to go, you can hit the ground running with a store months earlier than doing it all on your own.

OnlyGreen4Me stores carry a wide range of home and office products. For example, they lease Xerox printers using ink sticks instead of toner

TURNKEY ONLINE ECO-STORE, CONTINUED

cartridges, avoiding a great deal of waste, and carry eco-apparel made from bamboo and hemp, 100 percent biodegradable cleaning products and energy efficient do-it-yourself home kits. Green cleaning and break room supplies made from eco-friendly and recycled material and LED and CFL lighting are also part of the line.

They are also working with national solar and lighting integrators for the commercial market.

If you have an existing website drawing visitors, you could easily integrate an Eco-Store into it, plugging the OnlyGreen4Me system into your website. In addition to dealers having their own individual Eco-Store, they can market private label Eco-Stores to larger corporations. Larger corporations are often working on improving their sustainability and developing an Eco-Store internally can help. The Eco-Store and the larger corporation can share in commissions and use them to fund internal operations or sustainability initiatives. "For example, a school could have one of our Eco-Stores under their banner," says Green, "and students could use it for a 'Sally Foster' type fundraiser. The commissions they earned could be use to fund school sustainability projects."

When consumers and businesses are buying green, they increasingly look for products certified by a third party. OnlyGreen4Me works to include products for Eco-Stores that are from large companies and have been certified, where possible. "You will notice on our site that our products for the most part come from national manufacturers and they have their significant reputations on the line with their claims," says Green.

TURNKEY ONLINE ECO-STORE, CONTINUED

One of the concerns consumers and businesses have about green products is that they believe they are more expensive than other products. "We are finding that the cost of green products in general are coming down to traditional petro-based products rapidly, and in some cases like remanufactured ink and toner, of course, significantly below OEMs without sacrificing quality," says Green. "I believe pricing will continue to come down over time. It's important to note that our pricing is very competitive to the big power suppliers like Office Depot and Staples so that the end customers are getting great pricing. We're able to give that kind of pricing because we can offset the volume discounts that they get with a much lower cost structure, i.e., no inventory costs, no retail infrastructure costs and much lower employee costs."

The cost to get going with an Eco-Store with OnlyGreen4Me includes a setup fee that right now is $2,500 and includes the first year hosting and maintenance fee of $1,800 and ongoing hosting and maintenance fees of $150/month (paid annually in the subsequent years). As an Eco-Store dealer, you earn commissions on products sold, ranging from 5 to 35 percent. As of February 2009, in response to the economy, OnlyGreen4Me is helping out new dealers by waiving the usual setup fee and with a six-month commitment is getting dealers started for only a $150 per month hosting and maintenance fee.

There are hundreds of environmentally-friendly companies in existence today selling tens of thousands of worthwhile "green products" used in our everyday life—whether at work or home, for business or pleasure. There really is no turning back as this grass roots movement started by a few progressive, forward thinking individuals and entities

HOME PLANET OFFICE FURNITURE STORE BUSINESS PLAN*

Vision
Within the next 5 years, grow Home Planet Office Furniture into the leading California online retailer of eco-friendly and effective office furniture, with annual sales of $5 million.

Mission
We deliver productivity for green workspaces.

Objectives

- Grow sales to $10 million in Year 5, on 4,000 units sold, then 20% a year.
- Achieve 10% minimum net profit in Year 2 of operations.
- Reduce waste from packaging and production 35% by Year 3 and 60% by Year 5.
- Reduce production and shipping costs 25% by Year 5.
- Demonstrate overall customer satisfaction rating of 5/5 stars.
- Achieve 30% return business with commercial clients in Year 3.

HOME PLANET BUSINESS PLAN, CONTINUED

- Receive 5 major media mentions (print, radio, TV) in Year 2.

Strategies

- Build green reputation using FSC-certified wood, low waste, carbon offsets, and life cycle management.
- Develop world-class furniture with top talent, custom design, and assembly services.
- Build market by blogger relations and media attention to green story.
- Increase revenue with affiliate mktg program on internet and partnering with office products consultants.
- Reduce costs by computer-aided design, energy efficiency, and reducing waste.
- Attract/retain top talent w/ profit sharing, green operations, flexible hours, and telecommuting.

Plans

- Hire design team by February Year 1.
- Secure manufacturing facility and green product materials by April Year 1.
- Create profit sharing plan and implement by September of Year 1.
- Demonstrate pilot production by October of Year 1.
- Design website starting October Year 1 to launch website by April Year 2.
- Form relationship with office organization consulting firm by October Year 2.

Modeled after The One Page Business Plan by Jim Horan.

Green Retail Insights from Tom Larsen
RETAIL 101

Tom Larsen co-founded TD Innovations in 1995 and is president of GreenSmart, the company's line of laptop, messenger, and other bags made from eco-conscious materials. From his experience, he has learned what works and what doesn't when it comes to green retail, or retailing in general. You can read Tom's blog at tom larsen.typepad.com or find him in the Facebook or LinkedIn communities. When providing his insights, he referred to his lessons as "Retail 101," a quick compendium of his experience in the field, paving the way for others to succeed more readily.

People starting out with the green retail business are not always prepared for what is involved, says Larsen. "As a result, just as in the restaurant business, people enter into the business completely unprepared for the financial issues, running a business and making it succeed." Don't lose sight of providing economic sustainability in addition to providing environmentally sustainable products, Larsen advises, appreciating the diverse definitions of success people have. For some it's providing for their family, for others success is creating jobs in their community, and for many it is all about greening our world. Whatever your idea of success is though, your business needs to make money.

"Even if you're not in the business to create profits, you are in the business to pay your bills," says Larsen. "If you put up $100,000 of your own money, at some point later, you'll want to recover that money. Hopefully with interest—the rate of that interest is determined by the amount of smarts you bring to operating your business. To vastly

RETAIL 101, CONTINUED

improve your odds of staying open past three years, and be truly sustainable, follow these guidelines and get deeply educated on every one."

Blocking and Tackling—Marketing a Store

The first lesson Larsen drives home is the importance of marketing your store to get people through the door. "No matter what the retail concept, if no one knows about your fabulous store, no one will go there," says Larsen. "The absolute number-one reason that most retail businesses fail is that they do not create enough traffic in their store to remain viable. If the location draws traffic, then the opportunity to get some of them in the store goes up." But you can't count on location alone to do all the work. "On the other hand, location isn't everything, and neighborhoods and traffic patterns change. To win at any retail enterprise, just as in football, you've got to be really savvy about blocking and tackling, blocking out what you want and tackling the people in that sector to get them to your store."

Planning a schedule of marketing events can help, particularly when a store is just starting out. And once the plan is in place, make it happen. "Before you even open, create a Marketing Calendar—what you're going to do for the first 12 months in terms of getting the word out," says Larsen. "Fliers, radio, sponsor a Little League team, newspaper, web presence, local bloggers, host events, whatever it is, mix it up, commit to it early, and be passionate about making it happen."

The plan should be varied, to reach the most potential customers, and it should be flexible, allowing changes based on what works and what doesn't. "As the calendar progresses, analyze each of your efforts and

RETAIL 101, CONTINUED

modify it," says Larsen. "Doing the same thing all the time doesn't expand your market. If you advertise in the local paper, only the people who read the paper will see it. The same is true for a web ad or website."

Other events help build a network with local businesses that can help when you are new and getting off the ground. "You'll need to be a Rotary (or equivalent) and a Chamber member, and hosting an event of the Chamber or Downtown Business District or whatever is an early must. You only get to be new once. Since your business is you, you'll need to circulate in as many cooperative ways as possible. Be creative. There are many who want you to succeed and only need to be asked to assist."

And keep in touch with customers as they start to show up. Build a loyal customer base. "Capture all of the contact info from anyone who does venture into your store so that you can do follow-up marketing with them," suggests Larsen. "Whether you do a monthly e-newsletter or create a preferred shopper club, anyone who actually responds to your store is the most important person you can keep informed about your activities into the future. Cultivate this group and treat them special."

People—The Never-Ending Challenge of Retail

Workers are central to any retail store, of course, and the interaction with customers will have a great deal to do with your success. It's best to control this interaction rather than leave it to chance by laying out your expectations and providing training. "Who you hire and how they are trained says everything about your store," says Larsen. "Set your own standards from Day 1. Prescribe that smiles are mandatory.

RETAIL 101, CONTINUED

Prescribe how returns are handled and what will and won't be acceptable. Then, prescribe some more."

The interactions may not be perfect every time, but a great emphasis should be placed on avoiding upset customers. "Think back to any negative experience you've had, and find the way it could have been avoided and then write it up," as part of your manual, using these events to learn and avoid them in the future. "A negative experience in your store is nine times more likely to be shared with others than a positive story."

Feedback that is specific and constructive is probably one of the most valuable pieces of information that you can receive. "So when you actually have feedback, especially when it is negative, cherish it and presume that is the experience of dozens of people in your store. Address it if you choose, or live with it because it defines you. Either way, never think that any one customer experience is an isolated case."

Metrics—Keeping Track of Traffic

Drawing traffic is essential for retail success, green or otherwise, and it cannot be left to chance. In addition to marketing your store, you should collect data to see how well the marketing is working, measuring the foot traffic (the number of potential customers) who come through your door. "It is the fundamental number for all else that you will work to achieve," says Larsen. "In your budget, prior to opening your door for the first time, have a traffic counter in place. The whole thing is only a few hundred dollars."

Another tool to collect information on traffic is a calendar. It need not be fancy or expensive, says Larsen. "The second investment is a simple

RETAIL 101, CONTINUED

calendar. The boring paper kind with large squares for each day works just fine. In each day, you're going to note the number of people who entered the store, the number of sales you had, the total receipts for the day and whatever might have had an effect on the traffic or mood for the day."

The calendar is like your store's journal, helping you to see what is working and build on that success. "The journal will absolutely include any promotion that you have just put out and any event that you are having. I've seen store operators who include the weather each day. I've seen operators that include the promotion down the block. If you don't develop the habit of noting everything you can about what affects the traffic and the mood of the traffic, you can't begin to envision what you can do to enhance it."

The Fun Stuff—Product Selection Criteria and Sourcing

In starting your green store, you need to be specific about your concept; being green alone is not specific enough since it includes such a wide range of goods. "Organic produce is green. Organic cotton is green. Recycled paper notebooks are green. Fair Trade coffee is green. Disposable plates that biodegrade or are made from bamboo are green. Stainless Steel water bottles are green. You need to define the product categories and types of green criteria you plan to use that will allow your customer to understand your concept, a core product concept that will be easy for you and the consumer to understand."

The green concept for your store needs to be specific, but not overly restrictive. "If clothing is your mainstay, then clothing made from

RETAIL 101, CONTINUED

organic cotton, recycled PET polyester, bamboo, and many other fabrics are all options. You'll need to carry a number of different brands to make your Green Clothing store shoppable for the consumer.

"Maybe your store is more of a food associated store, green picnic supplies, organic jams and jellies, kitchen accessories, organic or sustainable textile table cloths," says Larsen. "Whatever it is, your product selections will define you."

And those product selections can be about more than just a type of object, but a message that the products all convey, something environmental they all share in common. "Be crystal clear in your mind about the criteria you want to use to define your store," says Larsen. Whether it's "social responsibility, product content, eco-consciousness, you'll need to find a position and stand by it. This position will define your entire purchasing plan.

"Become educated on how your suppliers define their green business or green product, and then ensure that this story is part of what the consumer can learn. You must know your story and communicate it to your staff well enough that all those who leave your business know 'why' you exist. Your action, in the form of inventory selection, will be the definer of your green store story."

The Best Part—Merchandising

With your store concept and the product selection around it, you need to display your store wares. "Whatever your store is, the customer walking in your front door needs to be able to understand your concept and the departments you've created for them to peruse. If the

RETAIL 101, CONTINUED

customer walks in and needs a guided tour of the store to figure things out, or your store is so cluttered with signage that it's a navigation challenge, they're not going to come back.

"However you choose to merchandise your store, see your store every day anew. Ask your staff for input," says Larsen. They are the ones on the floor everyday. Ask your friends, and insist they be brutally honest. Moving something from one area to another is awfully easy not to just do it and see what happens. Let the market influence you in the way it tells you it wants to see your product.

Tom Larsen's Ten Green Retail Dos and Don'ts

1. *Do invest in information.* Traffic counters, cash registers with departmental capability, and inventory tracking information identify bad areas early and great areas clearly.

2. *Do have a partner.* You can't do all this alone. Who manages the store on Sunday?

3. *Don't ignore the web.* Be sure your store has a domain and a story for why people should come visit you.

4. *Do social networking, develop a blog, and develop a newsletter.* The green community reads online incessantly. It is these people who will spread the word about your store to all their friends— at NO COST to you.

5. *Do always remember that almost everyone wants a green store to succeed.* The new auto repair shop, pizza place, or sandwich shop cannot get the kind of community support that you can.

---

*Starting **Green***

RETAIL 101, CONTINUED

6. *Don't set low goals.* Failure to meet low goals puts a business at survival risk. Choose big goals. Failure to achieve big goals will still meet low goal expectations and allow you to continue.

7. *Do be open to change.* Acceptance of change, and the discomfort it creates, is the true sign you're learning and growing.

8. *Do get free assistance from your suppliers.* They will happily assist you in your education. Ask them about best sellers, what's working, why and how?

9. *Do know your customer and who you want to attract.* That makes finding more of them so much easier.

10. *Most of all, do have fun.* You're about to create a new community. You're about to become a leader. If you accept that role, there is no limit to how much you will be able to accomplish.

11

Starting a Renewable Energy Business

The global energy industry is worth trillions of dollars each year, and it is changing, with production of solar and wind power expected to grow at a red-hot pace. Change always creates opportunities, and the shift in our energy use is a massive change, with governments, businesses, utilities, and consumers around the world moving away from fossil fuels and toward clean renewable energy.

The trends driving this switch include:

- The global fight against climate change, and putting a price on carbon
- Measures to reduce dependence on imported oil and increase national security
- Pollution-fighting measures
- Public opposition to coal mining methods and other forms of fossil fuel pollution
- The projected increase in the price of electricity from fossil fuels in the future
- Decreasing costs of renewable energy as production scales up
- Government incentives to reduce the cost of renewable energy and encourage its use

The bottom line is that economics drives almost everything when it comes to energy. Environmentalists were telling Americans to drive smaller cars for decades, with little success when oil was cheap. As soon as gas hit $4.50 a gallon in the United States in the summer of 2008, millions of drivers suddenly become new environmentalists by driving less and buying smaller cars. A small percentage of people will change their ways just because it's the right thing. Most people change when it hits their wallet.

Unregulated or unrestrained economic forces do not necessarily produce the most desirable result for all of us, but smart government policy drives economics in the right direction,

Power of Information

Studies have shown that information is another important driver of behavioral changes to use energy more efficiently and switch to cleaner forms of power. If people are not well informed about alternatives or if the alternatives are seen as expensive, their rate of uptake is low based on price alone.

reshaping the economic landscape to allow clean energy to compete. By putting a price on carbon and by providing incentives and information to support alternatives, we will shift the economy away from coal and oil and toward renewable energy. If you are investing, it's impossible to say what the stock market will do tomorrow but renewable energy seems like a good bet in the long term.

Solar Business Opportunities

When we think of solar power, we hear a great deal these days about the opportunities for green collar workers installing photovoltaic panels on residential rooftops. This is only one of a broad range of opportunities in the solar industry, however, with businesses contributing in many different ways, including the 14 listed here, with examples in parentheses of companies engaged in each.

1. Rooftop solar PV installation and integration for residential and commercial sites (like groSolar and Sun Power and Light)
2. Solar photovoltaic panel manufacturing (like Kyocera and Suntech)
3. Manufacturers of innovative new solar PV technology (like First Solar)
4. Utility scale solar electrical generation (like eSolar)
5. Residential solar hot water heating systems (like Heliodyne)
6. Solar pool heating (like Heliocol)
7. Solar gadget producers, like iPod chargers (like Innergy Power)
8. Solar mounting systems for rooftops (like SunLink)
9. Tools to help solar installers position panels (like Solmetric)
10. Monitoring systems for solar power (like Fat Spaniel)

11. Energy storage systems like batteries
12. Training and education for solar workers (like the Solar Living Insitute)
13. Installation of solar carports (like Envision Solar)
14. Building integrated photovoltaics (like altPower)

Although the solar industry has grown rapidly in the United States, it has grown even more rapidly in Germany and Japan due to long-term government commitments providing support for the installation of solar power systems. The on-again off-again nature of U.S. tax credits for solar in the past has hindered the growth of the industry, making businesses and investors uncertain about their long-term prospects. To change this, the federal government extended the tax credits for solar power by eight years in October 2008 and eliminated the $2,000 cap on the credit for installation of residential solar power systems. The eight-year extension helps businesses plan and invest for the long term, encouraging their growth around the country.

Even with this boost few businesses were left untouched by the economic crisis in 2008 and 2009. The American Recovery and Reinvestment Act of 2009 (the stimulus package) took support for renewable energy to another level with over $80 billion of support for clean energy. Grants and loan guarantees for renewable energy included in the package are particularly important for businesses that integrate and install solar power systems. Providing the option of grants to replace tax credits will attract investors back to fund the installation of solar

Green Markets

At West Coast Green (September 25–27, 2008) I spoke about the tax credits with Gary Gerber, the CEO of Sun Light and Power, a San Francisco Bay area solar installer. Although the solar industry has been highly concentrated in states like California with strong incentives for solar power installation, Gerber said he expected to see solar grow nationwide.

power systems, and more money from investors means more business for solar businesses across the board. "With the cash grant program you don't need to have a profit, so that will really spawn growth," says Lyndon Rive, CEO of SolarCity (*Entrepreneur*, March 9, 2009). "Instead of a 30 percent tax credit you can get a 30 percent grant. For every $10 you spend buying a system, you get $3 one way or another, getting a check back from a grant instead of a tax credit if you want." The stimulus also provides $6 billion in loan guarantees to make more credit available for solar, about the lowest risk investment around. If you put solar panels on a roof and the sun shines, they will produce power.

A broad array of renewable energy businesses will be big winners as the stimulus kicks in. "As the United States learns how to absorb the stimulus package, you will see tremendous growth and hiring in green collar jobs. In most states the businesses that will benefit are all renewable businesses in wind, solar, and geothermal, including manufacturers, distributors, installers, and the entire value chain," says Rive.

A variety of additional creative government measures are being implemented to provide further support for renewable energy. On-bill financing, which is being developed in California, allows business customers to finance certain energy efficiency projects with their utility and might be used to provide funding for solar energy projects in the future as well. Special financing districts being created in Boulder, Colorado; Berkeley, California; and other California cities provide low-interest loans for energy projects that are paid back over many years through property taxes (see the case study on page 184).

Solar Business Niches

The market for solar power is expected to grow enormously. The report *Clean Energy Trends 2009*, by Joel Makower, Ron Pernick, and Clint Wilder at Clean Edge, predicts that the solar industry

will grow from about $30 billion in revenues in 2008 to over $80 billion by 2018. Still, even with rapid growth in the industry, solar businesses will have to clearly define their core concept and find their niche.

To date, the solar power business has been highly focused in a few states like California, but new incentives and declining prices should expand the market to many more states. One opportunity is to expand into some of these new areas where there has not been a great deal of solar activity before. The market for solar in these new territories may start with the early adopters, the upper end of the market, and expand from there. Early adopters may be more attracted to the novelty of solar panels and their technology, and also may have greater interest in their environmental benefits. As the market expands, cost becomes more and more of an issue, driving the cost of solar down to grid parity and helping people save more money.

One way to break down the solar market is according to the size of projects. Different businesses and different technologies tend to be used in utility-scale projects at tens of megawatts or higher, midsize commercial projects of hundreds of kilowatts to a few megawatts, small commercial projects, and home residential systems of a few kilowatts. And there are also small portable systems, gadgets, or off-the-grid applications. The bigger the systems you are working with, the

Falling Costs

The cost of producing solar panels will fall as production volumes increase, until the cost of electricity from the panels will eventually be as cheap as, or cheaper than, the power from the electrical grid. This is what is called "grid parity" in renewable energy circles. Depending on the cost of power in a region, solar and wind may already have achieved grid parity. The expense of thin film photovoltaic systems is expected to keep falling in 2009 and 2010, making its use more widespread.

greater the capital required, so starting with small customers might help to get your foot in the solar door.

Another way to find a niche is by focusing on specific types of applications, such as taking advantage of the capabilities of rapidly evolving technologies like building integrated photovoltaics (BIPVs). Solar panels are a new material with a great deal of potential to become not just a functional part of buildings but also a design feature (see interview with Bob Noble at the end of this chapter). Focusing on military uses, government buildings, schools, hospitals, the developing world, nongrid-tied remote structures, or free-standing stationary objects (billboards?) might provide unique challenges and opportunities to start a focused solar business.

Solar Marketing

As solar becomes more common, with many competing businesses on the market, it will be more important for solar businesses to distinguish themselves with their brand. Having excellent customer service is probably going to play a larger role in developing a solar brand as competition intensifies.

The Greenest Americans (as described in *Strategies for the Green Economy*) believe in ethical consumerism and many have enough money to buy green even if it costs them more. Because they make the environment their highest priority, they spend their money on goods like solar power systems that reflect this. Building-integrated solar systems might be a good way to target this group; some customers find regular rooftop photovoltaic panels unattractive, creating a market for newer products that blend in better with the rest of the exterior home appearance, like roofing materials that have solar panels built right in.

Most people don't question the environmental benefits of solar power. They worry about its cost and reliability. For the

Starting Green

Compassionate Caretakers market group, a more mainstream market for solar, cost will be a big factor. Government incentives help to reduce the initial cost for those who have money. Creative financing solutions through power purchase agreements will, however, be important for many customers in this group. The most effective messages for this group are about the opportunities to save money and help their families and kids. Solar power cannot be viewed as a difficult and costly solution, but an easy one that fits into their busy lives and their tight budgets.

How to Compete

Businesses that install rooftop photovoltaic solar systems are often called "integrators" because they are taking components of solar power systems like inverters, mounting systems, photovoltaic panels, batteries, and wiring and integrating them together for each project. The beauty of this is they don't have to invent any new technology and assume the risk and expense of doing this. All they need to do is take components off of the shelf and piece them all together.

Solar integrators are one of the key types of businesses that will see rapid growth in many parts of the country. Areas that already have a strong business for solar integrators, like California, will see more growth, and new areas that perhaps had a small industry will see it become much larger. Even areas that have little solar power activity currently will start to see early adopters move to get started.

The downside to being an integrator is that if you face growing competition and don't have a technology advantage, you need to find some other basis on which to compete. You can compete on the price you charge, which means you either need to cut into your profits or find ways to reduce your costs. The costs for your business are going to be related primarily to labor and the cost of materials (like photovoltaic panels). If you are subcontracting, then the costs are mainly labor. To reduce the cost of components, you can negotiate with suppliers. To reduce the cost of labor, one direction people are taking is to increase the speed of panel installation by standardizing and using more rapid mounting systems such as the system from SunLink.

Of course, another way to go is to compete on quality. What can you provide that is value added and that avoids becoming a commodity with low profit margins? Can you include free panel monitoring and maintenance over the internet or by other wireless devices? Can you provide routine reports that customers can access about power production and greenhouse gases that they helped to avoid? Can you provide excellent service, with friendly knowledgeable field representatives? Rapid installation? Can you integrate solar power as part of the overall greening of a home? All of these would help to differentiate your business, seal the deal, and spread the word for future business.

Solar Resources

A solar integrator business may look simple, but there are some resources you will need to get started, including money, training, and marketing. The basic work involved is designing systems from various components, mounting solar panels on the roof, and then wiring the panels and inverter into the electrical system. If you have training in mechanical and electrical work and you have run your own business in these fields, you already have a jump on getting this business going.

A quick list of resources needed to start a solar integrator business includes:

1. Mechanical and electrical skills
2. Working capital for photovoltaic panel inventory for installation

3. Training and experience in solar installation
4. Solar certification (NABCEP), if you want a big plus
5. Transportation to carry materials and workers to work-sites
6. Tools for electrical work
7. Knowledge of applicable tax credits, rebates, or other financial incentives for solar in your state
8. Business insurance
9. Marketing to let customers know about your new service.
10. Connections with builders or other sources of leads

According to Scott Sklar, president of the Stella Group (a strategic marketing and policy firm for clean energy companies), there are opportunities to create solar businesses by people involved in a wide range of related businesses. Sklar notes that for people currently working as "plumbers, electricians, satellite dish or cable installers, battery bank or diesel backup installers, cellular or wifi system installers, or alarm and security equipment installers—setting up an energy efficiency, solar water heating, photovoltaics, or small wind business is not too different."

If you already have experience in the building trades, the steps to take include getting training and getting certified. You should have a contractor's license, including a solar installer contractor's license if this is available in your area. Becoming certified by the North American Board of Certified Energy Practitioners (NAB-CEP) can help provide further verification of your credentials to potential customers, reassuring them that you know your stuff and will get the job done.

If you have a background in electrical work and need to learn more

Resource Guide

Solar industry groups are an invaluable resource through their conferences, reports, news, and connections. See especially the Solar Energy Industries Association (SEIA.org) and the American Solar Energy Society (ASES.org).

about solar, classes are showing up in a wide range of training facilities. Local community colleges often have programs in solar installation today. The Solar Living Institute offers classes on an ongoing basis at its site and also travels to other locations to provide training. The California Center for Sustainable Energy (energy center.org) has frequent free workshops for consumers, workers, and businesses in renewable energy and energy efficiency.

The solar installation business is fairly capital intensive, but this does not have to stop you in your tracks if you don't have loads of capital to get started. The capital is to cover the cost of panel inventory. Even a small solar integrator could install two to three systems a week. With a typical residential system costing $30,000 or so, this means a cash flow of hundreds of thousands of dollars a month. If you work as subcontractor with a larger more established business, particularly at first, this will ease your entry into the business, reduce your initial costs, and drive more business your way if you already have some contacts in the field. Otherwise, you'll have to contend with generating your own leads, and coming up with more money to get started.

Solar Training

One challenge much discussed in the solar field is the potential difficulty in finding trained workers with rapid growth in the field. The February 2009 stimulus package provided for $500 million in training for solar and other green jobs, helping people find jobs and helping businesses to keep growing.

MAKING THE GRADE SOLAR
BUSINESS PLAN*

Vision
Within the next ten years grow Making the Grade Solar into the premier solar integrator for schools across the United States.

Mission
We give schools green power, and get kids ready for the future.

Objectives

- Install solar power at 10 schools by the end of Year 2.

- Make a 10% profit in Year 2 on sales of $2 million.

- Reach 50,000 students a year in Year 5 with educational programs.

- Achieve mention in 100 blog sites in Year 2.

- Reduce installation time per project 15% in Year 3.

- Negotiate 25% lower price on photovoltaic panels by end of Year 2.

- Complete 50 solar projects in Year 5.

- Save schools an average of 15% a year on electricity bills by Year 5.

Strategies

- Build market by meeting with schools, green blogging, and speaking at conferences.

MAKING THE GRADE BUSINESS PLAN, CONTINUED

· Differentiate business by providing solar teaching tools and curriculum.

· Develop pilot projects with visible and vocal school managers and communities.

· Add to client base by working with businesses in energy efficiency, water conservation, cool roofing, and organic landscaping.

· Reduce financing barrier by identifying grants, donations, and third party investors.

Plans

· Produce marketing materials by August Year 1 and distribute to 500 schools.

· Hire three field employees for installing solar power by October Year 1.

· Complete first installation project by January Year 2.

· Identify a funding source for solar power purchase agreements by March Year 2.

· Give talk at national educational conference in May Year 2.

· Develop solar curriculum in collaboration with others for grades 9-12 by February Year 3.

*Modeled after *The One Page Business Plan* by Jim Horan.

YES! SOLAR SOLUTIONS FRANCHISE OPPORTUNITY

Yes! Solar Solutions based on Roseville, California (yessolar solutions.com) is developing a unique approach to the solar industry, selling franchises for solar store outlets. The stores will sell photovoltaic solar power systems that franchisees will install in their area. Yes! is a subsidiary of Solar Power Inc., which makes its own panels and can provide a reliable source of panels for Yes! franchises. Compared to starting a business as a solar integrator on your own, a franchise provides a wide range of resources and training for installation and sales.

THE SUNTECH PERSPECTIVE: ROGER EFIRD OF SUNTECH AMERICA

The solar boom has room for businesses ranging from huge established companies to mom-and-pop solar shops. Solar photovoltaic panel manufacturers like Suntech play an important role in furthering the growth of the solar industry and as a resource for the many solar integrator businesses. Suntech is one of the world's largest solar companies, with production capacity steadily growing for both thin-film and crystalline silicon photovoltaic materials, and is moving to increase its U.S. market share. As part of Suntech's move into the U.S. market, industry veteran Roger Efird joined Suntech in 2006 as the

---

THE SUNTECH PERSPECTIVE, CONTINUED

president of Suntech America. I spoke with him at the Solar Power International 2008 about the opportunities for solar entrepreneurs.

Efird is very upbeat about the future of solar, predicting significant growth even before more recent support from the stimulus package and other programs that may be on the way, such as a national renewable portfolio standard. "Solar in the U.S. has been growing at 30 to 35 percent a year, and with the investment tax credit passed, the optimistic view is for 60 percent growth," says Efird, projecting performance in the year ahead. At the conference he said he expected the extension of solar tax credits for eight years to provide increased confidence in the market for investors and businesses. He also expected the removal of the $2,000 cap for residential solar power systems to have a big impact. "For the average American home this makes the tax credit go from $2,000 to $10,000. That's a big increase in the tax credit for residential, and we have to believe the residential market will grow dramatically as a result of that."

These stable incentives will allow the U.S. solar market to grow as it has in Germany. "Germany has a solar market eight times the size of the U.S. market, because they have a long-term incentive program and stability," says Efird. "The United States has been different, with incentives going up and down and up and down. We have something similar now, like Germany. The United States is by far the largest consumer of energy. Today about 10 percent of solar business is in the United States, but we are going to be the biggest market for solar, and the general feeling of the industry is that this rapid growth for solar begins immediately."

Although the solar market has been very concentrated in states like California, the increased federal support for installation of solar power

---

THE SUNTECH PERSPECTIVE, CONTINUED

should help solar to expand across much more of the United States. "There are a number of states that have an incentive program at the state level that was not large enough to stimulate solar growth, but with the new credit they will," says Efird. "North Carolina, Maryland, Pennsylvania, and maybe a dozen states will now have viable residential solar industries. The Mid-Atlantic region and the Northeast will see a big boost because most of those states have a solar program that has been up and running for a while, and this will boost those state programs to viability."

The expansion will extend even farther though, including regions that have little or no local support for solar. "Even in states with practically no solar, where the word 'solar' has never been used in their legislature," says Efird, "the 30 percent tax credit will spur the early adopters who love high tech, have high income, want to make a statement, and want to go green."

There is even a way of predicting how large the market growth will be in your area, by looking at the return on investment, the amount of time it takes for a system to pay for itself. The faster this happens, the greater the number of customers will be. "The rule of thumb has been that if a system will not pay for itself in ten years then you will not have the ability to build a viable market," says Efird. "For commercial systems the rule of thumb is a system needs to pay for itself in seven years to be viable. Now a lot of states move inside that ten-year window."

The changes taking place are not just for those in the residential solar business either. "Since 1978 utilities have not been able to take a tax credit of any kind for the installation of photovoltaic systems, but now

THE SUNTECH PERSPECTIVE, CONTINUED

that has been changed," says Efird. "At the far end of the spectrum are the huge solar farms, the big multimegawatt utility owned generating plant. This big solar farm business has been very slowly emerging. Now with this change in the law it will emerge rapidly."

The optimal position for photovoltaic solar may be in distributed power generation spread out across many sites. "That's where PV has no competition," says Efird. "You can't put concentrated solar on someone's roof. The only viable route on rooftops is PV." Concentrated solar power has its place in the market as well, although for larger scale power production like the large solar farms taking shape in the desert of the Southwest. "Several people have asked me if I see us competing with CSP (Concentrated Solar Power) systems. And the answer is no," says Efird. "CSP takes some pretty large economies of scale. They are viable at a certain size, in terms of megawatts. We're not going to compete—and there's going to be a rule of thumb. Up to a certain size, photovoltaic will be the best alternative, but for larger systems, CSP will be. It's going to be a matter of what the customer wants. If he wants more than 20 megawatts, maybe CSP, while smaller sites would be PV."

Among the many opportunities for solar entrepreneurs, Efird finds the residential solar integrator opportunity to be compelling. "I think the residential business is going to explode faster than the rest of the market," says Efird. "If I was going to start something, that's where I would start it."

Efird goes on to sketch out his vision of how a rooftop solar installer could get started, based on people who already have their own business in heating or electrical. "In my vision of the solar dealer I think of the

Starting Green

THE SUNTECH PERSPECTIVE, CONTINUED

guy who lives within a few miles of where you are," says Efird, someone like the Carrier air-conditioning guy. "He lives in your community and has a customer base of a few thousand people he has sold systems to and services them. He's got experience with electrical work, and experience with mechanical engineering. He's accustomed to getting up on a roof and he has a warehouse, tools, trucks, front office, secretary, and a database of customers who are happy with his work. And he has a son that is getting out of college and has a degree in environmental engineering."

For many trades, current work could provide the foundation for starting a solar business. "If I'm a homeowner and looking for a solar system, I want somebody I know, who will be around in the future, five to ten years down the road. I would imagine just like that HVAC guy who sells you an annual maintenance agreement, he can do the same for solar. You can say the same thing about a small electrical contractor and maybe a roofing contractor if he brushes up on electrical work."

Interview with a Green Leader:
Solar Parking Lots with Envision Solar and Bob Noble

While most people associate solar panels with rooftops, as the CEO of Envision Solar Bob Noble is developing solar solutions where others had not looked before, in parking lots. Envision Solar is designing, building, and installing solar trees for parking lots, an even greater opportunity perhaps than rooftops.

Noble got into the solar field from a background in architecture. While he was the CEO of Tucker Sadler Architects, a leading sustainable design architectural firm in San Diego, Kyocera America (also based in San Diego) asked them to design a solar carport. "We designed the elevated solar array which we named the first 'solar grove' with 25 solar trees that are structurally independent of each other, derived from nature: a tree with a trunk, branches, and a canopy," says Noble.

"I knew the opportunity was big the minute I heard 'solar carport,'" says Noble. "In early 2004 I Googled 'solar carport,' and there was virtually nothing. Like any entrepreneur working on large scale projects, I saw that this was potentially an enormous green commercial opportunity."

Coming from an architectural design background, Noble saw an opportunity to make the solar grove both beautiful and functional. "Have you ever hit a column with your car in a parking lot? From the architectural point of view, the cars and columns don't mix, so we reduced the number of columns in our solar grove, with only one column for each tree," says Noble. Thinking about photovoltaic panels as a building material and not just an electricity-producing surface opens up new possibilities. "It's not just about solar," says Noble. "It's about the built environment, functionality and form and texture, and light and dark, and shape and space. Solar needed to tell its own story, because it's beautiful. It's about taking beautiful material and transforming it into beautiful architecture."

People don't normally see opportunities in a parking lot. They see concrete and painted lines, a space to get in and out of. Noble sees it differently. "We are taking a blighted area, the parking lot, and making architecture truly start at the curb cut," says Noble. "There is an obligation to take the experience of design, architecture, and aesthetics out to people. Why wait for people to get into the building? Enhance your parking lots with a solar parking array."

Envision launched their business in 2006, and got going in 2007 with a project for the National Renewable Energy Labs in Golden, Colorado, a solar plug-in hybrid charging station demo. Things have grown from there. "We secured a pipeline of projects and did eight projects in 2008, in a variety of sizes, for a total of 1.3 MW on parking array projects for places including UCSD, Resmed, the City of Napa, Mesa College, Natomas east, and others," says Noble. "Things slowed down last year, but we started getting more work in Q4 (2008). And now (March 2009) work is cascading in, with very large scale funded projects coming in. This year we expect to see tremendous growth in the number and scale of projects."

Noble expects there to be a broad range of solar opportunities, many of them stimulated at the moment by the federal stimulus package. "The public agencies, cities, counties, towns, and the military have access to funds, either direct or under competitive environments, to fund solar projects. The number of solar projects coming directly from the stimulus package is extraordinary," says Noble.

With the growth of the industry, there are also opportunities for a broad range of people. "You could name a profession, and I can tell you how to carve out a piece. Any profession: If you are landscape architect, for example, you can work with our systems, because you are used to dealing with parking lots, traffic, and drainage." Graphic designers can find a role utilizing solar panels as an innovative material. "As a material, solar can be very attractive, and modules can be used like pixels to make beautiful patterns in different colors and different levels of translucency," says Nobel. The list goes on and on, with solar opportunities for everyone. "If you have a background in landscaping, construction, mechanical systems, or lighting, then this expertise can be translated into a solar business. People need to understand that they can cross over into solar. Even if they haven't worked in it before, they can jump in and grow a successful business."

In fact, sometimes the fresh perspective of coming from outside the industry can even be an advantage. "People can start something like Sunlink, where its founder just took a look and saw what was missing and reinvented how to do it, creating a better way to mount solar panels on rooftops without penetrating roofs," says Noble. "It's a great vision and product and the founder came out of another industry. The best thing you can do is to be an outsider and look at it with clear eyes. Bill Gross is another example of a visionary from another background; through Idealabs he has crossed over into a variety of businesses and industries, and now is building eSolar."

In designing its systems, Envision tries to avoid developing new technology for parts, focusing instead on innovative ways of assembling components that have already been well characterized. "We take the risk of assembling things, putting parts together, but we don't want the time delay, risks and asset allocation needed for new technology development for any one part," says Noble. "We are in the business of integrating things together, as is the solar integrated building system industry."

One facet of developing their business is reducing the cost of systems, in part by standardizing how they are produced. "We are producing solar integrated building systems that include a whole range of standardized products," says Noble. "Only with standardization can you lower costs, which includes lowering the cost of production, of shipping, of installation, design, and of laying in panels." In addition to lowering costs, they are getting more power out of the systems by designing them to follow the sun, increasing output by 18 percent. "We're on track to have the lowest cost installed system, and with tracking it will reduce the cost per watt of electricity produced by 15 percent," says Noble. "We're driving to a cost of $5 per watt for system installation. We call it our 'drive to five.' In California with rebates, and with other incentives, the cost will soon be below $6 per watt, which gets competitive with power from the grid."

The shade from the solar trees provides additional financial value. "If people pay for parking, they will pay $2 to $3 more for shaded parking, studies have found," says Noble. "Their cars are more protected, and cooler, and people are willing to pay more for this. We know shaded parking will be extremely valuable."

As an experienced entrepreneur, Noble has insight into many aspects of the startup process, including the ever-important task of raising money. "My best advice is to not be closed off to any direction," says Noble. "For a startup the place to start is with your own resources. Then there's friends and family. You can talk to people you have professional relationships with and they might invest. Then there are private placements, small retail rounds, which are a small offering of stock. The next step might be to have a private offering managed by a broker or investment banker with possibly a network selling the equity. You can turn to VCs [venture capitalists] if your model makes sense and fits with what the VC firm likes. A VC can bring management expertise as well as money, which is extremely important for a lot of early stage businesses."

Strategic partners are one option Nobel brought up that may have real advantages. "In my companies I've had excellent experience with strategic partners," says Noble. "They also typically have deeper pockets."

When it comes to grants, Noble suggests that the effort and distraction involved in getting the money may not be worth it. "When you get a grant, you must conform to what you wrote, and the work takes one to three years to be done, while young companies must move quickly. Be cautious about grants.

"And don't forget about getting to profitability," advises Noble. "That is the best plan, and it's our plan this year, to become profitable. It's within sight." That's a very good plan indeed.

12

Starting a Direct Sales Business

Small, Green, and Beautiful

While many people are seeking green opportunities, some budding entrepreneurs don't see how they can start something themselves. Some have limited time, while others have limited money, and some have little of either. They might be seeking a second income, working nights and weekends. They might be interested in furthering the green cause with their own business, but are put off by the prospect of setting up the infrastructure to run it. What these people are not lacking is motivation and commitment to positive change. If you are one of these people, there are a variety of possibilities for small green businesses that can be started at home, without a great deal of experience and with minimal cost.

Direct sales provides such an opportunity. Direct sales are a proven business model, as demonstrated by the success of businesses like Avon, Mary Kay, and Tupperware over the years, either as a one-on-one interaction between a representative and a customer in their home (like Avon), or a party plan, with the representative meeting with a group of people to demonstrate and sell products (like Tupperware parties). In addition, organizations can be flat in structure, or they can introduce multiple levels of hierarchy between sellers in a structure called multilevel marketing (MLM). In an MLM-based organization, a seller (or distributor, or associate) recruits others into the hierarchy and can earn income based both on what they sell themselves and a percentage of what their recruits sell. Amway is a well-known example of an MLM-based organization.

There is an ongoing debate about the relative merits of MLM-based sales vs. the flat organizational structure, and this debate is not restricted to the green world. I'm not going to say that there is one correct answer. Each opportunity should be judged based on its own merits. There are legitimate MLM-based opportunities which present real opportunities, including many green ones that have been around for many years, or that are newly emerging. One that deserves special mention is Shaklee, an MLM opportunity that has been around for many years with many nutritional supplement and cleaning products, including Green Seal-certified products and awards for their environmental contribution through reduced packaging.

There are a few ways to help distinguish whether you want to work with an MLM-based opportunity. Be wary of an MLM-based opportunity that talks about making easy money if you act now. Do not pay to become a member of an organization—this step takes you into pyramiding, which is a definite no-no. If it's legitimate, the organization should be interested in selling products, not making money off of bringing people into the system. And don't buy a garage full of soap because you are told it is necessary or to boost sales numbers—this is probably not a good idea, and can be indicative again of pyramiding.

There are some real opportunities today to work with direct sales organizations like those described in this chapter providing products that promote a sustainable lifestyle. The personal interaction between seller and purchaser can be a real advantage in the green world, particularly in this early stage of its development. The reason for this gets back to information. The interaction helps to dispel concerns, highlights the environmental benefits, customizes purchases for each unique situation, educates consumers about the use of each item, and provides the opportunity to talk about behavioral changes that go beyond buying products.

The bottom line is that if you're looking for a green business opportunity that you can start today, that allows you to work at home with a flexible schedule, that requires a minimum of time and money to start, and can allow for a good income, I suggest taking a look at these three to see if they are a good match for you.

Case Study
ZOLA GOODS COORDINATORS

One key that opens the door into the green business world is information. While a growing number of consumers have their hearts on board with going green, their heads are often less certain

ZOLA GOODS COORDINATORS, CONTINUED

about how to go about it in a way that fits in with the rest of their lives. Business models that combine great eco-friendly products for the home with information that makes the products relevant to daily life will help bring green to the masses. Zola Goods is working to do just this with Coordinators who arrange parties bringing green products to people in homes.

I often get asked, "What kind of green business can I start with very little money?" Zola Goods is one such opportunity. Founded by Beth Remmes, Zola Goods works through coordinators who organize parties for groups interested in going green in their homes. "There are many people who are interested in the environmental movement, but they don't really know where to start or how they can make a difference," says Remmes. With a mix of education and products that green the home, coordinators of Zola parties help to meet this need. Think of Tupperware parties, but for green products instead.

As a mother of two young children, Remmes has worked hard herself to balance her home life with her desire to earn a living and make a positive difference in the world. After considering a retail storefront providing green goods and information, she decided against it. "All of a sudden it occurred to me that if women were willing to gather to talk about and buy kitchen products or make-up, then I thought they would also be interested in learning how to help the environment and save money in the process. Also, this model allows people who are passionate about the environment to help spread the message in their community and earn a supplemental income."

ZOLA GOODS COORDINATORS, CONTINUED

Zola offers a wide range of affordable eco-friendly alternatives to everyday products. Items include those that reduce usage of some good (such as water and energy savers); items that are reusable (such as Wrap-n-Mats, shopping bags, to-go ware, stainless steel water bottles); and items that are made from recycled material (such as foil wrapper bags, or recycled paper note cards and journals). Zola also provides eco-friendly candles, fun family games, and other green gift ideas.

Coordinators are often moms seeking income and flexible hours, people who want to get involved in the green business revolution without turning their lives upside down. "This will be an ongoing process as I work to get the word out to anyone who may be interested in helping to bring about change in their communities. The only requirement is that someone wants to make a positive difference," says Remmes. "The most successful coordinators find a way to be of service in their community and become the hub for green information beyond Zola products." Coordinators also let people know about local recycling information, farmers' markets, or green festivals. The startup cost for becoming a coordinator is only $149 for a kit containing a number of items that can be used in daily life and for demonstrations at parties. The kit also includes all of the training materials needed.

"Most coordinators have parties for their friends and neighbors and then expand outward to include co-workers, parents/teachers from the local schools or other organizations," says Remmes. "Being green is something that so many people hear about, but they don't really know exactly what it means. So, when they have the chance to learn more

ZOLA GOODS COORDINATORS, CONTINUED

about it in a fun evening with others, people are happy to host or attend parties. From Tupperware to cosmetics—this is a model that has been successful for many years."

It's worth noting that while Zola is a direct sales company, it is not a multilevel marketing system and is transparent in its operations. Coordinators earn a commission directly of 20 percent on products sold, with no recruiting or sales requirements, no quotas, and no hierarchical pyramid. "The emphasis is on education and by offering the products for sale, the parties bridge the gap between hearing the information and then acting on it by purchasing eco-friendly alternatives," says Remmes.

The market for green is still wide open, barely scratching the mainstream. Zola's model may be one key to bringing green to more mainstream consumers and helping entrepreneurial individuals join the green business world as well.

Case Study
BE A GREEN IRENE ECO-CONSULTANT

Green Irene is a direct sales company, working through Eco-Consultants to bring green solutions directly into homes and offices across the country. People love saving money, but as more people seek ways to green their homes and businesses, they sometimes

GREEN IRENE ECO-CONSULTANT, CONTINUED

need help. The wide range of green products available and the lack of clear information about them can make going green a challenge for those who don't want to make a full-time job out of it, which is most of us. If you want to change your light bulbs to compact fluorescent bulbs, which ones will you buy? Which ones will work the best and provide the best value? They are not all the same, and some have more pleasing colors and warm up more rapidly.

To bridge the gap between growing interest in greening our homes and businesses, and the lack of knowledge of how to get there, Green Irene is creating a network of Eco-Consultants across the country who, for a modest fee ($99 as of this writing), go to people's homes and suggest a variety of green changes in a one-to-two-hour Green Home Makeover. There are (in mid-2009) over 400 Eco-Consultants in 45 states. Helping people green their homes is also an opportunity for the Eco-Consultants. Green Irene founders P. J. Stafford and Rosamaria Caballero Stafford provide the training and tools Eco-Consultants need, and Eco-Consultants find their clients. Working as an Eco-Consultant involves minimal startup costs (about $450) and does not require a great deal of prior knowledge. It also allows people to have a flexible schedule. People with full-time jobs can do eco-consulting in evenings and weekends. Stay-at-home moms can work around family commitments. Others can add eco-consulting to their complementary green business (green cleaning, interior design, professional organizing, energy auditing, and construction). Working as an Eco-Consultant does require the ability to be entrepreneurial, to get out in your community, make connections, and to learn.

GREEN IRENE ECO-CONSULTANT, CONTINUED

Green Office Makeover

The Green Office Makeover with a Green Irene Eco-Consultant can help entrepreneurs to reduce the environmental impact of their business and to save money. The Green Office Makeover costs from $250 to $450 for small businesses with 10 to 50 employees and requires two hours to a half day of consultation. This investment includes:

- A consultation and evaluation at your office

- Presentation of the Green Irene findings and recommendations during the visit

- Phone and e-mail follow-up with your local Eco-Consultant

- Three-month membership to "Ask Green Irene," which gives you access to the private green office database and free e-mail support from the central Green Irene Research Team

The founders of Green Irene started it in 2007, motivated by their values and their experiences in greening their own home, finding that even changing their lights to compact fluorescent bulbs was not trivial. "The 'lightbulb' lit up when we realized how difficult it could be to do something as simple as swap out the bulbs in our apartment to CFLs," says Rosamaria Stafford. "After all the visits to Home Depot and the buzzing and flickering results, we realized we would have gladly paid a green expert to come in and tell us what to do and how to do it! Even though they want to go green, most people don't have enough time to make 'going green' another time-consuming hobby."

In addition to helping people to green their homes, Green Irene is also providing opportunities to individuals to start their own small business

GREEN IRENE ECO-CONSULTANT, CONTINUED

earning a part-time income while working as a force for change in their community. "Our Eco-Consultants not only earn money through consulting and product sales," says Stafford, "but they also can be the person pushing for the new school to have green, toxic-free, and energy-saving features built in, or the person at the city council meeting making a case to tax plastic bags so people finally carry reusable bags to the store."

They see a broad demand for the services of Eco-Consultants. "Anyone who doesn't think we are entering a time where we have to change our wasteful living habits and adopt more sustainable ways to live is in denial," says Stafford. "As more people begin to adopt green practices at home, they want to see those values adopted in their workspace, too, so we have recently added our Green Office Makeover service for small businesses."

When the Eco-Consultants perform a Green Home Makeover or Green Office Makeover, they will often suggest products or improvements that can improve energy efficiency, improve indoor air, and reduce water use. To provide the best products, Green Irene does a great deal of work researching products before recommending them. "We research the product, seek out reviews, editorials and commentaries, and then we talk to the manufacturer and get clear answers to questions about specifications and ingredients to ensure that the products will meet our Eco-Consultants' and our customers' critical green eye," says Stafford. "On many products such as the CFLs, low-flow showerheads, toxic-free cleaners and detergents, we try and use the products ourselves at home to make sure that we believe in and can honestly recommend the

GREEN IRENE ECO-CONSULTANT, CONTINUED

products." The products can then be purchased through each Eco-Consultant's individual Green Irene website or in person during their appointments and workshops.

Simplifying choices is another way Green Irene helps clients. Left on our own, the number of choices for even simple items like shower heads can be daunting, but Green Irene generally offers only one product in a category. "We offer two low-flow showerheads because the aerating and laminar technologies have such different feels to achieve a full shower feeling," says Stafford. "We feel people have enough choices to make and don't need the stress of 10 choices across 30 or more categories of products. We also are looking for products with good value, though not necessarily the least expensive."

In addition to helping with product selection, Green Irene Eco-Consultants can help identify contractors that can do any work required in the home or office. "Most contractors are local business-people, so we count on and encourage our local Eco-Consultants to develop relationships with local contractors that they can refer clients to," says Stafford. "Toxicity-free home cleaning companies, landscapers who use native plants that use less water and few chemicals, certified energy auditors, etc. Initially, most of the folks are handymen, electricians, plumbers, etc., who may help with installation of thermostats, new low-flow toilets, and similar items since we don't sell installation services."

Though some might worry they don't know enough about eco-friendly choices to work as an Eco-Consultant, Green Irene helps Eco-Consultants get started with extensive training and ongoing support. "I would say

GREEN IRENE ECO-CONSULTANT, CONTINUED

that research and communication are at the heart of our business," says Stafford. "We provide online training that is designed to initially take about 20 hours, complete with quizzes and additional reference materials including videos. The training covers topics including energy efficient lighting, water conservation, energy conservation, toxic-free living, indoor air quality, reduced waste and recycling, and emergency preparedness."

Another resource that can help is a database called "The Ask Green Irene Greenbase." "This is an incredibly comprehensive and growing resource of information to help our clients green their lives as well as for our Eco-Consultants to grow and manage their local Eco-Consulting practice," says Stafford. "Researchers are adding content to the Greenbase daily, and we encourage our Eco-Consultants to e-mail material to us as well."

The Eco-Consultant's Perspective on Direct Sales with Green Irene

For the Eco-Consultant's perspective on this direct sales opportunity, I spoke with Ophelia Ramirez, a Green Irene Eco-Consultant in San Diego.

Ramirez got started in Green Irene after moving to San Diego from San Francisco and realizing that working as an Eco-Consultant would allow her to reinvent herself by working to help the environment. "The more I read about global warming, the more I believe that even if we make small changes in our lives they can add up to a meaningful difference for our planet," says Ramirez. "So looking around for opportunities I

GREEN IRENE ECO-CONSULTANT, CONTINUED

Googled 'green jobs' and saw an ad from Green Irene. Working as an eco-consultant is not a nine-to-five job. I work as an independent contractor, in control of my own time, which I like. And after e-mailing and talking with the co-founders and getting to know each other, I found that they have the same mentality as me, that small changes can make a big difference."

Green Irene takes care of many aspects of the business for each Eco-Consultant, but they must still connect with clients and identify contractors in their community. "Green Irene provides the foundation for the Eco-Consultants, but it's up to the consultant to build a network of vendors and clients," says Ramirez. "I've identified a handyman, a landscaper, and an energy efficiency auditor who I met and interviewed. With time people in this network can help each other with our businesses."

The clients they work with are typically just starting to adopt more eco-friendly habits, but need help to succeed. "The Eco-Consultant gets the process started, and from there it can go in many different directions," says Ramirez. "If they want a deeper level of work on energy efficiency in their home, for example, they can work with the energy efficiency auditor in my network who gets more technical, doing the blower test, for example, to look for leaks in the building envelope."

Resource Guide

To find out more about Green Irene and the potential for being an Eco-Consultant, you can check out GreenIrene.com and BeAGreenIrene.com.

GREEN IRENE ECO-CONSULTANT, CONTINUED

Ramirez has found working as an Eco-Consultant to be rewarding in more ways than one. "I love being around people and talking to them, and being a part of their education," says Ramirez. "It's not about wanting people to feel guilty. It's about saying 'Whatever you want to do, let me help you.' I would recommend it as a wonderful opportunity to be a part of doing something for the planet, while working at your own pace. For the mother who wants to develop her own income stream, on her own schedule, for example, it's ideal."

Case Study
GREEN COACHES WITH EMAGINE GREEN

Emagine Green was founded by Tonya Ensign after years of working in corporate America for companies from Honeywell to startups. She knew she wanted to create a business to help the environment, but wasn't sure what the business should be. "I thought through how I could get the message across," says Ensign. "For a website alone, I would need to generate a lot of traffic. For manufacturing, there are large upfront costs for new product development and branding. For a retail store, brick and mortar, I would have to deal with inventory expenses, retail space, and so on. If you are a consultant, once you stop consulting you are done. I wanted to create an opportunity where people have low startup costs, low risk, low inventory, and where we would take the hassle out of the business for people."

EMAGINE GREEN, CONTINUED

Emagine Green recruits people who join their organization as Green Coaches, doing direct sales with its products at home parties. The organization takes care of all the business basics for the Green Coaches, including getting a license, paying credit card fees, web hosting, and e-commerce setup, letting each Green Coach enjoy being an entrepreneur, setting his or her own calendar, his or her own schedule, without having to ask permission to take the day off. Emagine Green is focused on two missions, to help people go green and to create opportunities for entrepreneurial individuals.

To help people go green, it doesn't just provide information but also gets people to act on this information. "Every product we sell is hand-picked to change behavior," says Ensign. "If you don't change behavior, there's no point in buying different products. Why get a programmable thermostat if you don't program it?"

Joining the organization costs only $129 as of this writing. After signing up people for only the last 10 months (as of Feb 2009), it already has Green Coaches in about half of the states, with more signing up all the time. Not everybody will be right for the opportunity, so people are screened to make sure it's a good fit for both Emagine Green and for the potential Green Coach. To help them get started, Emagine Green provides training to help them learn about the green world.

Working with Emagine Green, Green Coaches earn residual income and management training. With a couple of levels in the organization, people can advance and get experience mentoring others. This opportunity has appealed to people from many backgrounds. "One segment is women who are stay-at-home moms, struggling to balance kids and

EMAGINE GREEN, CONTINUED

career," says Ensign. Another group joining is women who want out of the corporate America, who are seeking something they can be passionate about, something they care about. "They are very ambitious, and primed to be leaders and managers," Ensign says. "Another group is people who are entrepreneurial, and perhaps have started their own business before, like working in real estate. They see the potential of the timing for a business in the green world and know how to be a sole proprietor, how to market themselves."

As an executive coach, Ensign realized what it takes to make real behavioral change. Like Jenny Craig and similar organizations, change is not just information, but having a support structure, creating camaraderie. The key to change is meeting people directly, teaching them about the importance of environmental choices, demonstrating options for greener choices, and selling them directly. "Education and demonstration are the key," says Ensign. The model is a well-known one, like Pampered Chef, one of Warren Buffet's investments. Other examples are Rubber Stamper or Creative Memories, all of which are now large successful businesses in mature fields.

The difference for Emagine Green is that the field of green is still wide open for most people. "Most people still don't know much about green, so for these products it's still a big opportunity," says Ensign. "It will be ten years before it's really mainstream, and we're poised to take advantage.

"The key is to get into people's houses," says Ensign. "People just don't know that it takes seven bottles' worth of water to make every water bottle they buy in the store. They're shocked when they hear we use a

EMAGINE GREEN, CONTINUED

million plastic bags a minute. We talk for 20 minutes, then they say 'What can I do?' They can buy bottles, bags, or other products that fit what they are looking for, for their health, for the environment, or to save money. Which habits do you want to break?" When talking about the products with clients, they tie each product to a behavior to change. To reduce paper towel use, connect it to buying bamboo towels that are reusable.

In addition to knowing that Emagine Green is a direct sales party planning company, its also good to know what Emagine Green is not—it's not a pyramid or MLM (multilevel marketing) company. In MLM organizations, "about 3 percent of people are team leaders, and the rest are customers on auto-ship programs," says Ensign. "People think they're going to get rich quick, but very few do."

Emagine Green is ready to grow, says Ensign: "We're internally funded, no debt, and we've invested in the systems, people, and model so we can grow rapidly and take on a lot more people."

Thriving with Green in the Conserver Economy

As I finish up this book in early 2009, the economy is in the midst of dramatic upheaval that has left few of us untouched. Millions of people in the United States are unemployed, home and stock values have fallen dramatically, and a palpable sense of fear permeates the lives of many. With trillions of dollars of debt left in a crumbling house of financial cards, borrowers large and small are suddenly finding for the first time that further borrowing is no longer an option. We are witnessing a tectonic shift from the consumer economy we have known to a new conserver economy in which people and businesses are saving more, spending less, and thinking of the long term. And yet, even here in the midst of the biggest economic crisis of our time, there are opportunities for businesses in the conserver economy that is emerging, an overarching trend that reinforces the green economy in many ways.

Many economists believe that when the economy recovers it won't bounce back up, but enter a period of slow growth. Those who are waiting for a quick return to old spending habits may be disappointed. For years Americans have maintained a negative savings rate, spending more than they make, but you cannot keep this up forever. Much of this spending was fueled by refinancing to withdraw money from homes that rapidly escalated in value, but the dramatic declines in home values have taken this option off the table for most. We are entering a new era in which some of the excesses of consumerism are held in check by economic realities. This transition from consumer to conserver is creating new niches for businesses to move into. Finding the opportunities created by new trends and habits, businesses can thrive.

When I was growing up my Mom would tell us about her childhood in the Great Depression growing up on a farm, about driving to town with chickens to sell and eggs to trade for an ice cream cone. Her family lived simply because they had to. They were not hungry. All of their needs were cared for, but they were not shopping for sport or distraction. They wasted little, with every resource used and reused. When something broke, it was fixed. If it had a hole, it was mended. That was just the way it was.

For us kids the whole story sounded a little distant and irrelevant to our own lives. We lived in the suburbs after all, in the land of fast food and shopping malls, ground zero of the consumer economy—what did chickens and farming have to do with us? My mom's stories are sounding a lot more relevant these days. Those chickens are coming home to roost.

Despite the massive turmoil that we face, the conserver economy has some good things going for it. By forcing us to save more, waste less, and use resources more carefully, the impact of the conserver economy is green in many respects. It's also bigger than green trends have been in the past, and more closely connected to the daily concerns of most mainstream Americans like paying their bills, taking care of their kids, and providing for their future.

Change is often hard, but even as old opportunities shrink and disappear, new ones are emerging. Even as GM struggles, new automakers are emerging to produce the next generation of electric cars, and consumers are turning to carsharing, ridesharing, and other strategies for their transportation needs. Even as energy-intensive industries struggle with the steadily rising cost of power, businesses providing energy-efficient alternatives will thrive. New opportunities are emerging everywhere, if you know where to look for them.

Where are the new opportunities? The trends to look for in the conserver economy are sharing, repairing, reusing, renting, rebuilding, and rethinking.

- *Sharing.* Sharing is more than a nice thing for kids to do with their friends. Sharing gets more mileage out of resources we have already invested in goods, having two or more people share one object rather than everyone buying their own. This is good for the planet and for the pocketbook, helping people save money. Carsharing with businesses like ZipCar is one example, and sharing books, purses, clothes, and other goods and services are also eco-friendly solutions that are on the upswing in the conserver economy.

Starting *Green*

Repairing. While the consumer economy treated most goods as disposable, to be frequently thrown away and replaced by new goods, the conserver economy finds people returning to the old habit of fixing old appliances, electronics, and computers. Luxury clothing retail stores are not doing well at present, but tailors are thriving.

Reusing. Secondhand goods may not seem sexy, but they can be a real bargain. Used cars are not as exciting as new ones, but they can be a much greater value, and used car sales have been pulling some auto dealers through the current precipitous slump in new car sales. Used cars are also a very green option, particularly fuel-efficient used cars. Used clothing is another example. Consumers may not be flocking to the malls in the same numbers as before, but everybody needs clothes at some point, driving an increase in sales of quality used clothing.

Renting. We buy many goods not so much for the object itself, but for a service it performs for us. For example, we don't really care if we own an air conditioner, as long as we have cool air on a hot summer day. We don't want a refrigerator—we want cold food. Renting or leasing objects can avoid the unnecessary investment to purchase goods that may not be needed in the long term, and creative business models called servicizing that have been used in the green economy allow customers to buy a service (covering my floors) instead of buying a product (flooring).

Rebuilding. In many respects we have been living for the moment in recent years, and now we are finding that we need to return to old habits of investing in the future. We are retooling the economy to be more efficient, productive, and greener. We are updating the electrical grid, and investing in infrastructure projects. We are retrofitting millions of buildings to stop wasting billions of dollars worth of energy. Rebuilding our economy with measures like this is a solid investment for the long term.

🍃 *Rethinking.* As people come to terms with our altered economic landscape and their place in it, they are rethinking the actions, values, and priorities that got us into this mess. They are rethinking whether they need such large cars and homes. They are rethinking the assumptions of the consumer economy, that more is always better, and that we can easily buy today and pay whenever. They are appreciating that our actions have real consequences, for ourselves, for our economy, and for our planet.

How these trends play out and the direction the broader economy takes will play a big role in the direction of the green economy. If the conserver economy is a dominant influence in daily life for millions of people, as seems likely, then it will have a pervasive and lasting green impact on the opportunities for all of us.

Future Perfect

We have great challenges laid out before us, but the creativity and energy of entrepreneurs is leading the way to a greener economy and a greener world. With the courage, resourcefulness, passion, and commitment of people like those I interviewed for this book, we can make the change happen. We can create the world we want to see: one with a strong economy, good jobs, prosperous businesses, clean air and water, no climate change, and the natural world preserved, not just for today but for all of the generations ahead.

No matter where you are today, you can be a part of this change. You can join the move to change how business is done and create a prosperous and healthy world. You may not see it today and may not believe it, but you have everything you need to get started.

The choice is ours. Each of us has the power to choose our own destiny and to decide the type of world we want to live in. We have the power to choose one path or another, to choose a better world for ourselves and our children. Building your green business can be your contribution, your mark on the world for the future, and your path to success.

I think that we will do it, and I hope you'll be a part of it. The main reason I think that the green business wave will succeed and create a better and brighter world is that I don't really see another option. There's only one path forward, and it's a great way to go. Why would we do anything else?

The future is green—I'll see you there.

Resource Guide

The green business world is large and growing rapidly. Many wonderful websites and books are not included here, but this listing does provide a sampling of resources to get you started in the right direction.

Websites
Blogs, News, and Information

CaliforniaGreenSolutions.com. Providing business solutions green businesses need, arranged by business function, industry, training, and the natural resources that are impacted.

CleanEdge.com. Clean Edge provides information for investors and companies and on marketing and finance; includes the Clean Energy Trends 2009 report.

Ecopreneurist.com. Blog site with contributions from many individuals keeping the green entrepreneurial community up to date.

Fastcompany.com/blog/glenn-croston/starting-and-growing-green-businesses-0. Glenn Croston's expert blog on green business for Fast Company.

GreenBiz.com. One of the most widely read sites for the news and opinion on the green economy, including green business expert Joel Makower as the executive editor of Greener World Media, which produces GreenBiz.com and the related sites, including ClimateBiz.com.

GreenBusinessOwner.com. A wide-ranging information resource loaded with practical strategies, insights, and opportunities for green businesses and entrepreneurs.

LazyEnvironmentalist.com. Site for Josh Dorfman, author of *The Lazy Environmentalist,* and the founder and CEO of Vivavi.

LOHAS.com. Home of the *LOHAS* (Lifestyles of Health and Sustainability) journal, with info about this marketing group.

OrganicArchitect.com. Site for the design firm founded by architect, author, and educator Eric Corey Freed

75GreenBusinesses.com. Glenn Croston's website about his book *75 Green Businesses* providing green business opportunities for a wide range of people.

StartingUpGreen.com. Glenn Croston's support resource for green entrepreneurs and the companion site to this book; helping green entrepreneurs succeed with opportunities, strategies, and resources.

Stateofgreenbusiness.com. From the editors of *GreenBiz,* the annual State of Green Business Report lays out in clear language what progress is being made by the green business world and where things are lagging.

SustainableIndustries.com. The site for *Sustainable Industries* magazine, providing a business-oriented perspective of the green economy.

Energy Efficiency

climatesaverscomputing.org. For information about efforts to develop energy-efficient PCs.

eere.energy.gov/education/adult_education.html. Features information about training and education for renewable energy and energy efficiency.

energystar.gov. Information about energy efficient appliances and other efficiency moves the government is supporting.

EPEAT.net. A listing that rates computers according to environmental criteria, including energy efficiency.

resnet.us. The Residential Energy Services Network, the creator of the HERS Index for rating the energy efficiency of homes; information on how to become a certified rater.

rmi.org. The Rocky Mountain Institute, home of world renowned experts in energy efficiency such as co-founder Amory Lovins.

settosave.com. Palm Desert energy survey program.

Government

arb.ca.gov/cc/cc.htm. For information about the implementation of AB 32 in California, the landmark legislation to reduce greenhouse gas emissions in that state.

business.gov/expand/green-business. Billed as the "official business link to the U.S. Government," with a special section about green businesses.

EPA.gov. The site of the U.S. Environmental Protection Agency; not only is this site the place to look for updates on the changing regulatory landscape but it is also the home for a great deal of information, including the *Small Business Source Book on Environmental Auditing.*

epa.gov/sbo/pdfs/auditbook_500.pdf. EPA *Small Business Source Book on Environmental Auditing.*

green.ca.gov. California is a leader in the United States in the green movement. See what the state is up to, and where the rest of the United States is headed.

Small Business Administration (sba.gov). Working with all businesses, the SBA has information about how small-business loans work and many other practical resources for entrepreneurs.

Schools and Organizations

BuildItGreen.org. Build It Green is a nonprofit for green building in California, and the developer of the GreenPointRated green building certification system.

Coopamerica.net. Its name has changed but its domain name has not; but on this site for Green America, formerly called Coop America, you can look up green businesses in its listings, get news, information about conferences, and more.

Energycenter.org. The California Center for Sustainable Energy, a nonprofit based in San Diego, California, helping consumers, businesses, and workers with workshops, training, and assistance with energy-related projects.

Globalreporting.org/Home. The site for the Global Reporting Initiative (GRI); setting the standard for how sustainability reports are written.

GreenDrinks.org and ecotuesday.com. Organizers of green networking events.

NRDC.org. Site for one of the largest and most influential environmental information, action, and lobbying groups, the Natural Resources Defense Council.

Presidiomba.org. Site for the Presidio School of Management, which features a sustainability focused MBA program that launches students into a wide range of green business opportunities.

Sfgreenbiz.org. The site for the San Francisco Green Business Program, with checklists for going green.

Solarliving.org. The Solar Living Institute, which is a rich solar resource with frequent workshops both at the center in Hopland, California, and in many other communities.

Us-cap.org. The site for the U.S. Climate Action Partnership of businesses and nonprofits, looking for a consensus on how action on climate change might be structured so it will work best for all parties involved.

Usgbc.org. The site of the U.S. Green Building Council, the developer of the LEED green building rating system.

Business Partners

CO2Stats.com. To make your website carbon neutral by optimizing how it loads and offsetting the impact of any greenhouse gas emissions resulting from use of your site.

Ecoimprint.com. Provider of green promotional materials.

Environmentallyfriendlyhotels.com. To find a green hotel to stay at; compiled by Kit Cassingham.

Gaiahumancapital.com. For recruiting and building cleantech businesses, with Dawn Dzurilla the founder and president.

GreenBusinessInsurance.com. To insure your business in an eco-friendly way, with Pat Thompson of Dublin, Ohio.

Greenirene.com. To find out more about becoming a Green Irene eco-consultant or using its services to green your home or your office.

Greenpostcards.com and ecoprint.com. Green printing services.

Interfaceglobal.com. The site for the Interface floor covering company, which is making great strides toward becoming a truly sustainable business under the leadership of green business leader Ray Anderson.

K4forum.com. The site for the angel investors group Keiretsu Forum, which has groups in many cities.

Kpcb.com. Site for world renowned venture capital firm Kleiner Perkins, one of the biggest players in the cleantech community, with none other than former vice president Al Gore as a member of the team.

Natcapsolutions.org. The site for Natural Capitalism Solutions, co-founded by one of the co-authors of *Natural Capitalism,* Hunter Lovins; provides tools and strategies for businesses, nonprofits, and governments to do well and do the right thing for the environment.

Onepercentfortheplanet.org. Helping businesses give back a portion of what they make for green causes.

PickupPal.com. To set up ridesharing.

ProformaGreen.com. Website for Proforma Simonetta Freelance, provider of green promotional materials.

Pulsestaging.com. For eco-friendly event staging with Midori Connolly.

ShoreBank Pacific (Eco-bank.com). The site for the green bank ShoreBank Pacific, which helps green businesses and the communities they are a part of, helping both to succeed.

SignatureGreen.net. Green businesses need the help of many others, including those providing green PR and marketing help, like David Mleczko of Signature Green Public Relations and Marketing.

SolarCity.com. Provider of solar power installations and power purchase agreements with businesses, with no cost upfront.

Stonyfield.com. The site for organic yogurt producer Stonyfield Farm, with Gary Hirshberg the CE-Yo and president; provides interesting information and insights on what this green business leader is up to today.

SustainableSpaces.com. The site for the efficiency business Sustainable Spaces in San Francisco.

Terrapass.com or CarbonFund.org. Providers of carbon offsets to reduce the carbon footprint for your business and go the deepest shade of green.

TheFunded.com. Website for The Funded, founded by Adeo Ressi, in which business executives turn the tables on venture capitalists and rank their merits.

TheGreenOffice.com. Provider of green office supplies.

Wendel.com. The site for green law firm Wendel, Rosen, Black & Dean in Oakland, California.

ZipCar.com. To use corporate (or personal) carsharing.

Books
Starting a Green Business

Cooney, Scott. *Build a Green Small Business: Profitable Ways to Become an Ecopreneur* (New York: McGraw Hill, 2009).

Croston, Glenn. *75 Green Businesses You Can Start to Make Money and Make a Difference* (Irvine, CA: Entrepreneur Press, 2008).

The Green Business Leaders

Anderson, Ray. *Mid-Course Correction. Toward a Sustainable Enterprise: The Interface Model* (White River Junction, VT: Chelsea Green Publishing, 1998).

Hirshberg, Gary. *Stirring It Up: How to Make Money and Save the World* (New York: Hyperion, 2008).

Green Business Operations and Strategies

Esty, Daniel and Andrew Winston. *Green to Gold: How Smart Companies Use Environmental Strategy to Innovate, Create Value, and Build Competitive Advantage* (New Haven, CT: Yale University Press, 2006).

Freed, Eric Corey. *Green Building and Remodeling for Dummies* (Hoboken, NJ: Wiley, 2007).

Makower, Joel and Cara Pike. *Strategies for the Green Economy: Opportunities and Challenges in the New World of Business* (New York: McGraw-Hill, 2008)

McKay, Kim and Jenny Bonnin, with Tim Wallace. *True Green @ Work: 100 Ways You Can Make the Environment Your Business* (Washington, DC: National Geographic, 2008).

Savitz, Andrew W. and Karl Weber. *The Triple Bottom Line: How Today's Best-Run Companies Are Achieving Economic, Social and Environmental Success—and How You Can Too* (San Francisco: John Wiley, 2006).

Seireeni, Richard with Scott Fields. *The Gort Cloud: The Invisible Force Powering Today's Most Visible Green Brands* (White River Junction, VT: Chelsea Green Publishing, 2008).

The Big Picture

Friedman, Thomas. *Hot, Flat, and Crowded*: *Why We Need a Green Revolution—and How It Can Renew America* (New York: Farrar, Straus and Giroux, 2008).

Hawken, Paul, Amory Lovins, and L. Hunter Lovins. *Natural Capitalism: Creating the Next Industrial Revolution* (New York: Little, Brown and Company, 1999)

Hawken, Paul. *The Ecology of Commerce* (New York: HarperCollins, 1993).

Jones, Van. *The Green Collar Economy: How One Solution Can Fix Our Two Biggest Problems* (New York: HarperOne, 2008).

McDonough, William and Michael Braungart. *Cradle to Cradle: Remaking the Way We Make Things* (New York: Farrar, Straus and Giroux, 2002).

 *Starting Green*

Cleantech

Krupp, Fred and Miriam Horn. *Earth: The Sequel: The Race to Reinvent Energy and Stop Global Warming* (New York: W.W. Norton, 2008).

Pernick, Ron and Clint Wilder. *The Clean Tech Revolution: Discover the Top Trends, Technologies, and Companies to Watch* (New York: HarperCollins, 2008).

Starting Up Businesses

Caffey, Andrew. *Franchises and Business Opportunities* (Irvine, CA: Entrepreneur Press, 2001).

Horan, Jim, foreword by Tom Peters. *The One Page Business Plan for the Creative Entrepreneur* (Berkeley, CA: The One Page Business Plan, 2004).

Keup, Erwin. *Franchise Bible* (Irvine, CA: Entrepreneur Press, 2004).

Toolkit Media Group. *Start Run & Grow: A Successful Small Business* (Riverwoods, IL: Toolkit Media, 2008).

Index

Starting Green

Starting **Green**